Violence
in the U.S.

Volume 2

1968-71

Violence
in the U.S.
Volume 2
1968-71

Edited by Thomas F. Parker

FACTS ON FILE, INC.   NEW YORK, N.Y.

Violence in the U.S.

Volume 2

1968-71

Library of Congress Catalog Card Number 74-81146
ISBN 0-87196-230-6

9 8 7 6 5 4 3 2 1
PRINTED IN
THE UNITED STATES OF AMERICA

CONTENTS

Page

FOREWORD

THIS 2D VOLUME OF THE FACTS ON FILE chronicle of violence in the U.S. covers the period 1968-71. These were the years in which Martin Luther King Jr. and Robert F. Kennedy were slain, in which many black militants asserted that the nonviolent civil rights movement was giving way to an era of black violence, in which new ferocity battered the nation's city's and campuses and in which the activists opposing the war in Vietnam took increasingly forceful steps to bring their protest to public attention.

Troubled Americans examined the phenomenon of widespread violence with growing intensity, and their concern was deepened by the results of their study. The Advisory Commission on Intergovernmental Relations found in 1968 that the woes of the cities added up to a "major crisis threatening ... the whole fabric of American society." The National Commission on the Causes & Prevention of Violence warned in 1969 that U.S. cities might become divided into "fortified" residential compounds and ghetto neighborhoods, which would be "places of terror." It said that the nation's colleges were threatened by a "small but determined minority" seeking to destroy "existing institutions" or convinced that "violence and disruption may be the only effective way of achieving societal and university reform."

This volume records the conclusions of those who studied the nation's trial by violence as the U.S. emerged from the troubled 1960s into what appeared to be the equally dangerous decade of the 1970s. And it details the brutal events that led to these conclusions. The material of this book was taken largely from the record compiled by FACTS ON FILE in its coverage of world events. Despite the controversial nature of much that appears here, a conscientious effort was made to present all facts without bias.

1

ASSASSINS, EXTREMISTS & CAMPUS TURMOIL (1968)

U.S. System Threatened?

Americans were warned during 1968 that the growing violence in the U.S. might destroy their social and political order. In the aftermath of the unprecedented urban disorders of 1967, the Advisory Commission on Intergovernmental Relations asserted that the crisis in the cities threatened the U.S. political system and the fabric of American society. The President's National Advisory Commission on Civil Disorders, in its report on the 1967 racial disorders, warned of the deepening rift between white and black societies in the U.S. and called for a national commitment to reverse the trend.

A sniper shot the Rev. Dr. Martin Luther King Jr. to death Apr. 4. In the wave of grief and anger that swept the nation, rioting broke out in at least 125 cities in 28 states. 55,000 Regular Army troops and federalized National Guardsmen were called out to restore order as the number of dead and injured soared. Further controversy flared when Chicago Mayor Richard J. Daley instructed police to "shoot to kill" arsonists in future riots.

Sen. Robert F. Kennedy, Presidential candidate and brother of an assassinated President, was shot to death June 6. As the nation mourned, Pres. Johnson asked for tighter gun controls.

Urban disorders continued. Racial disturbances flared in Salisbury, Md. when Negroes rioted after a white detective had shot and killed a black burglary suspect. 11 people died in Cleveland, O. when black nationalists shot it out with police. Gary, Ind. was shaken by racial disorders. 3 people died in Miami violence that erupted during the Republican National Convention. Outbreaks of urban violence occurred in Akron, O.; St. Paul, Minn.; Newport News, Va.; Peoria, Ill., and the Chicago suburbs of Harvey and Dixmoor. Los Angeles police clashed with blacks at a festival held to commemorate the Watts riot of 1965. Police dispersed Negro protesters with tear gas in Washington, D.C.

During 1968 police departments across the nation made efforts to repair community relations in ghetto areas and to improve crowd-and-riot-control techniques.

Violence plagued the campuses. 3 black youths were killed in a confrontation with police in Orangeburg, S.C. Police clashed with students after activists closed down normal operations at

3

Columbia University. Gunfire, dynamiting and arson attempts accompanied violent student demonstrations in Berkeley, Calif. Students clashed with police repeatedly at San Francisco State College as Pres. S.I. Hayakawa adopted a hard line on student protesters.

Anti-war protesters demonstrating in Chicago during the Democratic National Convention were attacked by police with rifle butts, tear gas and chemical Mace. After Detroit area bombings, 11 youths were arrested in an anti-establishment bombing plot.

America Warned of Urban Crisis' Dangers

The Advisory Commission on Intergovernmental Relations warned in its 9th annual report Jan. 30, 1968 that the troubled cities constituted the "major crisis threatening the political system and, indeed, the whole fabric of American society." This crisis, the report noted, "was characterized by serious rioting, the breakdown of law and order, and, in a number of areas, the disappearance of any meaningful sense of community among the residents of blighted neighborhoods."

The policies and practices of government on the local, state and federal level, which "hardly satisfied the modest requirements of a bygone era . . . , are grossly unsuited to cope with today's urgent challenges," the report contended. It held that the manner of meeting current challenges—"seething racial unrest and civil disorder, burgeoning crime and delinquency, alarming differences in individual opportunity for education, housing and employment"—"will largely determine the fate of the American political system; it will determine if we can maintain a form of government marked by partnership and wholesome competition among national, state and local levels, or if, instead—in the face of threatened anarchy—we must sacrifice political diversity as the price of the authoritative action required for the nation's survival."

The effect of the 1967 summer riots on all levels of governments, the report said, was "to weaken 'welfare' measures and to toughen 'police' measures." There was a "tendency of local officials and news media to speak almost entirely in terms of remedial action by the federal government, occasioned perhaps by the feeling that only through access to federal financing could sufficient resources be mobilized." Paradoxically, the report said "much of the dissatisfaction of [urban] minority groups" was an outgrowth of the inadequacies of local government structure and fiscal arrangements and state constitutions and statutes. Specifically the report cited:

unbalanced patterns of state school aid, which tended to favor the suburbs over the central city ghettos; inadequate urban housing and the prohibitive costs of suburban housing, which created a "white noose" of the suburbs around the ghetto; "repressive restrictions upon the administration of public welfare."

The commission asserted that "the restoration of vitality in the nation's urban areas is an assignment surpassing the present capabilities of any one level of government and even of all levels acting collectively." It reported increasing agreement "that private enterprise must become more deeply involved in urban problems if these problems are to become manageable and if the metropolitan areas themselves are to remain governable."

Newark Riot Report Charges Excesses

The Governor's Select Commission on Civil Disorder in New Jersey charged Feb. 10, 1968 that National Guardsmen and state and local police had used "excessive and unjustified force" against blacks during the Newark riot of July 1967. The Commission recommended sweeping reforms in the city's legal, police and educational systems. The report said:

"There is no full or logical explanation for mass violence such as Newark experienced last summer." "There is evidence of deteriorating conditions in the ghetto; of increasing awareness of and frustration with these conditions among its residents; of the emergence of outspoken groups that focused these feelings; and of miscalculations, insensitive or inadequate responses by established authority." "The evidence that witnesses or interviewees were able or willing to provide . . . wouldn't support a conclusion that there was a conspiracy or plan to organize the disorders."

The Newark police were neither equipped nor psychologically prepared to cope with the outbreak of violence. Newark Mayor Hugh J. Addonizio and Police Director Dominick Spina were unable to recognize the bitterness of the city's Negroes, and Addonizio was incapable of making decisions. The city administration was "too hesitant to request state police assistance, despite the views of high officers in the Newark Police Department that such aid was needed."

The "amount of ammunition expended by police forces was out of all proportion to the mission assigned to them." Police Chief Spina had testified before the commission: "I think a lot of the report of snipers was due to . . . the trigger-happy Guardsmen, who were firing at noises and firing indiscriminately sometimes, it appeared to me." Although the Newark Police Department had said that 11 deaths were from shooting "from undetermined sources," "the location of death, the number of wounds, the manner in which the wounds were inflicted, all raise grave doubts about the circumstances under which many of these people died. . . . These homicides are matters of grave concern and should be quickly and exhaustively investigated and resolved by appropriate grand juries." The commission "strongly suggested" that policemen had engaged in senseless reprisal at the moment the disorders started to wane.

The commission made 100 recommendations covering the areas of city government, police, municipal courts, housing, schools, employment, welfare, health, anti-poverty and anti-riot procedures for the city. Among the commission's proposals:

(1) Abolition of the Municipal Courts and assumption by the "more politically insulated" state courts of their responsibilities. (2) The recruitment of black and Puerto Rican policemen and the promotion of qualified Negroes to positions of lieutenant and captain. (3) The appointment of a police commissioner's board "representing the total Newark community" to review complaints of police misconduct. (4) The utilization of the resources of the New Jersey business community in the hiring, training and upgrading of slum residents for jobs and the elimination of discriminatory practices in labor unions. (5) The creation by the state of a master plan for riot control. (6) The establishment of task forces to open lines of communication between City Hall and the ghetto. (7) Additional riot control training and extensive curtailment of the use of firearms. (8) Comprehensive summer jobs and recreation programs.

The commission said in the introduction to its report:

". . . Although violence has marked the path of many ethnic and social groups, the major issues that were in contention in those conflicts have long since been resolved. But one great issue remains unresolved: It is the place of the Negro in American society. It is this issue that almost tore the nation apart 100 years ago. It is this question that led to the Chicago riot of 1919, the Harlem riots of 1935 and 1943, and the mounting disorders . . . since World War 11. In the wake of the major racial conflicts of this century, commissions like this were established. They investigated . . . and made recommendations. Many chapters in these earlier volumes read much like some in this report. Poor housing, unemployment and inferior education of Negroes figure prominently in the report on the 1919 Chicago riot, just as they do in our analysis of the conditions in Newark in 1967. The mood in our cities clearly indicates that commissions like ours will have outlived their usefulness unless action is forthcoming from their recommendations. Our disadvantaged communities must see far more tangible evidence of a commitment to change than has emerged so far, or the summer of 1967 is likely to become a prologue to tragedy, and the time for study and planning will have run out. . . .

"There is a clear and present danger to the very existence of our cities. . . . The burden of responsibility weighs most heavily on those in positions of leadership, power and with control over the resources that will be needed to produce tangible results. . . . The fate of a city today is in the hands of the policeman on the beat, the landlord of a tenement building, the shop steward in the factory, the employer, the storekeeper, the social worker, the public employe behind his desk or the neighbor who will not be a neighbor. . . . We need . . . more respect by patrolmen for the dignity of each citizen. We need . . . more flexible hiring standards now. We need more principals, teachers and guidance counselors who want their students to succeed instead of expecting them to fail. We need more social workers who respect and foster a client's pride instead of treating him as an irritant or a child. Suburban residents must understand that the future of their communities is inextricably linked to the fate of the city, instead of harboring the illusion that they can maintain invisible walls or continue to run away. . . .

"If the events of last July had one effect, it was to show that we can no longer escape the issue. The question is whether we shall resort to illusion, or finally come to grips with reality. The illusion is that force alone will solve the problem. But our society cannot deliver on its promises when . . . disorder and lawlessness tear our communities apart. No group of people can better themselves by rioting. . . . Riots must be condemned. The cardinal principle of any civilized society is law and order. . . . Without it no one will succeed or endure. The primary responsibility of government toward a threatened riot or mass violence is prompt and firm action, judiciously applied and sufficient to restore peace and order. At the same time, we recognize that in the long run law and order can prevail only in conditions of social justice. Law enforcement in our country is neither designed nor equipped to deal with massive unrest. Our police establishments should not be forced into the role of armies of occupation. Therefore, reality demands prompt action to solve the long-neglected problems of our cities.

"Inherent in these problems is the virus of segregation. It must be attacked at the source. It is rampant in urban bodies no longer healthy enough to fight disease of any kind and which will increasingly suffer frustration and disorder unless old and outdated approaches are abandoned and new solutions sought in the metropolitan and regional context. . . ."

Anti-Riot Plans Developed

Army Secy. Stanley R. Resor said Feb. 16, 1968 that the National Guard had been given special training and equipment to handle civil disturbances. His disclosure was made at a closed session of the Senate Armed Services Committee. Gen. Harold K. Johnson, Army chief of staff, testified that the "active Army has 7 task forces, each of brigade size, specifically earmarked for civil disturbance duty." He said the forces totaled more than 15,000 men.

The *N.Y. Times* had reported Feb. 15 that the Army had established a 13-member Special Civil Disturbance Board Dec. 1967 and that the National Guard had strengthened a 227-man section and renamed it the Special Office for Military Support to Civil Authority.

Atty. Gen. Ramsey Clark had announced Jan. 12, in his year-end report to the President, that the Justice Department had installed a computer for its newly created Intelligence Unit to handle data on urban unrest.

An AP survey made public Mar. 1 revealed that police throughout the nation were stockpiling weapons and recruiting civilian reserves in preparation for summer riots. Among the survey's findings:

● Detroit police had stockpiled 100 pairs of binoculars, 2,000 tear-gas grenades and 1,200 gas masks; they had ordered 25 special anti-sniper rifles, 500 carbines, 300 shotguns and 150,000 rounds of ammunition; they had recruited 600 civilian reserves.

● The Monroe County (Mich.) sheriff, with a $50,000 riot-control fund, had bought a $13,500 armored truck, 15 walkie-talkies, 100 rifles, 15,000 rounds of ammunition, 500 tear-gas canisters and flak vests.
● Tampa, Fla. police had stocked 162 shotguns, 150 bayonets, 5 sniper rifles, 25 carbines and M-1 rifles, 300 gas masks.
● Chicago had bought helicopters and was training pilots. Cook County (Chicago) Sheriff Joseph I. Woods's effort to recruit 1,000 volunteers for a riot control posse for the summer had been ruled illegal Feb. 29 by a Cook County Circuit Court in the absence of an immediate emergency.
● The Los Angeles police had established 15 4-man special weapons and tactics (SWAT) teams and planned to train 30 more; a $45,000 mobile command post was bought to house the field commander in the event of a riot. The Los Angeles sheriff's office had bought a surplus Army M-8 armored car and had equipped it as a "rescue vehicle."
● The Newark police were testing a closed-circuit TV system.
● Philadelphia Police Chief Frank L. Rizzo had placed specially trained teams with shotguns and machine guns throughout the city, prepared to establish outposts on rooftops in riot zones.

Presidential Commission Blames White Racism

The President's National Advisory Commission on Civil Disorders (the Kerner Commission) warned Feb. 29, 1968 that America "is moving toward 2 societies, one black, one white—separate and unequal." Reporting after a 7-month study of the racial disorders of the summer of 1967, the commission asserted that "this deepening racial division is not inevitable." With adequate action, it said, "the movement apart can be reversed."

"White racism," the commission charged, was chiefly responsible for the "explosive mixture" of discrimination, poverty and frustrations in the black ghetto that was vented in violence. The report said: "What white Americans have never fully understood— what the Negro can never forget—is that white society is deeply implicated in the ghetto. White institutions created it, white institutions maintain it, and white society condones it."

The commission called for a "massive and sustained" national commitment to action. It recommended sweeping reforms in federal and local law enforcement, welfare, employment, housing, education and the news media. While the programs would require "unprecedented levels of funding and performance," the commission said, "there can be no higher priority for national action and no higher claim on the nation's conscience."

The 11-member advisory commission, headed by Illinois Gov. Otto Kerner, had been appointed by Pres. Johnson to answer 3 basic questions about the 1967 summer riots: "What happened ?" "Why did it happen?" and "What can be done to prevent it from happening again ?" The commission released a summary of its report Feb. 29; the full 1,400-page report was released Mar. 2.

In response to the question "What happened ?" the commission said: There were no "typical" riots. "The disorders of 1967 were unusual, irregular, complex and unpredictable social processes." The commission cited allegedly discriminatory police practices, unemployment and underemployment and inadequate housing as the most pervasive and intense of the specific grievances. The commission held that the 1967 disorders "were not caused by, nor were they the consequence of, any organized plan or 'conspiracy.'"

In answer to the question "Why did it happen ?" the commission declared that while the factors were "complex and interacting," "the most fundamental is the racial attitude and behavior of white Americans toward black Americans." The results of these white racial attitudes were: "Pervasive discrimination and segregation in employment, education and housing"; "black in-migration and white exodus," which "produced the massive and growing concentrations of impoverished Negroes in our major cities"; the converging of segregation and poverty on youth of the black ghettos "to destroy opportunity and enforce failure."

The commission presented nearly 160 recommendations to answer the question "What can be done ?" They included :

• The decentralization of city governments to make them more responsive to people's needs.
• "The creation of 2 million new jobs in the next 3 years"—550,000 in the first year.
• "On-the-job training by both public and private employers with reimbursement to private employers for the extra costs of training the hard-core unemployed."
• "Sharply increased efforts to eliminate *de facto* desegregation in our schools through substantial federal aid."
• "Substantial federal funding of year-round quality compensatory education programs."
• Establishment of "uniform national standards of welfare assistance at least as high as the annual 'poverty level,' " with the federal government paying "at least 90% of total payments."
• A "national system of income supplements based strictly on need."
• A "comprehensive and enforcable federal open housing law to cover the sale or rental of all housing, including single family homes."
• Efforts to "bring within the reach of low and moderate income families, within the next 5 years, 6 million new and existing units of decent housing, beginning with 600,000 units in the next year."
• A privately organized and funded institute of urban communications to train and educate journalists in urban affairs, to recruit more Negroes as journalists, to improve police-press relations and to review the press coverage of riots and racial problems.

"To maintain control of incidents which could lead to disorders," the commission recommended that local officials:

"Assign seasoned, well-trained policemen and supervisory officers to patrol ghetto areas, and to respond to disturbances.

"Develop plans which will quickly muster maximum police manpower and highly qualified senior commanders at the outbreak of disorders.

"Provide special training in the prevention of disorders and prepare police for riot control and for operation in units, with adequate command and control and field communication for proper discipline and effectiveness.

"Develop guidelines governing the use of control equipment and provide alternatives to the use of lethal weapons. . . .

"Establish an intelligence system to provide police and other public officials with reliable information that may help to prevent the outbreak of a disorder and to institute effective control measures in the event a riot erupts.

"Develop continuing contacts with ghetto residents to make use of the forces for order which exist within the community.

"Provide the machinery for neutralizing rumors, including creation of special rumor details to collect and evaluate rumors that may lead to a civil disorder, and to disseminate effectively the true facts to the ghetto residents and leaders."

The commission warned against trying to control urban disorders by equipping police with "mass destruction weapons," which were "designed to destroy, not to control." The commission said that "despite instances of sensationalism, inaccuracy and distortion, newspapers, radio and television tried on the whole to give a balanced, factual account of the 1967 disorders." The report charged, however, that "important segments of the news media failed to report adequately on the causes and consequences of civil disorders and on the underlying problems of race relations."

Richard M. Nixon, campaigning for the Republican Presidential nomination, said in a radio interview in Keene, N.H. Mar. 6: "One of the major weaknesses of the President's commission is that it, in effect, blames everybody for the riots except the perpetrators of the riots." "And I think that that deficiency has to be dealt with first. Until we have order we can have no progress." "I believe that we've got to make it very clear to potential rioters that in the event something starts next summer that the law will move in with adequate force to put down rioting and looting at the first indications of it." The commission had "put undue emphasis on the idea that we are in effect a racist society, white racists versus black racists." "There is a great deal of prejudice in the U.S. and there will continue to be a great deal of prejudice, and I think this talk that tends to divide people, to build a wall in between people, doesn't help in breaking down this prejudice. What we need is more talk about reconciliation, more talk about how we're going to work together."

The Kerner commission July 27, 1968 released several studies that found that urban riots were a form of social protest increasingly accepted by black Americans as justifiable because of conditions in the nation's ghettos. The studies, which supplemented the commission's earlier report, indicated that a significant minority of ghetto residents had participated in street violence occurring in their cities and that the rioters' behavior was greeted with ambivalence and tacit support, not condemnation, from other ghetto residents.

One study explicitly rejected the "riffraff" theory of riot participation, which held that riots were perpetrated by a small fraction of the black community composed of riffraff and outside agitators who were rejected by a majority of ghetto residents. A 2d study examined racial attitudes and reported that most Negroes, while still espousing integration, did not accept the "basic assumption of major improvement so seemingly obvious to many white Americans." A 3d study found that institutions serving the black slums were "insensitive" to the plight of ghetto residents.

The first study, entitled "Who Riots? A Study of Participation in the 1967 Riots," was conducted by Dr. Robert M. Fogelson of the Massachusetts Institute of Technology and Dr. Robert Hill of Columbia University. The authors said that the "riffraff theory" had been widely used by police chiefs to explain the riots. According to the report, the theory was accepted by the public because it reassured most white Americans that the problems of the U.S. city could be handled without "thoroughly overhauling its basic institutions or seriously inconveniencing its white majority." Since the riots could be seen as a function of poverty rather than race, they were regarded as "peripheral to the issue of white-black relations." The findings indicated that the 1967 urban riots were carried out by a "small but significant minority of the Negro population, fairly representative of the ghetto residents" and "tacitly supported by at least a large minority of the black community." The authors expressed the view that the riots were a "manifestation of race and racism in the United States," a reflection of and protest against the "essential conditions" of ghetto life and an "indicator of the necessity for fundamental change in American society."

Major findings of the study: There was a larger number of female participants in the riots than were indicated by arrest statistics. Where data was available, it showed that more than 2/3 of those arrested were 18 years of age and older. A plurality of those arrested were single. In 7 of 9 cities surveyed, 97% or more of those arrested were local residents. About 3/4 of those arrested were employed. 40% to 90% of those arrested had prior criminal records (not necessarily convictions), but this must be weighed against estimates that 50% to 90% of black males in the urban ghetto have criminal records. While an overwhelming majority of the black community deplored the violence in the riots, a majority felt that the riots would have "beneficial consequences for improving the Negro's social and economic conditions."

These findings were supported in part by the conclusions of the 2d study, "Racial Attitudes in 15 American Cities," conducted by Profs. Angus Campbell and Howard Schuman of the University of Michigan. Campbell and Schuman found that the riots were justified but "not recommended" by most Negroes. The authors collected data in more than 5,000 interviews of blacks and whites in 15 major U.S. cities. They found that most Negroes saw the riots partly or wholly as "spontaneous protests" against unfair conditions and economic deprivation. 1/3 of the whites agreed that the riots were a revolt against real grievances. 1/3 of the whites but only a very small percentage of the blacks defined the riots as "essentially criminal actions," to be suppressed by police action. 1/3 of the black respondents saw little real change in the position of Negroes since the 1954 Supreme Court decision on school desegregation.

(The results of a separate federally-financed study of police operations in slum precincts in Washington, Boston and Chicago were reported by the *N.Y. Times* July 5. The findings showed that 27% of the policemen studied were "either observed in misconduct situations or admitted to observers that they engaged in misconduct." 10% of the policemen observed were reported to have used "improper" or "unnecessary" force. The precinct studies were part of the broad investigation of the President's Commission on Law Enforcement & Administration of Justice, but the results were not published along with the commission's report Feb. 18, 1967.)

Police Slay 3 Black Students in Orangeburg, S.C.

3 black youths were shot to death and at least 34 persons were wounded in a confrontation between police and students at South Carolina State College in Orangeburg, S.C. Feb. 8, 1968. The deaths were the culmination of racial violence that had begun there Feb. 5 with student protests against the segregation of a local bowling alley; the disorders had resulted in the mobilization of the National Guard and the 2-week closing of the college.

The series of incidents began when students from the predominantly black adjoining campuses of South Carolina State College and Claflin College demonstrated Feb. 5 in front of the All-Star Bowling Lanes. They resumed the demonstrations Feb. 6, and 15 were arrested on trespassing charges. One policeman and 7 students were injured and hospitalized Feb. 6 as the disorders grew more violent.

Gov. Robert E. McNair Jr. mobilized a National Guard unit Feb. 6 and placed another on alert Feb. 7.

Students at State College began throwing rocks and bottles at passing cars Feb. 7, and about 100 helmeted highway patrolmen were sent to seal off the campus. Classes at State College were suspended Feb. 7, and M. Maceo Nance Jr., acting president of the college, protested against alleged police brutality. 200 National Guardsmen were brought to Orangeburg later Feb. 7, and 2 more Guard units were sent to Orangeburg Feb. 8.

The 3 students were killed late Feb. 8 in what was at first reported as an exchange of gunfire between police and students. According to an original report, Negroes opened fire on police and firemen who were trying to put out a grass fire. It was reported later, however, that the students did not shoot. Instead, a trooper was knocked down by a piece of lumber thrown by a student; the state troopers thought he was shot and opened fire. The 3 black students were killed, and 34 persons were wounded.

Gov. McNair proclaimed a state of emergency Feb. 9 and ordered a 5 p.m. curfew. 600 National Guardsmen were ordered to help seal off the college campuses, which were nearly deserted by early Feb. 9. McNair blamed the violence on "black-power advocates who represented only a small minority of the total student bodies" at the 2 schools. He said Cleveland Sellers, 23, state coordinator for the Student Nonviolent Coordinating Committee (SNCC), was responsible for the trouble. Sellers, wounded in the shooting Feb. 8, had been arrested.

800 local Negroes met in Orangeburg Feb. 11 and called for the immediate removal of the National Guard and suspension of law enforcement officers responsible for alleged police brutality. They announced plans for a boycott of white businesses. Dr. C.H. Thomas Jr., local NAACP president, said that 62.9% of the county population was black and that their buying power in Orangeburg (total population, 17,000) was 60% to 70%. The Negroes also demanded that the city make restitution to the families of the 3 dead youths. Their demands included: placing Negroes in appointive city and county jobs; the addition of "an

equitable number of Negroes" to local and state police forces; elimination of the county dual school system; busing of pupils for racial balance.

It had been announced Feb. 10 that Mayor E. O. Pendarvis and the City Council had established a biracial Human Relations Commission to find the causes of the violence and avert further outbreaks. State NAACP officials Feb. 13 criticized the commission on the grounds that its black members had been appointed without NAACP recommendation. (The South Carolina Task Force for Community Uplift, a biracial organization formed in the fall of 1967 and indorsed by McNair, urged all South Carolina municipalities Feb. 22 to form biracial groups immediately to deal with the causes of "possible racial upheaval in their midst.")

The Southern Regional Council said Feb. 24, in a 42-page report entitled "Events at Orangeburg," that the shootings showed the dangers of "get tough" police tactics. The report said: "The events also would at least suggest the implications of forces in motion not just in Orangeburg but across America in 1967-68, including black power and white overreaction to its emotional mood, the tendency to violence by Negroes dismayed by the failure of nonviolent and other peaceful protest against social injustice and inequity still enduring, the national tendency nearing public policy to a fear of riots amounting to phobia and a response to Negro unrest with massive police and military force." Although the governor had said that the police shot only after they thought they had been fired on, "no one has been able to find any weapons that the students might have used. No one . . . saw any students with guns." The report asked why police had not used "less lethal methods of riot control, such as tear gas or Mace," and why students had not been warned before the shooting. It said that SNCC coordinator Sellers apparently "had little influence on the campus" and had little effect in trying to encourage the organization of a Black Awareness Coordinating Committee.

Students returned to the State College campus Feb. 26, 1968. McNair announced Mar. 5 that he had rescinded his state of emergency order and that the National Guard had been withdrawn.

A federal grand jury in Columbia, S.C. Nov. 8 refused to indict 9 state highway policemen in the shooting of the 3 students. McNair Nov. 8 called the jury's decision "a conclusive and fair judgment of the incident." (The jury of 18 men and 5 women included 2 Negroes.) But the U.S. Justice Department insisted Dec. 20 that the 9 patrolmen be brought to trial, and it filed charges in Federal District Court in Columbia. The Justice

Department accused the policemen of violating the constitutional rights of the Negroes.

A federal jury in Florence, S.C. May 27, 1969 acquitted the 9 state patrolmen. The jury included 2 Negroes. The government had attempted to prove that the shootings were not provoked and that the police thus had violated an 1870 federal law that made it a misdemeanor for law authorities to deprive a person of his constitutional rights—*i.e.,* the right to life. Government witnesses testified that the troopers had issued no warning before firing. Warren Koon, then a reporter for the *Charleston Evening Post,* testified May 20 that "the first shots I heard were those fired by the troopers." 2 Orangeburg doctors testified the same day that there were several back and side wounds on the bodies of the slain students. The government introduced other testimony to show that 28 persons had been shot in the side or back. The defense, however claimed that a "highly explosive, extremely dangerous, riotous situation" existed on the campus and that the defendants "did what they had to do" to repulse "an armed mob of rioters who were shooting at them." FBI agent Nelson L. Phillips testified May 24 that he had heard small-arms fire immediately before the police had begun firing at the students. He said campus police had turned over to him molotov cocktails and other explosives after the shootings.

Martin Luther King Slain, Riots Shake Cities

The Rev. Dr. Martin Luther King Jr., 39, Nobel Peace Prize-winner and acknowledged leader of the nonviolent civil rights movement, was shot to death by a sniper in Memphis, Tenn. Apr. 4, 1968. James Earl Ray, arrested in London 2 months later, pleaded guilty to King's murder and was sentenced to 99 years in prison.

The news of King's assassination evoked expressions of dismay and shock across the U.S. and throughout the world. The killing precipitated rioting and violence in Washington, Chicago and some 125 other U.S. cities. At least 43 persons were killed, 2,600 injured and 21,000 arrested in the disorders. 21,000 regular federal troops and 34,000 National Guardsmen were sent to the troubled cities during the week after King's death as local authorities called for help to end the disorders.

Pres. Johnson, reflecting the nation's grief, delivered a nation-wide TV address in which he lauded the slain black leader and appealed to "every citizen to reject the blind violence that has struck Dr. King, who lived by nonviolence."

The bullet that killed King hit him on the right side of the neck at 6:01 p.m. CST as he leaned over a 2d floor railing outside his room at the Lorraine Motel in the predominantly black section in Memphis. He was pronounced dead at St. Joseph's Hospital at 7:05 p.m. after emergency surgery. King, who had returned to Memphis to lead a 2d march in support of the city's striking sanitation workers, most of them black, had been discussing plans for the proposed march with 2 of his aides, the Rev. Jesse Jackson and the Rev. Ralph Abernathy, before dinner.

Atty. Gen. Ramsey Clark flew to Memphis Apr. 5 with Justice Department officials on Pres. Johnson's orders. Clark said at a news conference that the FBI was looking for the assassin in several states. He reported that "all the evidence indicates that this was the act of a single individual."

FBI agents and Memphis police collected a small suitcase, a caliber-30.06 Remington pump rifle with a telescopic sight that had been discarded in a nearby doorway, and a number of fingerprints, all presumably left by the murderer. Memphis Police Director Frank Hollomon said that the evidence indicated that the shot had been fired from a bathroom used by upstairs occupants of the rooming house only 50 to 100 yards from King's motel room.

The Rev. Ralph David Abernathy, 42, was named Apr. 5 to succeed King as president of the Southern Christian Leadership Conference (SCLC). The SCLC's first activity under his leadership, Abernathy said, would be to carry out the Memphis march that King had planned to lead. This massive demonstration was held Apr. 8 with King's widow, Mrs. Coretta Scott King, taking her husband's place in the front rank ahead of an estimated 42,000 silent marchers, including thousands (estimated at 30% of the total) of whites. The march ended with a rally in front of City Hall, where Mrs. King urged the crowd to "carry on because this is the way he would have wanted it." But, she cried, "how many men must die before we can really have a free and true and peaceful society? How long will it take?"

The sanitation workers' strike, plagued by violence, had begun Feb. 12 over demands for a 33% pay raise, recognition of the American Federation of State, County & Municipal Employes as bargaining agents, a dues checkoff system, seniority rights, health and hospitalization insurance and other fringe benefits. Mayor Henry Loeb had broken off negotiations with union representatives Feb. 14. He contended that the strike was illegal under a 1966 State Supreme Court decision banning public employes' strikes. The garbage collectors Feb. 15 defied the mayor's ultimatum to return to work or be replaced, and the city began hiring new workers. The NAACP Feb. 16 and the Shelby County Democratic Club (a Negro political and social organization) Feb. 17 urged massive civil disobedience to demonstrate support for the strikers.

Violence erupted Feb. 23 during a march by 1,000 strikers after the City Council rejected the union's demand for a dues checkoff. Police said the outbreak began when the protesters tried to overturn a patrol car; witnesses said policemen knocked marchers to the pavement. Police moved in with nightsticks and cartridges of chemical Mace to quell the disturbance.

The Southern Regional Council (a foundation-supported research and information organization) Mar. 23 issued a report describing the strike as "merely a symptom of Memphis' larger problem." The report said the white community had failed to respond to black grievances, and it charged the police with "injudicious" acts. In Memphis, the report said, the record of police behavior "has not been a notably bad one," but "the police spark was present" in the recent disturbance. In fact, the report concluded, the Memphis disorder revealed that police departments "have become themselves direct and dangerous influences toward disorder."

Fresh disturbances began Mar. 28 when black students at the Hamilton High School, who were prevented from leaving school to join King's protest march, began pelting police with bricks. The march from the Claiborne American Methodist Episcopal Temple to City Hall had barely begun when 30 to 70 black youths darted alongside the procession and began smashing store windows along Beale Street and looting the store. 250 city and county police moved in with riot clubs and tear gas and sealed off one end of the street. Almost immediately 4,000 National Guardsmen armed with rifles and bayonets entered the area in armored personnel carriers. Another 8,000 were placed on alert. The Memphis Transit Authority stopped all bus service, and Mayor Loeb ordered a 7-p.m.-to-5-a.m. curfew.

At the outbreak of the rioting King was taken to a nearby motel. Most of the marchers returned to the church. After King left, police began firing tear gas at the Negroes, looters and bystanders alike. Several persons were reported beaten by police. Larry Payne, 16, was shot and killed when, according to police, he turned on a policeman with a butcher knife. About 60 persons were reported injured. More than 150 persons were arrested, about 40 of them on looting charges. It was said that of 155 stores with their windows smashed, only 35% had window displays damaged and only 5% had been entered.

Pres. Johnson declared in Washington Mar. 29 that federal assistance to Memphis, should it be necessary, would be available. But, he cautioned, "our system of government and our society depend on capable local law enforcement." The President said: "The tragic events in Memphis yesterday remind us of the grave peril rioting poses. This nation must seek change within the rule of law in an environment of social order. Rioting, violence and repression can only divide our people. Every one loses when a riot occurs."

Following the murder of King, Pres. Johnson, in his televised address Apr. 4, expressed shock and sorrow at "the brutal slaying" but hope "that all Americans tonight will search their hearts as they ponder this most tragic incident." "We can achieve nothing by lawlessness and divisiveness among the American people," Johnson said. "It's only by joining together, and only by working together, can we continue to move toward equality and fulfillment for all of our people."

The President spent most of Apr. 5 meeting with moderate black leaders, Congress members and officials of the District of Columbia and dealing with the violence that broke out throughout the U.S. in reaction to King's slaying. Federal troops were brought to Washington later that evening to restore order there.

The President Apr. 5 again went before the nation on TV to proclaim Sunday, Apr. 6, a national day of mourning for King and to announce that he had asked Congress, in adjournment over the weekend, to convene in joint session "at the earliest possible moment" to hear his proposals "for action—constructive action instead of destructive action—in this hour of national need."

King's death preempted the nation's attention: There were memorial marches and rallies throughout the U.S., many public school systems closed, public libraries and museums were shut, many businesses and the stock exchanges were closed, seaports from Maine to Texas shut down as longshoremen and seamen stopped work, the UN flag flew at half-mast, the opening of the baseball season (scheduled for Apr. 8) was postponed, the Stanley Cup hockey playoffs were postponed, the playoffs in the American and National Basketball Associations were postponed, Hollywood's Oscar-award presentation ceremony was postponed, the Presidential nomination campaign abruptly halted.

Most major black organizations and leaders paid high tribute to King and urged a continuance of his fight against discrimination in the nonviolent spirit. But militant black leaders said King's death marked the death of the nonviolent movement and urged retaliation in kind. Julius Hobson of Washington said Apr. 4 that "the Martin Luther King concept of nonviolence died with him. It was a foreign ideology anyway as foreign to this violent country as speaking Russian." United Black Front Chairman Lincoln O. Lynch called on black people Apr. 4 "to abandon the unconditional nonviolent concept expounded by Dr. King and adopt a position that for every Martin Luther King who falls, 10 white racists will go down with him. There is no other way. White America understands no other language." But Sen. Edward W. Brooke (R., Mass.), a Negro, said Apr. 4 that "the sorrow which all Americans of good will feel at this terrible loss must bind us together, not rend us apart." CORE National Director Floyd McKissick asserted Apr. 4 that King's philosophy of nonviolence had died with him. "White people are going to suffer as much as black people," McKissick said.

NAACP Executive Director Roy Wilkins warned Apr. 8 against retaliation. Despite the "talk about 'get whitey,' 'kill 10 whites for every Negro killed,'" he said, "the people who lose their lives are Negroes." He announced that the NAACP was mounting a nationwide drive against racial violence and stressing jobs for the unemployed and better community relations. King, he said, would have been "outraged" by the disorders following his assassination, and "millions of Negroes in this country" were opposed to violence. Wilkins Apr. 8 criticized black-power leader Stokely Carmichael. It was reported, he said, that Carmichael had responded in a reasonable manner on first hearing of King's death, but, "the next day, miraculously, as if somebody had come to see him and talked to him, comes that talk about 'get your guns.'" (Wilkins Apr. 4 had expressed concern about "a racial collision." He warned that "too many officials in key states and local positions are interpreting 'riot control' and 'law and order' to mean a crackdown racially on Negro Americans.")

The news of King's assassination and the widespread civil disorder that followed were received with shock in many countries around the world. The news was reported under banner headlines and forced the cancellation of many radio and TV programs. Government and religious leaders sent their condolences to Mrs. King and praised her husband as a man of peace who had sought to achieve racial harmony in the U.S. through nonviolent means; they described his death as a loss to all mankind. Memorial services were held in a number of foreign capitals, and moments of silence were observed by various parliamentary bodies. The *N.Y. Times* reported Apr. 6 that the assassination "evoked in Europe ... a reaction of intense horror at the deed and of fear for the stability of American society." Reporting on world reaction Apr. 7, the *Washington Post* said that certain countries, among them the USSR, Communist China, India and West Germany, viewed the murder and subsequent rioting as "a sign of deep sickness in American society, if not outright disintegration."

Rioting Follows Assassination, Rights Law Enacted

Baltimore, Chicago, Kansas City, Mo. and Washington, D.C. were the hardest hit of the cities rocked by the racial violence that swept the country Apr. 4-11 in the wake of King's assassination. At least 125 cities in 28 states suffered racial disturbances. With the exception of the Southwest, Northwest and Northern Plains, no area of the country was exempt from the disorders. The Justice Department Apr. 23 reported 46 persons killed in the rioting that followed the assassination.

In a clear response to the assassination and to the widespread civil disorders that followed, the House of Representatives Apr. 10, 1968 approved a Senate-passed civil rights bill prohibiting racial discrimination in the sale or rental of about 80% of the nation's housing. Pres. Johnson Apr. 10 called the action "a victory for every American" after "a long tortuous and difficult road." The President signed the measure Apr. 11. In a statement delivered at the ceremony, Johnson said: The assassination of King had "outraged" the nation, but "America is also outraged at the looting and burning that defiles our democracy." "We all know that the roots of injustice run deep, but violence cannot redress a solitary wrong or remedy a single unfairness." "The only real road to progress is through the process of law."

An attempt to put the Senate-passed bill before the House by unanimous consent had been blocked Mar. 14, and the bill was referred to the House Rules Committee. The House Democratic leadership sought to have the committee vote on acceptance of the Senate amendments, but the committee Mar. 19 voted, 8-7, to delay action on the bill until Apr. 9. Following King's assassination Apr. 4, there was a surge of demand for action on civil rights. By Apr. 9, with troops ringing the Capitol, the committee voted 9-6 to clear the bill for House consideration without change and with debate limited to one hour.

The bill provided a 3-stage reduction of racial barriers in about 52.6 million housing units. It also made it a federal crime to harm civil rights workers and to cross state lines to incite a riot or to instruct persons in the use of firearms or molotov cocktails in riots.

In the turmoil that followed King's death, Washington, D.C. Apr. 4-7 experienced the worst outbreak of racial violence it had ever known. 9 persons died. 1,202 persons were reported injured, including some policemen, firemen and military personnel. 6,306 persons were arrested. 1,130 fires were reported. And 13,600 federal troops were moved into the city before the disorders were quelled.

Looting and vandalism had erupted in Washington late Apr. 4 after Stokely Carmichael led about 50 youths down 14th Street to urge stores to close as a sign of respect for King. The group, shouting "Close the stores—Martin Luther King is dead," swelled to more than 400 persons about a mile north of the White House. Within an hour Negroes began smashing store windows and looting, despite a plea by the Rev. Walter E. Fauntroy, vice chairman of the City Council, to Carmichael to disband his group and go home. But Carmichael reportedly refused to stop his march.

According to the *N.Y. Times,* Carmichael urged members of the crowd: "If you don't have a gun, go home." "When the white man comes he is coming to kill you. I don't want any black blood in the street. Go home and get you a gun and then come back because I got me a gun." But the *Washington Post* reported that Carmichael simply urged rioters to stop looting and "go home." "Not now, not now," he was quoted as shouting to looters. Carmichael declared at a news conference the morning of Apr. 5: "When white America killed Dr. King last night she declared war" on black America. There was "no alternative to retribution." "Black people have to survive, and the only way they will survive is by getting guns."

Rioting in Washington Apr. 5 was generally held to 3 predominantly low-income black Negro sections of the city—a 10-block strip along 14th Street N.W., a 10-block strip along 7th Street N.W. and a 12-block strip along H Street N.E. The downtown area near the Capitol and the White House suffered minor damage.

At 4:02 p.m. Apr. 5 Pres. Johnson signed a proclamation declaring that "a condition of domestic violence and disorder" existed in Washington. He issued an executive order mobilizing

4,000 Regular Army and National Guard troops to supplement the city's 2,800-man police force. Police and troops were ordered to avoid excessive force. The troops were dispatched with the following orders: "I will, if possible, let civilian police make arrests, but I can, if necessary, take into temporary custody rioters, looters and others committing crimes. I will not load or fire my weapon except when authorized in advance by an officer under certain specific conditions, or when required to save my life." The President named ex-Deputy Defense Secy. Cyrus R. Vance as his special representative in the crisis.

A new wave of looting and arson broke out in Washington Apr. 6. An additional 8,000 federal troops were moved into the city; more than 9,500 troops were put on street patrol, and 3,000 were held in reserve. Serious food shortages began to be reported Apr. 6. Hundreds of persons were homeless.

A return to normality in Washington was reported Apr. 8. "Mayor" (Washington Commissioner) Walter L. Washington said that 35 distribution centers had been established to supply nearly 185,000 riot victims with food. Emergency housing and jobs were being provided at special centers established throughout the city.

2 more deaths were reported in Washington Apr. 9, and the total reached 10. (7 of the deaths were said to be unquestionably related to the rioting, the other 3 only possibly related.) Troops remained on duty Apr. 9, but the number of daytime patrols was decreased. A gradual withdrawal of troops from the city was begun Apr. 12.

In Chicago, 11 Negroes died in racial violence that swept the city Apr. 5-7. Federal troops and National Guardsmen were called in to quell the disorders, in which more than 500 persons were injured and nearly 3,000 arrested. 162 buildings were reported entirely destroyed by fire, and a score more were partially destroyed. The disturbances had begun Apr. 5 when black youths, released from school early in memory of King, began roving downtown streets and smashing windows. They swept through the Loop section and by nightfall had caused severe damage in the 2300 and 2400 blocks of West Madison Street. 4 deaths were reported: 2 looters were shot, one person died in a fire and a another was shot to death. One fireman was wounded by a sniper.

6,000 National Guardsmen joined Chicago's 10,500 policeman Apr. 6. They were instructed to shoot only in self-defense and then to shoot only at definite targets. Early Apr. 6 Mayor Richard J. Daley and Brig. Gen. Richard T. Dunn, in command of the Guardsmen, had made a tour of the riot area and declared the situation "under control." Later in the day, however, violence was renewed with increased vigor and spread from the West Side to the South Side and the Near North Side. 800 arrests and 125 major fires were reported during the day. 1,500 additional Guardsmen were called into the city. The Guardsmen and the police were ordered to take more "aggressive action" against lawbreakers.

In the evening of Apr. 6, after 9 Negroes had been killed in Chicago's disorders, Illinois Lt. Gov. Samuel H. Shapiro asked Pres. Johnson for federal aid to quell the "serious domestic violence in or near the city of Chicago." The first of some 5,000 federal troops ordered to the city began arriving at 9:30 p.m. The President also sent Deputy Atty. Gen. Warren Christopher to Chicago as his special representative. While troops took control in the North and West Sides of the city Apr. 6, the situation on the South Side deteriorated. Firemen trying to put out fires were under constant attack by snipers. By nightfall thousands of blacks were reported homeless.

Sporadic incidents of sniper fire, looting and arson were reported in Chicago Apr. 7 as federal troops continued to patrol the city. Police reported 11 Negro deaths, 7 of them directly and 4 indirectly related to the rioting.

Shapiro said at a news conference Apr. 8 that the Chicago emergency had ended. Troops, National Guardsmen and police, however, continued to patrol the city. Members of 2 major black South Side gangs, the Blackstone Rangers and the East Side Disciples, agreed to suspend hostilities and aid patrols to prevent further outbreaks of violence and destruction.

5 black militants were arrested in Chicago Apr. 8 on charges of conspiracy to commit arson. Those arrested were Frederick (Doug) Andrews, 29, founder of the Garfield Organization (announced purpose: the improvement of economic conditions on the West Side); Edward Crawford, 46, president of the National Negro Rifle Association; Andrew Brown, 24, of the Garfield Organization; Curlee Reed, 19, and Anthony Williams, 17.

The 5,000 federal troops left the city Apr. 12.

Chicago Mayor Daley announced at a news conference Apr. 15 that he was instructing policemen "to shoot to kill" arsonists and to "shoot to maim or cripple" looters in any future rioting. His orders, transmitted to police through Police Supt. James B. Conlisk, said: "Such force as is necessary including deadly force shall be used" to prevent the commission of such forcible felonies as arson, attempted arson, burglary and attempted burglary and "to prevent the escape of the perpetrators." Daley said that he had thought those orders were in effect during the Apr. 5-7 violence but that he had discovered that morning that policemen had been instructed to use their own discretion as to whether to shoot. Daley said he thought that arson was "the most hideous crime." He declared: "If anyone doesn't think this was a conspiracy, I don't understand."

6 persons died in the racial violence that erupted in Baltimore Apr. 6. More than 700 persons were reported injured Apr. 6-9, more than 5,000 arrests were made, and the number of fires reported exceeded 1,000. The National Guard and federal troops were called in to quell the rioting.

Gov. Spiro T. Agnew had declared a "state of emergency and crisis" in Baltimore Apr. 6 after black youths set at least 20 fires, smashed windows and looted stores in the predominantly black section of East Baltimore. Police temporarily gained control of the area when they sealed off a 5-block section of the commercial Gay Street section. But violence was renewed, and the governor called in 6,000 National Guardsmen and the state police at 10 p.m. to aid the city's 1,100-man police force. Guardsmen were armed with bayonets and tear gas and were instructed to carry their guns unloaded.

4 persons were killed in Baltimore the night of Apr. 6: one Negro and one white were victims of a fire caused by a firebomb; 2 Negroes were shot to death in 2 separate tavern incidents. More than 300 persons were reported injured. The level of violence rose during the night, fell by morning and then increased steadily throughout Apr. 7. Maj. Gen. George M. Gelston, Maryland adjutant general, kept the National Guardsmen under strict orders not to shoot unless fired on and to return fire only when given orders by an officer or when the source of attack could be definitely identified.

At nightfall Apr. 7 Agnew declared that he had "determined that federal reinforcements are necessary in the city." 2,995 federal troops were immediately dispatched to Baltimore, and Lt. Gen. Robert H. York, a paratroop officer, assumed over-all command from Gelston.

Despite a curfew, bands of youths roamed Baltimore streets, looting and setting fires. Fires were reported scattered over a wide area of the city and not concentrated in particular areas, as in other cities. By morning violence subsided.

Pres. Johnson sent an additional 1,900 federal troops to Baltimore Apr. 8 to reinforce 2,995 federal troops sent earlier, the

5,953 mobilized National Guardsmen and 1,500 state and local police on duty.

In sections east and west of Baltimore's downtown business district, troops used tear gas Apr. 8 to dispell mobs who were reportedly bombarding police and firemen with rocks and bottles and interfering with efforts to control fires. As looting and arson spread late Apr. 8, the first sniper fire was reported. The rioting's 6th fatality was reported early Apr. 9 when a Negro was found burned to death in an apartment over a grocery store that had been firebombed.

At the urging of civil rights leaders, military and police officials agreed Apr. 9 to permit blacks to patrol ghetto neighborhoods as "peacemakers" to try to end the vandalism. State Sen. Clarence Mitchell 3d, a Negro, had met with 150 slum residents that afternoon for a "peace rally" and to have them "pass the word" that the patrols would be out at night to ease the tension. After a 7-p.m. curfew took effect, 16 black "block leaders" under police and military escort toured the riot-torn areas, where they urged residents to clear the streets.

About 80 elected and appointed black officials walked out of a meeting with Agnew Apr. 11 after he charged them with failing to help enough in preventing the riots. He also accused militant young Negroes of inciting the black community to violence. Before the governor finished his remarks someone yelled: "Let's have a black caucus . . . it's an insult." They then walked out and held a meeting at a black parish church in west Baltimore. Agnew had also told the group: "It's no mere coincidence that a national disciple of violence, Mr. Stokely Carmichael, was observed meeting with local black power advocates and known criminals in Baltimore Apr. 3, 1968—3 days before the Baltimore riots began."

Agnew asked Washington Apr. 12 to withdraw the federal troops and defederalize the National Guard as soon as possible. 2,000 troops were removed immediately, and the remaining troops were removed Apr. 13. The National Guard was relieved of active duty Apr. 14 when Agnew lifted the state of emergency.

6 Negroes were shot and killed in racial violence that erupted in Kansas City, Mo. Apr. 9-11. 3,000 National Guardsmen were called to the city, and order was restored by Apr. 14. The violence had begun Apr. 9 after police fired tear gas into a crowd of about 1,000 blacks who had gathered at city hall to hear an address by Mayor Ilus W. Davis. The Negroes, mostly teenagers, had marched to the building to protest the city's decision to keep the schools open that day—the day of the funeral of Martin

Luther King—in contrast to the decision of neighboring Kansas City, Kan. to close its schools. The police said they, had fired the tear gas after a Negro threw a bottle at them. The crowd then dispersed but began a rampage in the black East Side area; they smashed windows, set fires and looted stores. By the end of the night one Negro had been shot and killed by police while he was looting a liquor store; 57 persons were injured (7 by gunfire) and about 270 arrested. About 75 fires were set, and 300 to 400 National Guardsmen were called in.

St. Louis' most serious violence broke out Apr. 10. The first incident occurred in the morning outside predominantly black Lincoln High School, where students were waiting for classes to begin. Police urged the students to go inside the building; when they apparently felt that the students were resisting, they fired tear gas into the crowd. The students ran into the school, and the police followed and fired tear gas again inside the building. The school was evacuated, and most students went home. Despite the incident, the city remained relatively calm most of Apr. 10.

The afternoon of Apr. 10, however, crowds of Negroes began roaming through St. Louis' East Side, and the situation quickly got out of hand. Rioters threw molotov cocktails at police and National Guardsmen, set about 70 fires, looted stores and harassed police and firemen with sniper fire. 4 Negroes were shot and killed by unknown persons in a 4-block area of sniper fire along Prospect Street. 22 persons were injured, about half of them by gunfire, and about 150 persons were arrested, most of them for destruction of property and curfew violations. Police reported that their command post was under sporadic sniper fire, and the police academy was severely damaged by fire. Davis ordered all police to duty, and the National Guard force was increased during the day to 3,000 men.

Although the violence, declined Apr. 11, Davis declared a state of emergency and imposed a dusk-to-dawn curfew. One Negro was shot and killed by police in a gunfight; his death raised St. Louis' 3-day toll to 6. Only 5 confirmed sniping incidents and minor arson were reported Apr. 12, and nobody was injured. Scattered sniping and firebombing continued Apr. 13, but the city moved the curfew back to 11 p.m.

Officials announced Apr. 14 that order had been restored in St. Louis and that about 2,500 of the National Guardsmen were being sent home.

Among other racial disorders that shook U.S. cities following the murder of Martin Luther King:

Cincinnati—Ohio Gov. James A. Rhodes ordered 1,200 National Guardsmen to Cincinnati Apr. 8 to quell rioting that erupted following a memorial service for King in the predominantly black suburb of Avondale. 2 people were killed in the disorders. The disorders spread after James Smith, a black guard, accidentally shot and killed his wife while trying to ward off youthful looters from the English Jewelry Store. Rumors spread, however, that Mrs. Smith had been killed by a frightened policeman. Fire-bombing, looting and window smashing followed.

In suburban Mount Auburn, black teen-agers dragged Noel Wright, 30, a white graduate student and art instructor at the University of Cincinnati, and his wife from their car Apr. 8. They stabbed Wright to death, and 3 black girls beat Mrs. Wright.

Detroit—4,000 National Guardsmen and 400 state policemen were sent to Detroit Apr. 5 to help 4,200 city police quell racial violence. Mayor Jerome P. Cavanagh proclaimed a state of emergency. 2 Negroes were killed by policemen in looting incidents Apr. 5. Gov. George Romney said one looter was killed "accidentally." 1,483 persons were arrested Apr. 5-9; 802 of the arrests were for curfew violations. 12 persons were injured. 378 fires were reported. Romney announced the end of the state of emergency Apr. 12.

Nashville—Sporadic incidents of looting, firebombing and vandalism were reported in Nashville's black sections Apr. 5-9. About 4,000 National Guardsmen were sent into the city Apr. 5-6. 2,000 Guardsmen sealed off the campus of the predominantly black Tennessee A & I State University Apr. 6 after 2 students were wounded in violence Apr. 5, and 50 Guardsmen dispersed a crowd of about 200 students with tear gas. After calm was restored, a curfew was removed Apr. 14.

Newark, N.J.—Sporadic looting broke out in Newark Apr. 9 after dozens of fires were set in the city's predominantly black Central Ward. 15 persons were arrested; 6 persons were reported injured in the fires, and 600 persons were left homeless. 500 black youths patrolled the streets in the evening urging the community to "cool it." Mayor Hugh J. Addonizio Apr. 10 praised the Negroes and whites for cooperating in trying to keep the peace. A fire described as the worst in Newark's history raged through the Central Ward Apr. 20. 35 buildings were destroyed and 500 persons were left homeless, but there were no deaths or major injuries.

N.Y. City—The disorders in N.Y. City Apr. 4-5 were considered relatively minor. The police followed a policy of using large numbers of policemen rather than firearms to restore and maintain order, and many black leaders, including militants, urged Negroes to "cool it" and forego rioting. Several fires were reported Apr. 4, however, and store windows were smashed and their contents looted.

Scattered incidents of looting were reported Apr. 5. Police Commissioner Howard R. Leary put the city's 28,788-man police force on an emergency basis. Police were instructed: "There will be no indiscriminate use of the gun. In these situations, a firecracker can get everybody to draw his weapon. You will not use your revolvers to pick off snipers. In case you see snipers, take cover, notify the command and a special sniper team will be sent. We want looters arrested, but . . . we don't want to hurt anyone." Police Apr. 5 reported 94 arrests, 30 persons injured, including 10 policemen, and 158 incidents of looting, arson and rock throwing.

Volunteer black peace-keepers who fanned out through ghetto neighborhoods in Harlem and Bedford-Stuyvesant Apr. 4-5 were credited with keeping violence to a minimum.

Oakland, Calif.—Bobby James Hutton, 17, an officer of the militant Black Panther Party, was killed and 4 other persons were wounded during a 90-minute gun battle between Negroes and police in predominantly black West Oakland Apr. 6. 2 policemen and Eldridge Cleaver, 32, Black Panther "education minister," were among those injured; 8 persons were arrested. According to the police, firing erupted when policemen stopped to question occupants of 3 parked cars. As the patrolmen stepped from their car, they reportedly were shot at without warning. Then the civilian occupants of the cars fled to a nearby building. Police reinforcements arrived, traded gunfire with the men in the house and then used tear gas. The men in the house finally agreed to surrender. Hutton emerged first. One report indicated that someone had shouted that Hutton had a gun; Police Chief Charles Gain said Hutton bent over and began to run. "The officers could not see his hands clearly and, assuming he was still armed, then ordered him to halt," Gain said. "Upon failure to do so, they fired at him." Black Panther Chairman Bobby George Seale, 31, asserted Apr. 7 that witnesses had "said that Hutton was shot when his hands were in the air." He added Apr. 12 that the police had ordered Hutton to run and then had shot him.

Pittsburgh—Violence swept black areas of Pittsburgh Apr. 4-8. 5,200 National Guardsmen and 375 state police were called in to assist the 1,500-man city police force. More than 1,100 persons were arrested. The police and Guardsmen were ordered not to shoot looters.

Scattered incidents of vandalism and firebombings were reported Apr. 5. The disorders spread Apr. 6 from the predominantly black Hill district to the North Side, where black gangs set fires, smashed windows and stoned cars. More than 90 persons were reported injured. Gov. Raymond P. Shafer Apr. 7 declared a state of emergency and called in the state police and National Guard. 2,200 Guardsmen and 300 state police moved into the city immediately. Among the 24 persons reported injured Apr. 7 were 2 Guardsmen, 3 firemen and 4 policemen.

The number of fires reported since Apr. 4 rose Apr. 8 to 190. But Pittsburgh was generally reported calm Apr. 9, and the National Guardsmen were withdrawn from the city Apr. 11-12.

Trenton—Harlan M. Joseph, 19, a black member of the Mayor's Youth Council and divinity student at Lincoln University (Oxford, Pa.), was shot to death in Trenton Apr. 9 by Michael A. Castiello, a white policeman. The shooting took place during the 2d night of sporadic outbreaks of racial violence. State police were called in to aid city policemen. More than 235 persons were arrested Apr. 9-12, in most cases for violating a 9-p.m.-to-6-a.m. curfew imposed by Mayor Carmen J. Armenti Apr. 9. 30 persons were injured; dozens of stores were looted and/or damaged by fire.

According to police, Joseph was one of 5 black youths who smashed the display windows of a haberdashery store across the street from Trenton's city hall and stole apparel. Police said Joseph was "a looter, and loot was recovered from his person." Detective Capt. Leon Foley said that Patrolman Castiello had fired a warning shot in the air and then had tried to wound one of the fleeing youths in the leg. "But his gun was jostled by the crowd just as he fired," Foley said, "and the bullet struck the Joseph kid in the back." Other witnesses said the Joseph youth was trying to stop the looters and was not looting.

Hughes withdrew the Guard Apr. 12.

Memphis Strike Settled

Pres. Johnson sent Labor Undersecy. James Reynolds to Memphis Apr. 5,1968 to meet with representatives of the city and the sanitation workers union in hopes of breaking the deadlock of the 8-week-old strike that had culminated in King's death. The U.S. District Court in Memphis Apr. 3 had enjoined King from leading his 2d protest march in Memphis Apr. 8, but after King's death, Bayard Rustin, executive director of the A. Philip Randolph Institute, the Rev. James Bevel and the Rev. James Lawson, chairman of the Congress on the March for Equality (COME), announced plans to hold the march as a memorial tribute as well as a demonstration of support for the strike.

During the night of Apr. 4-5 more than 30 persons were injured in rioting in Memphis. At least 3 major fires were reported and dozens of stores looted. There were reports of sniper fire. The first death resulting from violence was reported Apr. 6. Gov. Buford Ellington (D., Tenn.) immediately ordered 4,000 National Guardsmen into the city.

Mayor Henry Loeb said Apr. 5 that "in view of the tragic circumstances" the city would withdraw its objection to the march (it took place Apr. 8) and he would meet with the strike mediator to "get this thing behind us and find a solution to our differences." A settlement of the strike was reached Apr. 16. The agreement included a 2-step 15¢-an-hour salary increase, city recognition of the union as the "designated representative" of the city's public works employes; a dues checkoff; promotions on the basis of seniority; a "no-strike" clause. (The workers had been paid $1.60 and $2.25 an hour.)

'Shoot-to-Kill' Controversy

There was widespread controversy over Chicago Mayor Richard J. Daley's instructions to Chicago police Apr. 15, 1968 to "shoot to kill" arsonists and to "shoot to maim or cripple" looters in future rioting.

New York Mayor John V. Lindsay said at a news conference Apr. 16: "We happen to think that protection of life ... is more important than protecting property or anything else. ... We are not going to turn disorder into chaos through the unprincipled use of armed force. In short, we are not going to shoot children in New York City." "There were incidents last summer when persons thought to be looters were killed, but it turned out upon later investigation that they were not looters."

At a news conference in Trenton, N.J. Apr. 16, Gov. Richard J. Hughes scored the shooting of looters and arsonists. "My own judgment is that the sanctity of human life is such that an intelligent response by the police will result in arrests rather than shootings," Hughes declared.

Following an address to the American Society of Newspaper Editors in Washington Apr. 17, in response to a question from the audience, Atty. Gen. Ramsey Clark repudiated Daley's instructions as "a very dangerous escalation of the problems we are so intent on solving." "I think that to resort to deadly force is contrary to the total experience of law enforcement in this country," Clark asserted. He said: "I do not believe it [the use of deadly force] is permissible except in self-defense or when it is necessary to protect the lives of others." Earlier in his speech, Clark had sharply criticized the indiscriminate use of force since it could provoke counterattack by rioters and encourage "terrorist and guerilla tactics" and risk "permanent alienation among minorities." He said that the FBI manual prohibited the use of "deadly force" except for self-defense or to "protect the lives of others."

Justice Department officials acknowledged Apr. 13 that methods of riot control in the violence that followed Martin Luther King's death had been based on a "humanitarian" plan of restraint and a minimum use of gunfire, the *N.Y. Times* reported Apr. 14. The policy, largely the work of Atty. Gen. Clark and ex-Deputy Defense Secy. Cyrus R. Vance, called for the use of "overwhelming law enforcement manpower" coupled with military and police restraint. The heavy use of tear gas was substituted for gunfire. A department official said: "That old stuff about 'looters will be shot on sight' is for the history books and maybe the movies. It's for people who don't know how it is to be in a riot where, if you shoot, they shoot back and you've got a lot of dead cops and troops along with the dead citizens." "We have drawn back from all that the law allows because it is our duty to stop riots, not to kill rioters."

Daley, in a statement Apr. 17 to the City Council, revised his comment. He said: Arsonists and looters "should be restrained if possible by minimum force" but could not be given "permissive rights" for their criminal behavior. Residents of the West Side, where most of the violence occurred, "had one universal demand— protect us from the arsonists, from the looter, from the mob and its leaders." "We cannot resign ourselves to the proposition that civil protest must lead to death or devastation, to abandonment of the law that is fundamental for the preservation of the rights of the people and their freedom."

Pres. Johnson, in a letter to Defense Secy. Clark M. Clifford (made public Apr. 23), praised the "wise and restrained use of force" by federal troops and National Guardsmen in the rioting following King's death. The President noted that not one death had been caused by military forces. He said that the more than 26,500 Army troops and 47,000 National Guardsmen had "fulfilled with distinction an assignment that was regrettable but unavoidable."

Assassin Captured & Convicted

James Earl Ray, 40, was arrested by Scotland Yard detectives at Heathrow Airport in London June 8, 1968. Ray had been the subject of a an intensive manhunt organized after the murder of Martin Luther King.

Ray was apprehended when he went to the airport to board a plane for Brussels. Arrested on charges of possessing a fraudulent Canadian passport and of carrying a revolver without a permit, Ray was arraigned on the London charges June 10 under the name Ramon George Sneyd (the name on his passport). The same day, at the request of the U.S. embassy, a provisional warrant was issued for his extradition to the U.S. to stand trial for murder.

The search for Ray was said to have been the most extensive in police history. The FBI issued a federal fugitive warrant in Birmingham, Ala. Apr. 17 charging Eric Starvo Galt, 36, with conspiracy in the assassination of King. The warrant charged that Galt—later revealed to be Ray—had conspired with a man "whom he alleged to be his brother" to "injure, oppress, threaten or intimidate" King. A Tennessee warrant charging Galt with first-degree murder was issued in Memphis the same day. The FBI announced Apr. 19 that Eric Starvo Galt was an alias of Ray, who had escaped from the Missouri State Penitentiary Apr. 23,

1967 after serving 7 years of a 20-year sentence for armed robbery and auto theft. He had been arrested and/or convicted on 5 occasions between 1949 and 1959. Ray was indicted under the name of Eric Starvo Galt in Memphis Apr. 23 on charges of murder and conspiring to violate the civil rights of King. He was reindicted May 7 under his real name.

The likelihood that King's murder was the work of a conspiracy had been discounted by Atty. Gen. Clark in Memphis Apr. 5 immediately after the slaying. At an impromptu news conference, Clark said that there was no evidence of a "widespread plot—this appears to have been the act of a single individual." He reiterated Apr. 7: "We have evidence of one man on the run. There is no evidence that more were involved." But as evidence accumulated, a widespread feeling grew that more than one person had been involved in the slaying and that Ray might have been a hired killer. The day after Ray's capture, however, Clark, interviewed on the ABC-TV program "Issues and Answers," again held that Ray had acted alone. "We have no evidence of any other involvement by any other person or people," he said.

Ray was extradited by a London court July 2 and returned to the U.S. July 19. On arraignment in Memphis July 22, he entered a plea of not guilty; he was charged with murder and carrying a dangerous weapon. But Ray pleaded guilty Mar. 10, 1969 to the murder of King. He was sentenced the same day to serve 99 years in prison. Judge W. Preston Battle ordered Ray to the Tennessee State Prison in Nashville after brief court proceedings during which Ray indicated that he disagreed with the prosecution's theory that there had been no conspiracy.

Poor People's Campaign Continues Despite King's Death

The Poor People's Campaign, planned by the late Martin Luther King in Aug. 1967, brought 9 caravans of poor people to Washington, D.C. beginning May 11, 1968. As proposed by King, the campaign was marked by massive lobbying by the nation's poor in Washington to pressure Congress and the Administration to enact legislation to reduce poverty. Thousands of participants encamped in a canvas-and-plywood "Resurrection City U.S.A." in the capital and took part in demonstrations. The caravans, started from various parts of the country May 2-17, held rallies and picked up additional participants along the way to Washington.

Mrs. Martin Luther King Jr. May 12 led a 12-block Mother's Day march of "welfare mothers" from 20 cities to the Cardozo High School Stadium in the center of Washington's black ghetto. Mrs. King declared at the rally, attended by 5,000 participants, that she would try to enlist the support of "all the women of this nation in a campaign of conscience." She stressed the need for nonviolence but admitted that it was "not an easy way, particularly in this day when violence is almost fashionable, and in this society, where violence against poor people and minority groups is routine." But, she continued, "I must remind you that starving a child is violence. Suppressing a culture is violence. Neglecting school children is violence. Punishing a mother and her family is violence. . . . Ignoring medical needs is violence. Contempt for poverty is violence. Even the lack of will power to help humanity is a sick and sinister form of violence."

Robert Kennedy Assassinated, Study of Violence Ordered

Sen. Robert F. Kennedy, 42, was shot to death by a Jordanian Arab youth in Los Angeles June 5, 1968 shortly after Kennedy had won the California Democratic Presidential primary. Kennedy died June 6. The assassin, Sirham Bishara Sirhan, 24, was seized on the spot. Kennedy was buried in Arlington National Cemetary near the grave of his brother John F. Kennedy. In the mood of national mourning, Congress passed an anti-crime bill and, after urging by Pres. Johnson, a bill to curb the mail-order purchase of firearms. Sirhan was tried and convicted in 1969 of Kennedy's murder.

Kennedy was shot as he was leaving a rally in celebration of his victory in the California primary. He was gunned down less than 5 years after the assassination of his brother Pres. Kennedy and only 2 months after the assassination of the Martin Luther King. As a wave of sorrow, shame and indignation engulfed the nation, Pres. Johnson announced that he was creating a special commission to study violence in the U.S. with a view to finding out "how we can stop it."

The attack occurred at about 12:16 a.m. PDT June 5 about 3 minutes after Kennedy left the victory rally in the Ambassador Hotel. In the press of a happy throng, Kennedy entered a kitchen passageway en route to a press conference in another room. As he shook hands with the kitchen workers, his assassin suddenly opened

fire with a .22-caliber pistol. 8 shots were fired, and Kennedy fell
to the floor, hit in the head by one bullet and in the back of the
right arm pit by 2 others. 5 other persons were wounded, none
fatally, by the shots.

Accompanied by his wife, Ethel, who was with him when he
was shot, and campaign aide Fred Dutton, Kennedy was rushed by
ambulance first to Central Receiving Hospital, where Dr. Vasilius
F. Bazilauskas reported later that Kennedy arrived almost dead.
After external heart massage, adrenalin and use of a heart-lung
machine, Kennedy revived slightly. The dying man was then
speeded to the better-equipped Good Samaritan Hospital, where
surgeons worked for almost 4 hours to remove bullet fragments
from his brain. The fatal bullet had entered the cerebellum after
penetrating the mastoid bone behind the right ear. Kennedy died
at 1:44 a.m.

Sirhan, an unemployed clerk, resident alien and Christian
Arab, was seized with a revolver in his hand moments after Kennedy was shot. Roosevelt Grier, 287-pound defensive tackle for
the Los Angeles Rams football team, wrestled the gun from the
suspect while Kennedy lay on the floor. Grier sought to save the
suspect from assault by the crowd until Los Angeles policemen
carried the prisoner out by his arms and legs. The then-unidenti-
fied suspect, refusing to give police any information about
himself, was arraigned at 7 a.m. June 5 in municipal court
as "John Doe." He was charged, in a complaint by District
Atty. Evelle Younger, with 6 counts of assault with intent to
murder.

Los Angeles Mayor Samuel W. Yorty revealed June 5 that 2
notebooks had been discovered in the defendant's home and that
one of them contained "a direct reference to the necessity to
assassinate Sen. Kennedy before June 5 [the first anniversary of
the 1967 Israeli-Arab war]."

After Kennedy's death, Sirhan was indicted June 7 by a Los
Angeles County grand jury on a charge of first-degree murder. He
was also indicted on 5 counts of assault with intent to kill the 5
other persons injured. Sirhan entered no plea. His counsel, Deputy
Public Defender Wilbur Littlefield, was granted a delay for psychiatric examination of Sirhan.

Sirhan was found guilty of first-degree murder Apr. 17, 1969.
The jury decided Apr. 23 that the penalty should be death in the
gas chamber, but the penalty was never actually imposed.

Pres. Johnson pleaded with Americans June 5, 1968 to "put an end to violence and to the preaching of violence." He ordered Secret Service protection for all the announced Presidential candidates of major parties. (Authorizing legislation for such protection was passed immediately by Congress June 6 and signed by the President a few hours later.) In a TV broadcast the evening of June 5, Mr. Johnson announced his creation of the commission to "examine this tragic phenomenon" of violence in the nation's life. It would be "wrong" to "conclude from this act that our country is sick" and had lost "its common decency," he said. But the murders of John and Robert Kennedy and of Martin Luther King gave "ample warning that in a climate of extremism, of disrespect for law, of contempt for the rights of others, violence may bring down the very best among us."

Johnson appointed the following citizens as members of the commission to probe violence: Milton Eisenhower, ex-president of Johns Hopkins University; Archbishop Terence J. Cooke of New York; attorney Albert Jenner of Chicago; ex-Amb.-to-Luxembourg Patricia Harris; philosopher-longshoreman Eric Hoffer; Sens. Philip Hart (D., Mich.) and Roman L. Hruska (R., Neb.); Reps. Hale Boggs (D., La.) and William M. McCulloch (R., O.); and U.S. Judge Leon Higginbotham.

Johnson met June 10 with his new Commission on Violence and, in a televised statement, posed the principal questions the panel would attempt to answer. He charged the commission "to undertake a penetrating search for the causes and prevention of violence—a search into our national life, our past as well as our present, our traditions as well as our institutions, our culture, our customs and our laws." One of every 5 U.S. Presidents since 1865 had been assassinated (Lincoln, Garfield, McKinley and Kennedy) and attempts had been made on the lives of 3 others (Theodore Roosevelt, Franklin Roosevelt and Truman), Johnson said. He noted that guns were involved in more than 6,500 murders each year in the U.S. "This compares with 30 in England, 99 in Canada, 68 in West Germany and 37 in Japan," he said. The President asserted that the commission must weigh whether American society could "any longer tolerate the widespread possession of deadly firearms by private citizens."

Among other questions Johnson put to the panel: "Does the democratic process, which stresses exchanges of ideas, permit less physical contact with masses of people, as a matter of security against the deranged individual and obsessed fanatic?" "Is there something in the environment of American society or the structure of our institutions that causes disrespect for the law, contempt for the rights of others and incidents of violence?" "Has permissiveness toward extreme behavior in our society encouraged an increase of violence?" "Are the seeds of violence nurtured through the public's airwaves, the screens of neighborhood theaters, the news media and other forms of communication that reach the family and our young?" "What is the relationship between mass disruption of public order and individual acts of violence?"

Congress passed and sent to the President June 6, about 12 hours after Kennedy's death, an omnibus anticrime bill (HR 5037), the Crime Control & Safe Streets Act, barring the interstate shipment and out-of-state purchase of handguns. But public pressure was mounting for Congressional enactment of stricter gun-control legislation. In a gun-control message to Congress June 6, Johnson had referred to HR5037 as a "halfway measure" that "leaves the deadly commerce in lethal shotguns and rifles without effective control." (He also urged each state governor June 6 to review his state's gun laws and "amend them where necessary . . . to fully protect the citizens . . . from the deadly weapons that are now in dangerous hands.") The Administration June 10 sent Congress its proposals to ban the mail-order sale of rifles, shotguns and ammunition, the over-the-counter sale of such firearms to out-of-state residents and the sale of rifles and shotguns to minors. (The measure was passed by the Senate Oct. 9 and by the House Oct. 10.) Johnson asked Congress in a message June 24 to require national registration of every firearm and licensing of every gun-owner. The registrations would go into a computer listing at the FBI's National Crime Information Center. The licensing program should be carried out by the states, Johnson said, but he suggested that minimum federal standards be established and federal licensing be required for states not meeting the standards within 2 years.

Rioters Battle Police in Miami During GOP Convention

While speakers at the 1968 Republican National Convention in Miami were decrying violence and lawlessness in the nation's cities, racial tensions exploded in Liberty City, a black section of northwestern Miami several miles from Convention Hall. The disorders grew into 2 days of looting, fire bombing and shooting in which 3 persons were killed and scores injured. Gov. Claude Kirk called in the National Guard Aug. 8.

The violence reportedly erupted at a black "vote power" rally the evening of Aug. 7 when a white newsman refused to show his credentials. 52 persons were arrested that night, and an 8-square-block area of Liberty City was cordoned off by police. Mayor Steve Clark of Miami toured the area appealing for calm, as did Kirk and the Rev. Ralph D. Abernathy, president of the Southern Christian Leadership Conference. Abernathy broadcast a TV appeal to Miami's citizens to stay off the streets and help restore order. The acting Miami police chief, Lt. Col. Paul Denham, reported that calm had returned to the troubled area by 10 p.m., 4 hours after the rioting began.

More serious violence broke out the afternoon of Aug. 8 when black crowds battled police at the site of a meeting that both Kirk and Abernathy had promised to address. Neither appeared. As the rioting continued, 1,000 armed National Guard troops were sent to the area, and the Florida Highway Patrol riot wagon, an armored truck that spewed tear gas, went into action. Motorists driving home from work were dragged from their cars and beaten. Several liquor and grocery stores were looted, and fires were set. A curfew was imposed over a 250-block area. Kirk warned that "whatever force is needed" would be used to quell the violence. By 4 p.m., Sheriff E. Wilson Purdy reported that the situation was "under firm control," though Guardsmen and police continued to patrol the streets.

During the course of the Aug. 8 rioting, 3 Negroes were killed in gun battles with police. The dead were J. J. Austin, 28, thought by police to have been a sniper, Moses Cannon, 27, and Ejester B. Cleveland, 45, a passerby who had been caught in the cross-fire. At one point the disorders spread to within a mile of the Miami Beach convention area. Dade County Mayor Chuck Hall accused "people from out of town" of instigating the trouble. "It is no accident," he said, "that the first race riot in recent Miami history broke out during the Republican National Convention, when the city was swarming with newspaper, wire-service and television reporters."

City and county officials agreed Aug. 10 to release without bond about 250 of those arrested during the riots; the officials also sent medical teams into black areas to treat persons suffering from the effects of tear gas. In return, black Miami leaders promised to work to cool the tempers of Negroes angered at the police force's alleged brutality in quelling the violence.

The President's Commission on Violence was told Feb. 11, 1969 that the Aug. 1968 riots in Miami had "originated

spontaneously and almost entirely out of the accumulated depriva-
tions, discriminations and frustrations of the [Miami] black
community."

Violence in Chicago During Democratic Convention

The 38th Democratic National Convention, held in Chicago
Aug. 26-29, 1968, was beset by violence as opponents of U.S.
policy in Vietnam demonstrated and clashed with police outside
the convention hall.

Mayor Richard J. Daley had expressed his determination to
keep tight control of his city during the convention, and he used
forceful methods to do so in the face of an influx of youthful demonstrators and threatened violence. The 34-year-old International
Amphitheatre, which housed the convention, was turned into a
virtual fortress. A barbed-wire and chainlink fence was built to
enclose the building. On one side all entrances were closed, and
owners of nearby buildings were ordered to keep windows shut.
All persons entering the building were required to show credentials at a series of checking points, and policemen were posted on
the roof. A dummy portico was built at the main door, reportedly
to block the aim of any would-be sniper.

Thousands of antiwar, hippie, Yippie (Youth International
Party) and other protesters converged on the city and called for
mass demonstrations, marches and sleep-ins in city parks. (Demonstrators originally estimated that 100,000 protesters would come
to Chicago, but it was reported that only about 10,000-15,000
actually arrived) The major coordinating group for the demonstrations was the National Mobilization Committee to End the
War in Vietnam, a coalition of about 100 antiwar groups ranging
in outlook from leftwing militance to center moderation. Almost
all of the protesters were in their teens or 20s, and almost all were
white.

Daley placed Chicago's entire 11,900-man police force on 12-
hour shifts. On his request. Gov. Samuel H. Shapiro called up
5,649 Illinois National Guardsmen Aug. 20. And about 7,500
Regular Army troops were placed on stand-by duty.

A week of tensions and sporadic violence before and during
the convention blossomed into full-scale rioting Aug. 28 when
police and National Guardsmen battled youths in downtown Chicago. At least 100 persons were injured, including 25 policemen;
more than 175 were arrested. The Aug. 28 violence followed an
afternoon rally when protesters tried to leave Grant Park and

march towards the Loop area in an attempt to reach the International Amphitheatre. To keep the demonstrators from the amphitheater, security forces chased them along downtown streets and attacked them with clubs, rifle butts, tear gas and chemical Mace. Much of the action took place in front of the Conrad Hilton Hotel, convention headquarters, where delegates' wives, tourists and bystanders looked on and were sometimes drawn into the violence. Newsmen estimated that 2,000 to 5,000 youths were involved in the disorders Wednesday (Aug. 28) night. Some protesters threw bottles and rocks at the police; many carried the flags of anarchy and of the Viet Cong.

A series of marches Aug. 29 involved thousands of demonstrators, some of them led by Democratic delegates; each demonstration was an attempt to march on the International Amphitheatre, but all were turned back by the police and National Guard. One march, beginning with 200 persons and swelling quickly, was organized and led by the Wisconsin delegation as a protest against police "brutality" in suppressing demonstrations the night before. The marchers walked $1\frac{1}{2}$ miles before they were met by a solid police line backed by Guardsmen. At this point, most of the demonstrators turned back. Black comedian Dick Gregory Aug. 29 led about 3,000 persons along Michigan Ave. towards the convention site. The protesters, halted by police, insisted that they had the right to continue through the police barrier, and they stepped through one by one. More than 150 were arrested, including Gregory, Tommy Fraser, a delegate from Oklahoma, and columnist Murray Kempton, a New York delegate. Guardsmen used tear gas to disperse the remaining demonstrators.

The Aug. 29 marches also followed a Grant Park rally attended by 2,000 to 3,000 youths. Tom Hayden, leader of the National Mobilization Committee to End the War in Vietnam, said at the rally: "It may be that the era of organized, peaceful and orderly demonstrations is coming to an end and that other methods will be needed." He urged the youths to return home and create "one, 2, 300 Chicagos." Rennie Davis, another Mobilization Committee coordinator, advocated a U.S. National Liberation Front whose slogan would be: "There can be no peace in the United States until there is peace in Vietnam."

During the week's intermittent eruptions of violence, brutality charges were repeatedly leveled at the Chicago police. Demonstrators and newsmen charged that police had covered or removed their badges to prevent identification. Mayor Daley defended the city's police Aug. 28. "Security is what we need here for a decent convention," he said. At a news conference Aug. 29 he described the demonstrators as "terrorists" who had come to "assault, harass and taunt the police into reacting before television cameras." "In the heat of emotion and riot," he conceded, "some policemen may have overreacted, but to judge the entire police force by the alleged action of a few would be . . . unfair." The Democratic Presidential nominee, Vice Pres. Hubert H. Humphrey, backed Daley Aug. 31 with a denunciation of those who resorted to "planned" and "premeditated" violence during the convention. He declared that he had "little or no time" for those who reject the normal political system in the belief that "all they have to do is riot and they'll get their way." He added that it was time to "quit pretending that Mayor Daley did anything that was wrong" in ordering strong police action in Chicago. Vice Presidential nominee Edmund S. Muskie, questioned on NBC's "Meet the Press" program Sept. 1, said he had an "impression" that the police in Chicago had "overreacted." He said that there had been "trouble-makers" bent on disruption and that Daley had been forced to "organize to take care of the situation." But he asserted that the police, as "human beings, moved by events," had sometimes gone too far, and "a lot of innocent people were hurt."

The Chicago police reported Aug. 30 that more than 650 people had been arrested during the week's disturbances.

Reaction of the news media to the alleged police brutality was especially strong, and 5 newspapers, 2 news magazines and 3 TV networks sent a joint protest to Daley Aug. 31, asking him to order "an investigation by a responsible group of distinguished and disinterested citizens." The protest said: "Newsmen were repeatedly singled out by policemen and deliberately beaten and harassed. Cameras were broken and film was destroyed. The obvious purpose was to discourage or prevent reporting of an important confrontation between police and demonstrators which the American public has the right to know about."

Daley Sept. 3 asked the 3 major TV networks to make available an hour of prime program time "for the purpose of balancing the one-sided portrayal of the controversial events that were telecast during the meeting of the Democratic National Convention." "Certainly, under all principles of fairness," he stated, "the background and planning for the purpose of disrupting the city and the national convention, the tactics used by the demonstrators, the biographies of the organizers and leaders, the role of the law enforcement agencies and grave implications of these events to the cities of America, which were not portrayed during the convention coverage, should be presented to the American public." NBC replied with an offer to let Daley appear on a special one-hour edition of the interview program "Meet the Press," an offer which Daley rejected Sept. 4; ABC Sept. 5 made a similar offer of time on its interview program "Issues and Answers," but Daley rejected this as well. CBS turned down the mayor's request Sept. 5.

Daley, however, accepted an offer of prime time from the WGN Continental Broadcasting Co., based in Chicago, and from Metromedia, which had TV and radio outlets in New York, Los Angeles, San Francisco, Washington and Kansas City. The one-hour program, broadcast Sept. 15, defended the police force's role in the demonstrations, asserting that it had been ordered to clear the streets and protect the Conrad Hilton Hotel, convention headquarters, and its guests. Included in the film was a display of "weapons" said to have been used by the demonstrators—bricks, broken glass, a molotov cocktail, beer cans, rocks and slats from park benches. Interviews referred to "tremendous" provocation of the police by the youths. Daley appeared briefly Aug. 29 in an interview filmed with Walter Cronkite in which he justified the use of the National Guard because of the danger of assassination of the Presidential candidates. He accused "hard-core radicals" of causing the disorders.

Daley Sept. 6 issued a report defending the Chicago police force. The report said that the action taken by the police had been provoked by out-of-town "revolutionaries." It said that 60 persons had required emergency treatment at hospitals. (The Medical Committee for Human Rights, which had more than 400 doctors, nurses and medical students on duty in Chicago during convention week, reported different figures Sept. 10. Dr. Quentin D. Young, former national chairman of the organization, said that 125 persons had been treated in the emergency rooms of 7 Chicago hospitals. He said: 425 others had been treated at aid centers for injuries from billy clubs and for the effects of tear gas and chemical Mace; more than 200 persons were treated on the streets by roving medical teams, and 400 were given first aid for the effects of tear gas and Mace.)

David Ginsburg, director of the National Advisory Commission on Civil Disorders, criticized both the demonstrators and the Chicago police Sept. 9. He said: "The demonstrators had a right to demonstrate—peacefully—and they should have been allowed to do so. Facilities, even protection and possibly food, should have been provided." Ginsburg added that "some demonstrators deliberately tried to provoke the police," and "police were injured and wounded." "Obscenity and profanity, coupled with attacks—using weapons ranging from broken glass and rocks to lye—were used." Criticizing newsmen for biased reporting on the disorders, Ginsburg said: "The police undoubtedly reacted, but the media must also bear the burden of guilt in failing to portray the true nature of the organizations and the degree of provocation." "A balanced picture was not presented to the country."

James Ridgeway reported in the *New Republic* Sept. 7 that "the clashes between police and demonstrators began as calculated maneuvers" of the Mobilization Committee and Yippies, whose leaders "talked enthusiastically about little acts of violence . . . to provoke the police and manipulate the liberal McCarthy youths into their own ranks."

A Gallup Poll released Sept. 17 reported that 56% of a national sample of adults had approved of the way Chicago police handled the demonstrations, while 31% disapproved. 47% of the sample's young adults (aged 21-29) approved and 41% disapproved. Only 18% of the blacks sampled supported the police action, compared with 59% of the whites; 63% of the Negroes and 29% of the whites polled disapproved of the action.

A report issued Dec. 1 by a special panel of the National Commission on the Causes & Prevention of Violence sharply criticized members of the Chicago police force for excessive brutality in their handling of the demonstrations. The 233-page report, entitled "Rights in Conflict," charged that the actions of some of the police had amounted to a "police riot" that far outweighed the demonstrations as a source of the violence that swept the convention city. The report was published by the commission without evaluation or comment. The report's summary charged that some Chicago policemen had responded to provocation by demonstrators with "unrestrained and indiscriminate police violence . . . often inflicted upon persons who had broken no law, disobeyed no order, made no threat." It concluded that the loss of control and discipline of some of the police under "exceedingly provocative" circumstances "can perhaps be understood, but not condoned."

The special panel's investigators said that the police had been conditioned to expect that violence "against demonstrators, as against rioters, would be condoned by city officials." Mayor Daley's controversial "shoot-to-kill" order to police during the riots that followed the death of Martin Luther King was cited as an example of the attitude displayed by Chicago officials.

The report included a section describing police assaults on newsmen covering the convention. Investigators found that of the 300 newsmen covering the parks and streets of Chicago during convention week, 63 reporters and photographers had been physically attacked by police. The behavior of both the demonstrators and police was said to have been substantially influenced by the presence of the news media.

The report was the work of a 212-member study team set up by Daniel Walker, 46, president of the Chicago Crime Commission.

Walker, acting at the request of the national commission, assembled the team from among members of the Chicago commission, backed with lawyers and investigators loaned for the project by Chicago banks and law firms.

Chicago Police Superintendent James B. Conlisk said Dec. 3 that the term "police riot" used in the report was a distortion. He noted that 9 policemen had been suspended, one had resigned and 4 others had been recommended for dismissal because of their actions during the disorders.

Dr. Milton S. Eisenhower, chairman of the national violence commission, said Dec. 1 that the Walker report had been released promptly due to the "widespread interest" in its subject. He added that the commission neither approved nor disapproved the study. (At its opening session Sept. 18, the commission had heard conflicting testimony about the Chicago disorders from Atty. Gen. Ramsey Clark and FBI Dir. J. Edgar Hoover. Clark had warned of the dangers of police violence while Hoover had said that the Chicago police had had "no alternative but to use force.")

Urban Disorders, Police Become Targets

Racial disturbances shook Salisbury, Md. May 18-20, 1968 after the fatal shooting of a black burglary suspect by a white detective. Gov. Spiro T. Agnew declared a state of emergency May 18 and ordered National Guardsmen—ultimately 1,200 of them—into the city to put down the violence. 14 persons were arrested, and 12 persons suffered minor injuries. The trouble began May 18 when 300 blacks gathered in front of the police station in protest against the 3 p.m. shooting of deaf-mute Daniel Kenneth Henry, 22, by a white policeman, Jerry Mason, 26. Henry, it was reported, was being questioned when a struggle started, and he was shot when he seized a policeman's pistol, ran, disregarded a warning shot and failed to hear a police order to stop. News of the incident spread to the black sections of the city, and Negroes gathered at the station at about 6 p.m. to demand an explanation. Mayor Dallas G. Truitt promised a full investigation and announced that the detective had been suspended. (Mason was charged with manslaughter May 19).

Truitt May 18 ordered a curfew. By 7:30 p.m., however, gangs of Negroes swept down Main Street, smashing windows, throwing stones, looting, and setting fire to buildings. The riots, involving an estimated 1,000 blacks in groups of 200 to 300, lasted for 3 hours. National Guardsmen were called into action, and the police battled the crowds with dogs and tear gas. Fresh violence flared May 19 when a crowd gathered and Negroes threw stones at firemen fighting a fire in a black neighborhood. The police used dogs and tear gas and were aided by heavy rain in their efforts to protect the firemen. Dogs were also used by the police to disperse 20 Negroes in front of a civil rights leader's home. A brief clash erupted May 20, and Guardsmen used tear gas to break up a group of 25 to 30 Negroes blocking an intersection. But after several days of comparative calm, Agnew ended the state of emergency May 26, and released the remaining 100 Guardsmen.

More than 100 persons were arrested by police and National Guardsmen during 2 days of rioting in Akron, O. July 17-18. Mayor John Ballard declared a state of emergency and imposed a dusk-to-dawn curfew July 18 after fire bombs and looting disrupted the city's major black section in Southwest Akron. At one point a crowd of up to 100 Negroes charged a group of National Guardsmen and threw chairs and bottles before they were repelled by tear gas. After a stricter curfew had been imposed and more National Guard patrols had been added, relative calm was reported in the city July 22.

Violence broke out in the black district of Gary, Ind. after 2 policemen tried to arrest 2 black rape suspects late July 27. Order was not restored until July 30. The disorders began when members of a black motorcycle gang, the Sin City Disciples, reportedly tried to prevent the arrest. Windows were smashed at nearby stores, and looting and arson began. Mayor Richard G. Hatcher declared a state of emergency July 28 and ordered a curfew. Shooting incidents were reported the nights of July 28 and 29. Hatcher announced July 30 the formation of a commission of 14 black community leaders to serve as liaison between the black citizens and the city officials.

10 policemen and a reporter were wounded by gunfire in a predominantly black neighborhood in Peoria, Ill. July 30. They

were shot after a rock-throwing incident involving about 50 youths escalated into an exchange of shotgun fire with police.

4 policemen were wounded in 2 sniping incidents near the same street corner in the Crown Heights section of Brooklyn (N.Y. City) in August and September. Patrolmen Thomas Dockery, 31, and Leonard Fleck, 28, were wounded by shotgun blasts Aug. 2 as they left their car to answer a false call for help. Sgt. Peter Kunik and Patrolman James C. Rigney were injured Sept. 12 by shots fired from the top of a 4-story apartment building when their car stopped for a red light.

A curfew was imposed in 2 adjacent suburbs of Chicago—Harvey and Dixmoor—following a disorder Aug. 6 in which 6 policemen were injured by shotgun pellets, Cook County Under-sheriff C. Bernard Carey Aug. 7 blamed the disturbance on a group of young Negroes, the Black Elephants, said to be an affiliate of the city's Blackstone Rangers. The shots were fired as about 150 policemen were restoring order after some 200 young blacks had begun stoning cars along a street dividing the 2 suburbs. The area had been tense following the fatal shooting of a black youth by a policeman several weeks earlier.

A state policeman and a black youth were killed and 2 policemen were wounded in the Detroit suburb of Inkster Aug. 7-8. In the opening incident, a passing motorist and 2 policemen in a patrol car, one black and one white, were shot and slightly wounded by snipers Aug. 7. Detective Robert R. Gonser, 34, investigating in the area in an unmarked car early Aug. 8, was killed by a shot fired by an occupant of another car. James E. Matthers, 16, was killed, reportedly by police, when he ran during questioning after Gonser's death.

3 Negroes were killed and about 44 persons, including 6 policemen, were injured Aug. 11-12, 1968 when a 3-hour clash between police and blacks brought to a violent close the 3d annual Watts Summer Festival in Los Angeles. A week previously 2 incidents at the beginning of the festival had left 3 Negroes killed and 6 persons injured. The Watts festival was held to commemorate the Watts riot of Aug. 1965. The Aug. 11-12 clash took place after an angry crowd began throwing rocks and bottles at several policemen who were arresting a black woman on a drunken driving charge late Aug. 11. Soon after police reinforcements arrived, gunfire came from the crowd of several thousand people who were leaving the festival. A police officer said that he had seen people in the crowd being hit by shots. Police Chief Thomas Reddin said Aug. 12 that "there were indications" that one of the 3 Negroes killed had been

shot by police but that the other 2 were not shot by police. During the violence that followed, shops were broken into, guns were stolen and fire-bombs were thrown. 35 people were arrested.

In one of the earlier Watts incidents, Stephen K. Bartholomew, 21, Robert Lawrence, 22, and Thomas Melvin Lewis, 18, had been killed Aug. 5 and 2 white policemen, Norman J. Roberge, 29, and Ruby Limas, 25, had been injured in a gunfight at a gas station about 8 miles northwest of Watts after the police had stopped the men for questioning. Reddin told newsmen Aug. 6 that 2 of the 3 men killed had been Black Panthers members. (The festival had been closed temporarily Aug. 6 after 4 persons in the crowd were wounded by men firing from moving cars. Police said that some shots had been returned from the crowd.)

2 nights of violence began in St. Paul, Minn. Aug. 30 at a teenage dance. It resulted in 12 arrests and injuries to 52 persons, including 4 policemen wounded by gunshots. The violence started after 2 off-duty policemen had taken a gun away from a youth at the dance. They were quickly surrounded by a number of other youths who began throwing rocks, bottles and chairs at them. About 10 shots were fired, and police reinforcements dispersed the crowd with tear gas. Stores were firebombed Aug. 31, and vandalism was reported in the Summit-University section, where most of the city's 10,000 Negroes lived.

The fatal shooting Sept. 1 of Floyd D. Price, 55, a Negro, by a white policeman, James F. Sims, sparked a riot that caused an estimated $2 million worth of damages in a predominantly black business district in Newport News, Va. According to Police Chief W. F. Peach, Price had been shot after he had fired on Sims with a gun he had taken from a patrolman who had been beaten unconscious by 15 Negroes who were preventing the arrest of a woman on a drunkenness charge. About 20 minutes after the shooting, small bands of blacks began to swarm through the streets, setting off firebombs, smashing windows and looting. 200 local and state police sealed off the neighborhood at sundown Sept. 2 to prevent new violence.

Violence flared in Washington, D.C. following incidents in which Negroes were shot by white policemen. In the wake of rising criticism of police action, city authorities took steps to remove officers involved in slayings from active duty pending investigation and to limit police use of firearms.

Following the fatal shooting of a black pedestrian by a Washington motorcycle policeman Oct. 8, some 250 young Negroes protesting the incident blocked traffic and set fires until they were dispersed by police using tear gas. Elijah Bennett, 22, the victim, had been shot to death earlier in the day by Pvt. David Allen Roberts as the 2 men struggled after Roberts had stopped Bennett for an alleged jaywalking violation. A willful homicide verdict was delivered against Roberts by a coroner's jury Oct. 16, but a federal grand jury cleared Roberts of the charge Nov. 13. A grand jury Oct. 14 had also refused to indict 5 policemen involved in the fatal shooting July 14 of Theodore R. Lawson, a Negro, and 2 policemen involved in the shooting and wounding of another Negro, Marvin D. Vincent.

A disorder was set off in Washington Nov. 2 by the wounding of 2 black women by a white policeman, Pvt. Thomas Snow, 24. Snow had shot Mamie B. Haskins, 53, after she reportedly threatened him with a knife. Eva Loretta Walker, 18, was wounded by a stray bullet. Rumors that the women had been killed sparked a disturbance in which 3 cars were burned, several persons beaten and 13 persons arrested. At a ghetto intersection, black youths threw bricks at cars driven by whites, and 3 white men were pulled from their cars and beaten.

The Black United Front had voted July 18 to seek community control over policemen in Washington's ghetto areas. The front had said earlier, citing 7 incidents in the past year of citizens killed by police bullets in Washington, that the shooting of a district policeman would be "justifiable homicide." The National Capital Area Civil Liberties Union Aug. 1 called for more citizen control over police policy. After conferring with members of the City Council on ways to respond to ghetto unrest after shooting incidents involving police, Mayor Walter E. Washington Oct. 9 announced a new policy whereby a policeman involved in a slaying would be removed from duty pending preliminary investigation of the incident.

After 2 more shootings, one when a white policeman mistakenly shot and killed undercover black policeman Willie C. Ivery, 25, Mayor Washington Nov. 30 pleaded with the city to end "these senseless shootings." He called on the City Council to take action to curb the use of firearms. The council Nov. 21 had adopted guidelines to limit police use of guns.

11 Die in Cleveland Police-Black Nationalist Battles

A band of armed black nationalists fought Cleveland police with rifles in the city's Glenville ghetto district the night of July 23-24, 1968. It was the first reported case in which black extremists had carried out threats to mount an attack in a major city.

7 persons were killed in the first wave of shooting between the nationalists and police. 3 of the fatalities were nationalists, 3 were white policemen, and one was a Negro who had attempted to aid the police. 3 more Negroes were killed in other Cleveland shooting incidents the same night; an 11th person, also a Negro, was killed by a sniper in suburban Cleveland Heights July 26. 23 persons were wounded, more than 15 of them in the initial gunfight.

The shooting led to an explosion of racial tension, arson and lootings. Although 3,100 National Guardsmen were sent to Cleveland, the relatively rapid restoration of order was widely credited to the efforts of the city's black mayor, Carl B. Stokes.

The initial attack was attributed to a small militant group called the Black Nationalists of New Libya, led by Fred (Ahmed) Evans, 37, an astrologer and currently the head of an antipoverty project in the Glenville area. Evans surrendered to police late July 23, reportedly after his carbine had jammed during the fight. Although police said they had received prior warnings that coordinated extremist attacks would occur in Cleveland, Detroit, Chicago and Pittsburgh July 24, the 3 other cities remained calm. It was reported later (July 28) that Evans had instigated the attack after being informed that he was being evicted from his home and that his antipoverty project would not be permitted to move into premises promised to it.

Although reports conflicted as to exactly how the shooting began, press and news magazine accounts asserted that the first shots were fired by Evans' followers. According to a police summary of the events, issued July 31, a group of armed nationalists fired on police in a squad car outside Evans' headquarters. The police, who had been keeping the headquarters under surveillance, radioed for reinforcements and then fled. A municipal tow truck attempting to remove an abandoned car from the section was then fired on, and the driver was wounded.

Police reinforcements, armed with semi-automatic weapons, arrived and returned the fire. The black band, believed to number 7 men, occupied several Glenville buildings. The 3 policemen, the Negro aiding them and one nationalist were killed early in the gunfight. The bodies of 2 more extremists were found later in the ruins of one of the buildings; they had been killed by police bullets before the building was set afire and burned to the ground.

Acting while the Glenville gunfight was still underway and as rioting was beginning to spread to other nearby black communities,

Mayor Stokes asked Ohio Gov. James A. Rhodes to send National Guardsmen. Rhodes complied late July 23, and by the early morning hours of July 24 the first Guard units had entered Glenville. The gunfire and rioting had already halted, at least partially because of heavy rain that swept the city that night. 48 persons were arrested July 23-24 in connection with the violence.

Stokes conferred July 24 with black Cleveland leaders, primarily from the Hough and Glenville ghetto areas, and announced late in the day that he had accepted their requests for withdrawal of National Guardsmen and white police from the ghettos. The sections were cordoned off, and responsibility for the maintenance of order was entrusted to the city's 125-odd black policemen and to hastily-organized black citizens' patrols. The Rev. de Forest Brown, president of the Hough Development Corp. and spokesman for the black leaders, said July 24 that "we . . . have accepted the responsibility to restore law and order out of a chaotic situation."

But National Guardsmen were sent back into the black sections July 25 after scattered violence and looting had begun again late in the day. Announcing the measure in a televised message to the city, Stokes said that the 24-hour withdrawal of the troops had helped to restore calm and that the black volunteers had done their work "admirably" but that the renewed violence required the return of the troops. Stokes ordered a 9-p.m.-to-6-a.m. curfew in the section.

Few incidents and only a very few arrests were reported July 26-27, and the 400 Guardsmen actually sent to the black districts were withdrawn and returned to their armories July 27. With the restoration of calm, Stokes lifted the curfew and ordered resumption of routine police protection in the area.

Commenting on the Cleveland violence July 27, Stokes was reported by *Time* magazine to have said: The Glenville outbreak was "uniquely different from any other in any other city in the country. The others were a spontaneous reaction to an unresponsive environment. But this was a small group of determined men who planned an attack on the police." (Phil Hutchings, newly-named program director of the Student Nonviolent Coordinating Committee, told a New York press conference July 27 that the Cleveland eruption was "the first stage of a revolutionary armed struggle.")

A report released by Stokes Aug. 9 said there was no "tangible" proof that the policemen murdered by snipers July 23 had been lured into a trap. Stokes said that the trouble had started as the result of a "spontaneous action" and that there was no evidence to connect the shootings with recent sniping incidents in other cities.

5 black nationalists were indicted by a Cuyahoga (county) grand jury Aug. 26 on charges of first-degree murder in the July 23 shooting of the 3 policemen and a civilian. Indicted were Fred (Ahmed) Evans, Lathan Donald, 20, Alfred Thomas, 18, Leslie Jackson, 16, and John Hardrick Jr., 17. Evans May 12, 1969 was found guilty of murder and was sentenced to die in the electric chair.

A study of the Cleveland rioting, released May 29, 1969 by the President's Commission on Violence, said that the violence on the city's East Side might "have marked the beginning of a new pattern" in urban disorder. The report, contracted by the commission, was written by Louis H. Masotti, associate professor of political science at Case Western Reserve in Cleveland, and Jerome R. Corsi, a Harvard graduate student. As opposed to other recent urban riots, which the authors said began as attacks against property in ghettos, the researchers found that the Cleveland riot "began as person-oriented violence, blacks and whites shooting at each other, snipers against cops." They said a small group of black extremists had attacked white policemen as "symbols of the white society." Although they could not determine whether the police or the black nationalists fired the first shots, the authors contended that the armed nationalists were immediately responsible for the violence and had provoked the police into firing. The report criticized Cleveland newspapers for stories that allegedly increased racial tension.

Decline in Rioting Reported

Atty. Gen. Ramsey Clark said Oct. 3, 1968 that there was a "clear and significant decline in the number and severity of riots and disorders this summer." Clark's conclusion came from a comparison of statistics gathered by the Civil Disturbance Information Unit of the Justice Department for the months June-Aug. 1968 with data from former years. Clark noted, however, that riots following the death of Dr. Martin Luther King Jr. "made Apr. 1968 the 2d worst month of rioting in recent years."

The Justice Department data, released with Clark's statement, showed 29 deaths recorded in 1968 summer civil disorders, compared with 87 during the summer of 1967. The National Guard was called for assistance 6 times during the months studied and 18 times during the same period in 1967. Disturbances listed as "major or serious" by the Information Unit dropped from 46 in 1967 to 25 in 1968. Clark said that, in his opinion, "effective police action" accounted for much of the improvement.

Clark had said in an interview July 25 that there was less evidence of "militant agitation or conspiratorial efforts" in the outbreak of riots in major cities than there had been in the past few years.

Clark warned in a speech in Chapel Hill, N.C. Aug. 15 that current "loose talk of shooting looters" was likely to "cause guerrilla warfare in our cities and division and hatred among our people." Observers assumed that his remarks were intended to answer a statement made July 30 by Spiro T. Agnew. Agnew, in a speech delivered in New York before his Vice Presidential nomination, had called "the agonizing of a police officer who couldn't bring himself to kill a looter over a pair of shoes" an example of "the insidious relativism" that had entered American thinking. He had said that the guilt of a looter could not be measured by the value of property stolen. Agnew had criticized the Kerner commission report for blaming white racism and excusing individual responsibility in the cause of riots.

Grants, Police Reforms & Job Promises Follow Riots

The Justice Department announced Sept. 3, 1968 that it had awarded $3.9 million for riot control to 40 states, the District of Columbia and Puerto Rico. The grants were given under the 1968 Crime Control & Safe Streets Act to provide special training and equipment for police and pay for police-community relations programs.

During 1968, many of the nation's police departments instituted programs to reform police methods in ghetto communities, train police in the handling of crowds and improve the "image" of the policeman. Many of these reforms reflected recommendations of the National Commission on Civil Disorders in its summary report released Feb. 29.

Concern about police violence was voiced by many authorities, among them Dr. Nelson Watson, staff psychologist of the International Association of Chiefs of Police. Watson was quoted by the *N.Y. Times* July 7 as saying that the "very fact that police are the only group authorized by the state to use force tends to attract the occasional man who likes to use it." However, 2 other psychiatrists asserted Nov. 16 that police departments in major cities had been recruiting men shown to be better adjusted and to display better judgment then members of the general population. Drs. Margaret H. Peterson and Fred D. Strider of the University of Nebraska School of Medicine presented these views at a Chicago conference on violence attended by 1,000 psychiatrists.

In Los Angeles, where hostility to policemen was pronounced in the predominantly black Watts section of the city, the police department had instituted an intensive program to improve the police-citizen relationship. Los Angeles Police Chief Thomas Reddin said in a *N.Y. Times* interview published Nov. 18 that big city police forces had become so "motorized and mechanized" that they had lost touch with the community. "We have to find a way to humanize the policeman again," he added. One part of the program was based on revival of the "cop on the beat," familiar to the specific neighborhood.

The police department of Sausalito, Calif. was reported Nov. 29 to have instituted mandatory group therapy sessions in an effort to develop its staff's maturity and strength to withstand provocation.

The N.Y. City Police Department's 28,000-member Patrolmen's Benevolent Association called for greater public understanding and cooperation with police in advertisements carried in the city's 3 major newspapers May 27. Community councils had been established in each of the city's 76 residential-area precincts to enhance the policeman's image by developing recreational and skill-training programs and providing neighborhood forums for airing grievances.

N.Y. Mayor John V. Lindsay Aug. 4 made public a program under which the city's police and courts could handle up to 12,000 arrests daily in case of mass disorders. The plans were described in a 33-page report of the Mayor's Committee on the Administration of Justice Under Emergency Conditions. The procedures to be used included the rearrangement of detention and court facilities to handle large numbers of arrested persons without tying-up the police. The plans were made in response to the Kerner commission's recommendations for emergency action during civil disorders.

The formation of a new police group, a 220-member Special Events Squad (SES), was announced Aug. 9 by N.Y. City Police Commissioner Howard R. Leary. The SES was trained to handle crowds gathering at demonstrations, rallies or sporting events. Another mobile crowd-control unit, the Tactical Patrol Force, had already been assigned to work in high crime areas at night.

The Washington, D.C. Police Department Aug. 12 issued guidelines for the handling of disorderly individuals and crowds by methods short of arrest. The new police rules followed the recommendations of the Kerner commission, which found that indiscriminate disorderly-conduct arrests were instrumental in touching off riots. After several incidents in which police bullets had wounded innocent persons, the Washington City Council initiated a policy restricting police use of weapons except if needed to stop an escaping suspect witnessed committing a felony. The new guidelines otherwise forbade police use of guns except in self-defense or when lives were in danger.

The Labor Department and the National Alliance of Businessmen announced May 22 that private industry had pledged to find 106,000 jobs for the "hard-core unemployed." Labor Secy. W. Willard Wirtz said that 603 firms in the country's 50 largest cities had submitted contract proposals to hire and train 61,000 persons. The government was to reimburse the businesses for the extra costs necessitated by the hiring and training of unskilled workers. But the National Committee on Employment of Youth July 29 reported the results of a nationwide survey showing that business and government had failed to generate a large number of summer jobs for ghetto youth. In releasing the report, a spokesman for the group declared: "There is no indication that private industry has generated any new summer jobs this year."

Several large banks and life insurance companies announced plans during 1968 to make loans and mortgage funds available for housing and redevelopment projects in minority group neighborhoods and urban slums. The life insurance companies acted in partial fulfillment of a pledge made Sept. 13,1967 by the nation's major life insurance companies to Pres. Johnson that they would invest $1 billion in ghetto real estate.

Ex-Sen. Paul H. Douglas (D., Ill.) predicted Nov. 10 that the nation would "run into great difficulties" and more riots unless the public lost its hostility to government-subsidized housing for the poor. Speaking as chairman of the National Commission on Urban Problems, Douglas released a commission research report calling for the elimination of much of the red tape required of non-profit sponsors of low-income housing. The report, prepared by Nathaniel Keith, president of the National Housing Conference, noted that only 1/6 of the public housing units authorized by Congress since 1949 had actually been built. Douglas attributed this to middle-class hostility to low-income housing.

Inadequate housing could not be blamed for recent urban unrest and riots, the National Commission on Urban Problems concluded in a study issued Dec. 5. The report, written by Dr. Frank S. Kristof of the N.Y. City Housing & Development Administration, asserted that the U.S. had made "steady and unremitting progress" in housing since the Federal Housing Act of 1949 was passed. 20½ million additional housing units had been needed in 1950. But the need would be cut to about 10.8 million in 1970, Kristof estimated. Factors Kristof listed among the causes of the urban disorders: (a) the movement of blacks "from a scattered and inarticulate rural status to a crowded, increasing political and socially conscious force"; (b) the difference in status between Negroes (and other minority-group members) and the great majority of Americans in an affluent society. Kristof said great improvements were needed in the environment of poor neighborhoods. The improvements included better streets, lighting, draining, play areas, schools, garbage collection and transportation.

Rap Brown Arrested & Convicted

Chairman H. Rap Brown of the Student Nonviolent Coordinating Committee (SNCC) was arrested by federal agents and local police in New York Feb. 20, 1968 on a New Orleans bench warrant for alleged violation of court-imposed travel restrictions. He was also served with a warrant to appear in Richmond to show cause why bail there should not be revoked for similar reasons. Brown, who had addressed black-power rallies with Stokely Carmichael in Oakland, Calif. Feb. 17 and in Los Angeles Feb. 18, had been released on $15,000 bail in New Orleans Sept. 8, 1967 with permission to move freely between New York and Atlanta and to meet 15 speaking engagements on specific dates around the country. The California rallies had not been among those approved. Brown had been released on $10,000 personal recognizance bond in Richmond, Va. Sept. 18, 1967. The terms of the Richmond release restricted Brown to the Southern District of New York—Manhattan and the Bronx.

At the Los Angeles rally Brown proposed that any assassination of Negro leaders be followed by coordinated, "selected, protracted and swift retribution on police stations and power plants."

During a hearing in New Orleans Feb. 21, Brown was arrested on a new charge of threatening black FBI agent William H. Smith Jr. and his family. In the charge, Brown was quoted as telling Smith: "We'll get you. You better get your hat cause I'm going to

beat you back to the Coast. We better not find out where your
house is. If you have any kids we'll get them too." Brown pleaded
not guilty to the intimidation charge Mar. 13.

Federal marshals took Brown to Richmond Feb. 22. Federal
Judge Robert R. Merhige Jr. ruled Feb. 23 that Brown had violated
the travel restrictions of his bond. He ordered him to pay the
$10,000 immediately and ordered him returned to New Orleans.

Brown was released on $10,000 bond in Cambridge, Md. Apr.
18 after 8 weeks in various state and federal prisons for bond violations. The terms of the bail limited Brown to New York and New
Orleans, but he was permitted to enter Maryland to consult with
his lawyers on his pending trial.

Brown was convicted in federal court in New Orleans May 22
on one count of violating the Federal Firearms Act. He was sentenced to 5 years in prison and fined $2,000. A jury of 3 white men,
6 white women and 3 black women found Brown guilty of carrying
a .30-caliber carbine on a plane trip from New Orleans to New
York Aug. 18, 1967 while under indictment. He was found not guilty
of violating the firearms act during a flight from New York to New
Orleans 2 days earlier because he was not aware that he was under
an arson indictment in Maryland when he carried the gun across
state lines. U.S. District Judge Lansing Mitchell imposed the maximum sentence. Brown was released on $15,000 bond.

A memo, prepared for the National Advisory Commission on
Civil Disorders and leaked to the press Mar. 4, had blamed over-
reaction by white local officials to a "revolutionary" speech by
Brown for the racial violence in Cambridge, Md. during the summer
of 1967. The report said: "Brown was more a catalyst of white
fears than of Negro antagonisms, the disturbance more a product
of white expectations than of Negro initiative." "To the extent that
Brown encouraged anybody to engage in precipitous or disorderly
acts, the city officials are clearly the ones he influenced most.
Indeed, the existence of a riot existed for the most part in the minds
of city officials. . . ." Brown's speech was "unequivocally militant,
radical and revolutionary." But the triggering incident was a sheriff
firing a shotgun without warning and wounding Brown. Cambridge
Police Chief Brice G. Kinnamon "went on an emotional binge in
which his main desire seems to have been to kill Negroes." "The
response to Brown's exhortations were not universally favorable,
with some Negroes in attendance being very much turned off by
his strident and militant stance." (The memo was prepared by a
team of social scientists headed by Dr. Robert Shellow, assistant
deputy director for research at the National Institute of Mental

Health. Alvin A. Spivak, information director of the commission, said that it "was only a raw memo . . . never passed upon by the commission . . . [and] based on limited information.")

RAM Suspects Convicted

Black militants Herman B. Ferguson, 46, and Arthur Harris, 22, members of the Revolutionary Action Movement (RAM), were convicted in New York June 15, 1968 on charges of conspiracy to murder moderate black leaders Roy Wilkins of the NAACP and Whitney Young Jr. of the National Urban League. Ferguson and Harris were sentenced Oct. 3 to prison terms of $3\frac{1}{2}$ to 7 years each. But State Supreme Court Justice Joseph M. Conroy ruled Oct. 17 that there was "reasonable doubt" that the 2 defendants had received a fair trial, and he authorized their release on bail. Conroy's ruling was based on the fact that the prosecutor had mentioned, in the jury's presence, the assassination of Sen. Robert F. Kennedy.

Panther Founder Newton Convicted of Slaying

Since its formation in Oct. 1966 by Huey P. Newton, 26, and Bobby Seale, 31, in Oakland, Calif., the militant Black Panther Party had become part of the national Negro movement. Its membership had swelled from a few hundred to several thousand persons with chapters in major U.S. cities.

National interest in the Black Panthers was generated by Newton's trial and conviction for manslaughter in California and by the Presidential candidacy of Eldridge Cleaver, Panther "minister of information." Violent confrontations between Panthers and police had occured in California, New York and New Jersey and, charging police harassment and brutality, Panther leaders had issued repeated calls to blacks to arm themselves for a struggle for liberation.

Newton was convicted of manslaughter Sept. 8 in the Oct. 28, 1967 fatal shooting of Oakland Patrolman John Frey, 23. Newton was sentenced Sept. 27 to 2 to 15 years imprisonment. Oakland's Alameda County Courthouse, where the 7-week murder trial took place, was the scene of extensive "free Huey" demonstrations during the early days of the trial. 2,500 sympathizers marched on the courthouse July 15 when the trial began. Officials searched spectators and newsmen for weapons before they were allowed to enter the courthouse.

In addition to the murder charge, Newton had been indicted for assault with a deadly weapon against Patrolman Herbert Heanes, 25, who was wounded in the arm, and on charges of kidnaping a black motorist, Dell Ross, near the scene of the shooting. (Newton had been shot in the abdomen by Heanes during the gun battle.) Deputy Prosecutor Lowell Jensen questioned Heanes on the 1967 shooting at the opening of the prosecution's case Aug. 5. According to Heanes, he had joined Frey shortly after Frey had stopped a car identified as a Panther-owned vehicle. The driver, whom Heanes identified as Newton, was told by Frey that he was under arrest. Shots were then exchanged, and Heanes fired at Newton. Heanes was wounded and Frey was killed in the gunfire. Under cross-examination by defense attorney Charles R. Garry, Heanes admitted Aug. 6 that he did not remember seeing Newton with a gun in his hand. Heanes denied Garry's suggestions that he was the one who had shot Frey. A black prosecution witness, Henry Grier, 40, testified Aug. 7 that he had seen Newton shoot Frey. Garry pointed out discrepancies between Grier's initial statement to the police and his testimony in court. The prosecution submitted ballistics evidence Aug. 14 to show that the bullets that killed Frey had not come from Heanes' gun. The kidnaping charge was dropped Aug. 20 after Ross claimed to have suffered a loss of memory about the incident.

Newton took the stand Aug. 22 to deny that he had shot Frey. Most of his testimony was his explanation of his resentment against white society.

The jury, which elected its only black member as foreman, arrived at a guilty verdict after 4 days of deliberation.

Eldridge Cleaver Sought as Parole Violator

Eldridge Cleaver, 33, author, Black Panther Party co-founder and recent Presidential candidate of the Peace & Freedom Party, was sought as a parole violator on a fugitive warrant issued Nov. 27, 1968 in San Francisco.

Cleaver had been free on parole after serving 9 years of a 14-year sentence on a 1958 conviction for assault with intent to kill. He had been rearrested Apr. 6 after being wounded in a Panther shootout with Oakland police. (Panther member Bobby Hutton was killed in the shooting.) Cleaver's parole was immediately rescinded, but he was released June 12 on $50,000 bail by order of Superior Court Judge Raymond J. Sherwin, who criticized the cancellation of parole. Sherwin said that the cancellation had stemmed not from a failure of Cleaver's "personal rehabilitation" but from his "undue eloquence in pursuing political goals . . . offensive to many of his contemporaries." The State District Court of Appeals in San Francisco ruled Sept. 27 that Sherwin had acted beyond his authority in the case. This ruling was upheld by the California Supreme Court Nov. 20 when it refused to hear an appeal by Cleaver. U.S. Supreme Court Justice Thurgood Marshall Nov. 26 denied a request for a stay to prohibit officials from taking Cleaver into custody. The fugitive warrant was issued after Cleaver failed to surrender as ordered Nov. 27, and a federal warrant was issued Dec. 10.

Panthers Clash with Police on both Coasts

Black Panthers and police fought 2 gun battles on California streets in November. Unlike 2 earlier Panther-police shoot-outs in California, no one was killed in the November shooting.

In the first of the November gunfights, a Panther member and a policeman were wounded in Berkeley, Calif. Nov. 13. Reginald Forte, 19, and Ptl. Daniel Wolke, 22, were injured in the shooting, which began after Forte's car had been stopped for a traffic violation. Forte and his companions, John L. Sloan, 32, and William Kitt, 21, surrendered and were booked for attempted murder.

3 policemen were wounded Nov. 19 in a San Francisco gunfight with 8 Negroes whose panel truck had been stopped in connection with a service station robbery. The truck bore a sign reading "The Black Panther Black Community News Service." Lt. Dermott Creedon, Sgt. Robert Flynn and Inspector Michael O'Mahoney were injured when 3 blacks identified as William Lee Brent, 47, Wilford M. Holiday, 35, and Samuel Napier, 30, allegedly jumped from the truck and opened fire. A grand jury Dec. 2 indicted Brent and Holiday in connection with the shooting.

2 Oakland policemen had been dismissed and jailed Sept. 10 after firing more than 12 bullets into the headquarters of the Black Panthers and a neighboring restaurant. No one was injured. Police Chief Charles Gain said that the 2 men, Richard V. Williams, 28, and Robert W. Rarrell, 26, had been drinking on duty during the early morning incident. The shots seemed to have been aimed at an enlarged picture of Huey Newton in a window of the Panthers' headquarters.

Conflicts between Black Panthers and N.Y. City police had led to an incident in which police allegedly attacked 8 or 9 Panthers and a few white sympathizers in a hallway of the Brooklyn Criminal Court building Sept. 4, 1968. The assault was made by more than 150 white men, many of whom were identified as off-duty policemen in civilian dress, in the courthouse to attend a hearing for 3 Panthers arrested Aug. 21 for assaulting a policeman. The attack was made by whites who could not find seats in the courtroom. Swinging blackjacks, shouting "Wallace, Wallace" and proclaiming themselves "the white tigers," they converged on the small group of Panthers when they appeared in the hallway near the courtroom. Brooklyn Panther Chairman David Brothers said later that he had been kicked more than 20 times. Some of those attacked required medical treatment.

No arrests were made. At least 2 of the New York policemen involved were members of the Executive Board of the Law Enforcement Group (LEG) of New York, a dissident group of young, rightwing policemen. The LEG had been organized in August to voice resentment against Criminal Court Judge John F. Furey, who was alleged to have allowed Black Panthers to misbehave in his courtroom.

The Black Panther Party filed suit in U.S. District Court in New York Sept. 10 to obtain injunctions forbidding police to harass Panthers and asking for community control of the police. An attorney for the Panthers, Gerald B. Lefcourt, said Sept. 12 that recent arrests of members of the party indicated that police planned "a general roundup of the Panthers."

New Jersey Black Panthers and police exchanged accusations over 2 recent incidents—the machine-gunning of a Jersey City police station Nov. 29, 1968 and a firebomb attack on the Newark Panther headquarters Dec. 1. Jersey City Police Sgt. John Gerraghty said that Panther members were suspected of the shooting in retaliation for the Nov. 28 arrest on weapons charges of 7 Newark Negroes identified as Panthers. 3 members of the Panther party were arrested Dec. 5 in connection with the machine-gun attack. Panther spokesman Anthony Kaiser contended Dec. 1 that the bombing of the party's headquarters was in response to the attack on the Jersey City precinct house. Carl C. Nichols, 36, the party's chief organizer in New Jersey, and 2 other Panther members were injured when the bombs exploded outside their storefront office. The victims said that the bombs were hurled by 2 men in "police-type" uniforms. Newark Deputy Police Chief Kenneth Melchior said Dec. 1 that any link between the 2 incidents was "pure speculation."

3 Killed in Gun Battle at Boston Self-Help Office

3 Negroes were shot to death and 2 others wounded Nov. 13, 1968 when 5 other blacks invaded the headquarters of the New England Grass Roots Organization (NEGRO), a ghetto self-help association, and opened fire in the Roxbury District of Boston. The *Boston Globe* reported Dec. 8 that 3 arrested suspects and 2 of the victims were involved in a consortium of black organizations that had received a $1,969,425 Labor Department contract for job training.

Those slain were: Guido St. Laurent, 38, the blind founder of NEGRO; Carnell S. Eaton, 33, salaried director of the Roxbury-Dorchester-South End-Greater Boston Consortium (NEGRO was a member of the consortium), which had received the $1,969,425 contract in July (2 weeks before his death Eaton had been promoted to national sales director for Woolman Systems, Inc. of New York; Woolman Systems had contracted under the federal program to employ the consortium's training staff); and Harold King, 50, chairman of a Cleveland job training consortium advised by Woolman Systems.

A Suffolk County grand jury Dec. 3 indicted Alvin Campbell, 35, his brother Arnold, 33, and Dennis Chandler, 29, for the murders. All were consortium employes hired by Eaton, and Alvin Campbell had become director when Eaton was promoted by Woolman Systems.

(The *Boston Globe* reported Dec. 29 that the Labor Department had canceled the $1,969,425 contract. The FBI had been investigating the program for possible fraud. The *Globe* reported that only 12 trainees had been hired by the consortium and that no federal funds had been spent through the program. All salary and other expenses had been borne by Woolman Systems.)

Columbia University Disorders & Cox Report

Normal operations at Columbia University (N.Y. City) were virtually ended for the academic year after a group of leftwing students and a group of black students and non-students seized and occupied 5 university buildings Apr. 23-24, 1968. The seizures were in protest against the university's construction of a gymnasium in city-owned Morningside Heights Park, and in protest against the university's ties with the Institute for Defense Analyses (IDA). The demonstrators held the buildings until Apr. 30, when the university administration asked the city police to clear the buildings. The police were called in after efforts to negotiate an end to the take-over had failed. About 700 persons were arrested and 148 injured as the police ended the occupation.

The use of police on the campus provoked additional protests at the university. A general student-faculty strike was called. The focus of the new protests, uniting diverse groups, extended to questions of the structure of the university and the role of faculty and students in determining university policy.

The initial protest had involved members of the leftwing Students for a Democratic Society (SDS), members of the Students' Afro-American Society and a number of residents of Harlem, the black community adjacent to the university. At noon Apr. 23 Mark Rudd, 20, president of SDS' campus chapter*, led about 150 persons to Low Memorial Library in protest against the gymnasium project and against Columbia's ties with a 12-university research consortium, the IDA. The demonstrators protested that IDA aided in the war effort in Vietnam. The gym project was denounced as racist and a symbol of Columbia's usurpation of neighborhood land without regard for neighborhood residents. (Columbia had planned 2 gyms on 2.1 acres of the 30-acre park—one for Columbia College undergraduates and the other for the Harlem community. The university had agreed to finance services and heat for the community building. The university had acquired the land from the city in Aug. 1961.)

The demonstrators marched to the site of the new gym and tore down a section of fence around the site. They then marched to Hamilton Hall, headquarters of Columbia College, the men's undergraduate school. There they held Acting Dean Henry S. Coleman and 2 other officials as prisoners for more than 24 hours. On the orders of the black students, the white students, led by Mark Rudd, left Hamilton Hall at 5 a.m. Apr. 24 and marched to Low Library, where they occupied and ransacked the office of Dr. Grayson Kirk, president of the university. The Negroes in Hamilton Hall released Coleman Apr. 24.

2 more buildings were seized Apr. 25, when about 100 white students took Fayerweather Hall, a social science building, and

---

*The AP reported May 11 that in Oct. 1967 Rudd had drafted a plan entitled "Position Paper on Strategy for Rest of School Year—University Complicity." The plan called for: Mass action in April, including "a sit-in at Low Library which, after one day, turns into a general student strike. University capitulates." Rudd's goals were quoted as: "The radicalization of students . . . showing them how our lives really are unfree in this society and at Columbia, getting them to act . . . and striking a blow at the federal government's war effort."

about 100 white students seized Avery Hall, the architecture building. Early Apr. 26 students seized a 5th building, the mathematics building. This brought the number of people in 5 seized buildings to about 700.

All classes were canceled Apr. 26, and the campus was sealed off after about 250 black high school students, shouting "black power," invaded the campus in support of the black demonstrators. The university administration announced Apr. 26 that it had suspended work on the gym (in response to a request from the mayor).

H. Rap Brown, chairman of the Student Nonviolent Coordinating Committee (SNCC), and Stokely Carmichael met with students in Hamilton Hall Apr. 26. Brown said that the demonstrators were "fighting against the racist policies" of Columbia. As for the gym, he said: "If they build it up, people in Harlem should blow it up."

The university administration finally requested the night of Apr. 29-30 that the police end the seizure of the buildings. In response to this request, 1,000 city policemen, armed with nightsticks, moved onto the campus at 2:20 a.m. Apr. 30 and cleared the occupied buildings. 132 students, 4 faculty members and 12 policemen were reported injured in the forcible removal of the white students, but the 85 black students in Hamilton Hall were removed without incident. Dr. Kenneth Clark later praised police control at Hamilton Hall as "an extraordinary professional job."

The Police Department May 6 issued an 11-page interim report charging that "violence against the police was on a large scale." The report said: "Objects were thrown on them [the police] even before they entered the buildings and again while inside the buildings from persons above them. Police were punched, bitten and kicked, with many attempts to kick policemen in the groin. A pattern was seen in the use of females to bite and kick the policemen. . . . [Many demonstrators] resisted arrest and had to be carried bodily from the buildings. . . . In some buildings, demonstrators hurled furniture, bottles and miscellaneous objects at the police. . . ."

Students and police clashed again May 1 during a student rally. 5 policemen and 6 students were reported injured. Police were withdrawn from the campus May 2, but support for a student strike grew. The faculty of Columbia College voted May 5 to end formal classes for the term and to cancel final examinations. They asked individual teachers to meet with their students and to determine their own policy on grades and exams.

The 12-member executive committee of the university faculty May 5 appointed a 5-member commission, headed by ex-Solicitor

General Archibald Cox, professor of law at Harvard Law School, to investigate the disorders.

In a statement issued May 8 the 12-member faculty executive committee announced that it was "recommending changes in the basic structure of the university with the participation of students, junior faculty and senior faculty." The committee charged, however, that some of the student strikers were "seeking to escalate conflict, which may in fact prevent these changes."

Kirk announced May 8 that "important actions" had been taken to meet strikers' demands and to "provide a basis for assurance about Columbia's immediate and long-run future." He cited a general consensus on the need to reexamine the structure of the university. He said the trustees had agreed to withhold a decision on the gym pending "full consultation and negotiation with community and city representatives."

The Columbia disorders led to proposals in Congress and in the N.Y. State Legislature to withhold federal and state education-aid funds from students who participated in such disturbances. The proposals were denounced by Kirk May 11 after the N.Y. State Senate had voted May 8 to bar aid to any student convicted of a crime committed "on the premises of any college."

A 2d student invasion of a Columbia campus hall occured May 21 following the suspension of 4 radical students for failure to answer a summons to the dean's office; the students had been charged with participating in the April disruptions. Police quietly cleared the building early May 22; but as they began to clear the campus, violence erupted. Several fires were set; students were accused of hurling bricks, kicking, biting and swearing; police were accused of drawing guns, unnecessarily using nightsticks, and dragging students from buildings and beating them.

Kirk announced May 25 that he would not deliver the traditional commencement speech at the June 4 graduation exercises. In Kirk's place, Richard Hofstadter, De Witt Clinton Professor of American History, spoke at the ceremonies. Hofstadter said that "the technique of the forceable occupation and closure of a university's buildings with the intention of bringing its activities to a halt is no ordinary bargaining device—it is a thrust at the vitals of university life." More than 300 students and 15 faculty members staged a walkout as Hofstadter began his address. They attended a "counter-commencement" at Low Library, where more than 2,000 persons heard speeches by Dr. Harold Taylor, ex-president of Sarah Lawrence College; Dr. Erich Fromm, psychoanalyst and author; Columbia economics Prof. Alexander Erlich; and Dwight McDonald, critic and essayist.

Kirk, a principal target of the campus revolt, announced his retirement as Columbia University president Aug. 23. He was succeeded by Andrew W. Cordier, 67, dean of the university's School of International Affairs, who served as acting president. Cordier, former UN undersecretary for General Assembly affairs, stipulated that he would not be available for permanent appointment as president.

The beginning of the university's autumn academic session was characterized by conciliatory moves on the part of the Cordier administration and an unsuccessful SDS attempt to recreate the mood of the spring rebellion. As the fall session approached, SDS staged several rallies and demonstrations but was not able to mobilize the support it had gained during the spring rebellion. A demonstration by 150 students halted registration briefly Sept. 18, 1968, but no arrests were made and no police were summoned to the campus.

The Cox commission, appointed to investigate the April campus disturbances, issued a report Oct. 5 that was strongly critical of the Columbia administration, city police and "disruptive tactics" of rebel students. The commission concluded that the roots of the uprising lay not in the agitation of a small group of revolutionary students but in a "deep-seated dissatisfaction with Columbia life" among a large proportion of non-radical students and professors. The dissatisfaction was attributed largely to the administration's resistance to change and the fact that it "too often conveyed an attitude of authoritarianism and invited mistrust." The report found that the major conditions that set the stage for the rebellion were the Vietnam war; the university's connection with the IDA; racial strife; the university's relations with the surrounding community, and its insistence on construction of the gym.

The report criticized the police for using "excessive force," though it admitted that there had been incidents of student provocation and that under the conditions then existing on the campus, "violence was unavoidable." The commission emphasized, however, that it felt that the students' behavior "was in no way commensurate with the brutality of the police and, for the most part, was its consequence." The report continued: "Although the police force may have been excessive, a share of the responsibility for the injuries they inflicted fall upon those students and faculty who by resisting the police, either actively or passively, made it necessary for the police to use force with the inherent risk that it might easily get out of hand. This does not excuse or even mitigate the blame resting upon the police for using excessive force, nor does it exculpate the administration of its faults."

In criticizing the "disruptive tactics" of the rebels, the commission warned that "the survival ... of the free university depends upon the entire community's active rejection of disruptive demonstrations." Such a decision, it added, "rests with the liberal and reform-minded students. They can save or destroy the institution."

San Francisco State Disorders

A year of disturbances on the campus of San Francisco State College culminated in student clashes with police in Dec. 1968. Acting College Pres. S.I. Hayakawa closed the college for the Christmas holidays Dec. 13, one week earlier than scheduled, after 2 weeks of violent campus disturbances involving up to 3,000 students and 600 policemen.

Hayakawa, 62, who had become acting president Nov. 26, had taken a hard line towards student agitators and had brought police on campus to quell the uprisings and keep classes open. The college had been in constant turmoil since Nov. 6, when dissident students, led by the Black Student Union (BSU) and supported by the 3d-World Liberation Front (non-black minority groups) and Students for a Democratic Society (SDS), called for a student strike. The students had announced 15 demands, among them the reinstatement of a suspended black instructor, George Mason Murray, the establishment of a virtually autonomous department of black studies and the admission of any black student who applied, regardless of his qualifications.

In advancing the Christmas recess, Hayakawa noted his concern for the "safety and welfare of the young people who might be attracted to our campus. . . ." (High schools in the area officially began their holidays Dec. 13, and the college Student Strike Committee had announced plans to involve high-school students in its demonstrations the next week.) Hayakawa also cited the need for time to plan a new black studies program scheduled to begin in the spring semester. In addition, Local 1352 of the American Federation of Teachers had planned to start a strike Dec. 16.

At a news conference Dec. 13 Hayakawa reiterated his conviction that campus order should receive primary attention. He said he refused to allow student government a role in college disciplinary courts because of the "utterly irresponsible and rebellious body of student officers who now claim to represent the student body." He added: "I will not try to come to terms with anarchists, hooligans or yahoos."

The disturbances on the 18,700-student campus had begun more than a year previously. A racially-inspired violent outbreak Dec. 6, 1967 had resulted in intense criticism of Pres. John Summerskill by trustees of the state college system for his refusal to call the police. Summerskill Feb. 22, 1968 announced his resignation (effective Sept. 1) and condemned the state administration of Gov. Ronald Reagan for failure to "give higher education the constructive leadership it requires and deserves from that quarter." In the wake of continued demonstrations, Glenn Dumke, chancellor of the California state college system, announced May 24 that Summerskill's resignation would become effective immediately. He was succeeded May 30 by Robert Smith, 52.

Smith also met the opposition of the state trustees when he refused to assign English instructor Murray to a nonteaching position. Murray, a Black Panther member and BSU leader, had allegedly urged black students to bring arms to campus; his supporters argued that he had merely urged Negroes to defend themselves. (The *Los Angeles Times* had quoted Murray as saying in an address to about 1,000 students in the college amphitheater Oct. 24: "If students want to run the college—if the administration won't go for it—then you control it with a gun." "We are all slaves. The only way to become free is to kill all slave masters." Asked whom the slave masters were, Murray replied: members of boards of education and "the people in the Statehouse, the White House, the Pentagon, the Supreme Court and Chase Manhattan Bank.") When Chancellor Dumke ordered Murray's suspension Oct. 31, Smith complied but suspended him with pay. The strike called Nov. 6 was in response to his suspension.

Continued disorder and violence led Smith to officially close the college Nov. 13 "until we can rationally open it"; the faculty had voted that day to suspend classes. The state trustees Nov. 18 ordered the immediate reopening of the college and stipulated that there was to be "no negotiation, arbitration or concession" to the students involved in the disturbances; the board was headed by Gov. Reagan, an *ex-officio* trustee of the state college system.

Citing inability to resolve the conflicts between the students, the faculty, the administration and the state trustees, Smith

submitted his resignation Nov. 26. Hayakawa, an interna-
tionally known semanticist, was immediately named acting
president.

With the support of San Francisco police, Hayakawa opened
classes Dec. 2. But clashes built up during the week and climaxed
Dec. 5 when police used chemical Mace and drew guns to keep 400
demonstrators away from the administration building. 25 persons
were reported arrested, one for carrying a cocked and loaded .45-
caliber automatic pistol. More than 85 persons were arrested
in demonstrations throughout the week; about a dozen were
injured.

Hayakawa fulfilled some of the students' demands in announcing Dec. 6 that: (a) a black-studies program, including 11 teaching
positions, would be started immediately; (b) the 128 unused places
in a newly instituted special admissions program for 426 educationally deprived students were to be filled in the spring; (c) a nonwhite
director of student financial aid would be appointed to deal with
nonwhite student problems. Hayakawa did not yield to the strikers'
demand for amnesty for suspended students. He added that the
police would remain on campus to keep order. Militant student
leaders labeled his proposals unacceptable and vowed new resistance.

Clashes with police took place Dec. 9 as a rally turned into
an attempt to break into a classroom building. That night, on
recommendation by faculty members, Hayakawa temporarily lifted
the suspension of 44 students. Conflict continued, however, and
another week of demonstrations brought on the announcement of
the early Christmas recess.

Gov. Reagan Dec. 17 commended Hayakawa's strong action
in handling the crisis at San Francisco State. Asserting that police
would ring the campuses in California "if that's what they must
do," he said that "there is no longer any room for appeasement
or give." Reagan suggested the formation of "concerted plans to
get rid of those professors who've made it apparent that they are
far more interested in closing the school than in fulfilling their
contracts to teach, and likewise, ridding the campus of those part-
time students or those non-students who are the militant leaders
there."

College Student Disorders Nationwide

Disorders swept U.S. colleges and universities throughout 1968's spring and fall sessions. Among developments reported:

Berkeley, Calif.—After 2 nights of violent demonstrations in which about 12 people were arrested and 30 injured June 28-30, acting Berkeley City Manager William Hunrick June 30 declared a state of emergency and a 7-p.m.-to-6-a.m. curfew for a 50-square-block area near the Berkeley campus. The demonstrations, held in "solidarity" with recent French student protests, were sponsored by the Young Socialist Alliance and several other radical student groups. Police used tear gas to break up the demonstrations June 29-30.

Demonstrations continued through July 2 as students sought permission from the Berkeley City Council to block off a section of Telegraph Ave. for a July 4 rally. Permission was granted July 3, and an orderly rally took place July 4.

Fresh violence broke out Aug. 30-31 during demonstrations against U.S. policy in Vietnam and Chicago police tactics during the Democratic National Convention. City Manager William C. Hanley Sept. 2 declared a state of civil disaster resulting from 3 days of continued violence, including "sporadic gunfire, dynamiting of private property, the shooting of an officer and several arson attempts." More than 35 people were arrested and a dozen injured.

Boston—About 300 black students barricaded themselves inside Boston University's Administration Building for more than 12 hours Apr. 24. The students, members of an Afro-American group, demanded the admission of more black students, financial aid for black students, the employment of more black faculty members and courses in black history. They also demanded that the university name the building housing the School of Theology in memory of the Rev. Dr. Martin Luther King Jr.

Bowie, Md.—About 300 of the 500 students at predominantly black Bowie State College in Bowie, Md. boycotted classes Mar. 27-29 in a demand for better housing, educational facilities and teachers and for courses in black history. Students seized the administration building late Mar. 29 and closed off the campus. But after Gov.

Spiro T. Agnew Mar. 30 refused the student demand for a meeting with him until they relinquished control of the campus, they vacated the building. About 225 Bowie students were arrested in Annapolis Apr. 4 when they refused to leave the State House after a sit-in there in a demand for a meeting with Agnew.

Cheyney, Pa.—400 of the 1,800 students at predominantly black Cheyney State College in Cheyney, Pa. occupied the campus administration building May 6-8 in a demand for improved curriculum, better teaching and an investigation of administration handling of student money. The vice president of the board of directors announced May 10 that Dr. Leroy Banks Allen, president of the college, had submitted his resignation. Cheyney had been closed Mar. 22-24 after 100 state troopers were called in to quell 300 students who were protesting the expulsion of an undergraduate for disciplinary reasons.

Chicago—Students at Roosevelt University in Chicago demonstrated May 6-10 in protest against the school's refusal to give a full-time job to part-time Prof. Staughton Lynd, 39, a former Yale history professor who visited North Vietnam and Communist China in 1965. 24 undergraduates were suspended May 9 (effective June 8) after they were arrested in a clash with police. 16 students who barricaded themselves in the office of university Pres. Rolf A. Weil May 9 were expelled May 10. The expulsion prompted further protests: 11 students who refused to leave the president's office were arrested and charged with trespassing.

Cornell—About 60 of the 150 black students at Cornell University seized the Economics Department office Apr. 4 and held the department chairman captive for 6 hours in protest against alleged racist remarks of another professor, the Rev. Michael McPhelin, a Jesuit priest. An investigation commission reported May 1 that "if individual 'blame' is to be assigned, many must bear its burdens, including faculty and administration as well as students." It recommended against severe punishment for the demonstrators.

Hartford, Conn.—200 Trinity College students in Hartford, Conn. occupied the school's administration building Apr. 22-24 in a demand that the trustees approve a $150,000 scholarship program for Negroes. The demonstration was led by the new Trinity Association of Negroes, which included nearly all of the school's 20 nonwhite students. (The total enrollment was 1,160 students.) The demonstrators also called for courses in black history, "the psychology of the ghetto" and community development. At the start of the demonstration Apr. 22, the students held Trinity Pres. Albert C. Jacobs and 6 other trustees captive in the building for more than 3 hours. The demonstration ended Apr. 24 when the trustees pledged $15,000, to be matched by student fund raising, and promised to "go as far beyond that as the budget of the college will allow" for new scholarships. Dr. Jacobs also promised that "Trinity will admit as many qualified Negro students as are available and will provide adequate financial aid for them."

Howard University—Several thousand Howard University students in Washington participated in a sit-in demonstration in the campus administration building Mar. 19-23 and forced the halting of all school operations. The demonstration was triggered by threatened disciplinary action against 39 students, but it extended also to such issues as student control over school affairs and curriculum and criticism of the alleged "Uncle Tom" attitude of the administration. The demonstration was ended by agreement on a compromise plan offered by "liberals" among the university's trustees. (Howard was a private, predominantly black university. It had 8,600 students and received more than half of its funds from the federal government.)

The sit-in started late Mar. 19 when 500 to 1,000 students took control of the administration building after the administration refused to drop charges against 39 students who had disrupted the Charter Day ceremony Mar. 1. The students had swarmed onto the stage at the end of the program when the school's president, Dr. James M. Nabrit Jr., failed to announce promised changes in the university's disciplinary and academic procedures. Student Council Pres. Ewart Brown explained Mar. 21: "We want Howard University to begin to relate to the black community the way Harvard and MIT relate to the white community."

University officials warned the students Mar. 22 to evacuate the building by Mar. 25 or face possible arrest. After a series of meetings with representatives of the board of trustees, including

Dr. Kenneth C. Clark, psychology professor at City College in New York, the students Mar. 23 accepted a compromise settlement and ended the demonstration. Under the agreement: the university would resume normal operations, and the administration promised to "enter into immediate meetings with students and faculty in order to establish a judicial tribunal, in which students would have the major responsibility to hear and determine the charges lodged against the 39 students recently charged with misconduct"; demonstrators would be granted amnesty.

Northwestern—More than 100 black students seized the Finance Building at Northwestern University (total enrollment, 8,785) in Evanston, Ill. May 3. They surrendered the building May 4 after the administration granted many of their demands. The demonstration was sponsored by the Afro-American Student Union and a black student group called For Members Only (FMO). Demonstrators issued a list of demands that included: a university policy statement "deploring the viciousness of white racism"; more scholarships for Negroes and an increase in the number of black students; separate living quarters for black students by the fall; courses in black history, literature and art; black counselors provided by the university "to help us cope properly with the psychological, mental, and academic tensions resulting from dualism of our existence as black college students."

About 15 white students seized the office of the dean of students in another building May 3 in sympathy with the black students.

The Negroes ended their 36-hour sit-in May 4 after the administration agreed to most of their demands. The university said: It "recognizes that throughout its history it has been a university of white establishment—not to gainsay that many members of its administration, faculty or student body have engaged themselves in activities directed to the righting of racial wrongs. ... This university with other institutions must share responsibility for the continuance over many past years of these racist attitudes."

Ohio State—About 150 students—half of them Negroes—seized the administration building at Ohio State University in Columbus Apr. 26 and held 2 vice presidents and 4 staff members for several hours. The demonstration was ended after the university president,

Novice G. Fawcetts, announced that the school would establish an office of black student affairs.

San Fernando, Calif.—In a 3-hour demonstration Nov. 4, 300 students at San Fernando Valley State College occupied 2 floors of the administration building and held captive Acting Pres. Paul Blomgren and about 35 other persons. The seizure ended after Dr. Blomgren agreed to "amnesty" for the demonstrators. The students, members and supporters of Black Students Union and SDS, were protesting alleged racial discrimination in campus athletics and pending reductions in the Federal Educational Opportunities Program. Blomgren Nov. 5 canceled the amnesty, which he called "null and void" because it had been signed "under duress" and to insure the safety of personnel being "held hostage." A Los Angeles County grand jury Dec. 20 indicted 28 students on charges ranging from kidnap to assault in connection with the demonstration. (Blomgren's office was destroyed Dec. 8 in a fire. Officials reported evidence of arson.)

San Mateo, Calif.—Violence erupted at the College of San Mateo Dec. 13 as about 150 minority-group students smashed windows, doors and TV cameras in a 20-minute rampage through the campus. More than a dozen white students were beaten by the rioters with metal pipes and tire irons. The clashes followed a rally sponsored by the 3d World Liberation Front and the New Black Generation to support their demand for an autonomous ethnic-studies division. Pres. Robert L. Ewigleben, 40, ordered the school opened for classes Dec. 16 "as an armed camp with riot police on campus to maintain order." More than 300 policemen guarded all buildings and admitted only authorized faculty members, students and employes to the campus.

(The College of San Mateo, in a 2-year-old program to provide college education for nonwhites, had already increased its enrollment of such students from less than 100 to about 1,000. Almost 7,000 of its students were white.)

Santa Barbara, Calif.—Protesting against alleged racial discrimination, 20 members of the Black Student Union at the University of California at Santa Barbara seized a classroom building and held it for 9½ hours Oct. 14. They left after 7 of their 8 demands

had been approved by Chancellor Vernon Cheadle. The demands
included the hiring of more Negro coaches, professors and administrators; the establishment of a college of black studies and a
graduate program in Afro-American studies, and establishment of
a racial grievance commission.

Southern Illinois—About 500 students at Southern Illinois
University in Carbondale, Ill. failed May 8 in an attempt to seize
the office of the university president. Delyte W. Morris, in an effort
to gain student control of the school's newspaper and radio station
and to win a larger student voice in university affairs. 5 students
were arrested.

Tuskegee—About 250 black students at Tuskegee Institute in
Tuskegee, Ala. held 12 of the school's trustees captive in the
college guest house for 12-13 hours Apr. 7 in protest against the
trustees' refusal to grant student demands for reform. After a
confrontation with Sheriff Lucius Amerson, a Negro, who threatened to bring in the National Guard, the students released their
captives. The trustees included retired Gen. Lucius Clay, Rep.
Frances Bolton (R., O.), Tuskegee Institute Pres. Luther H. Foster
and National Foundation Pres. Basil O'Connor. Students had
boycotted classes Mar. 25-26 to demonstrate grievances against
the administration. They called for the abolition of the compulsory Reserve Officers Training Corps program, the awarding
of athletic scholarship grants, changes in the compus curfew
regulations and improvements in housing and dining-hall conditions.
Tuskegee Pres. Foster announced Apr. 12 that the school
was abolishing the compulsory military training program and
would offer athletic scholarships. Students would be charged a
special fee of $10 to help meet the costs of the financial aid
program.
After a 2-week shut-down ordered by the trustees as a result
of the student demonstrations, classes were resumed Apr. 22.

Urbana, Ill.—About 250 black students were arrested in Urbana, Ill. Sept. 10, following a 2-day sit-in in the University of
Illinois Student Union. The youths, most of them students in the

university's Project 500 for the educationally disadvantaged, were protesting "discrimination" in campus housing and "bad faith" by the university in providing financial aid. Approximately $5,000 damage was done to the Student Union during the demonstration. 213 black freshmen involved in the sit-in were given "reprimands of record" Dec. 12 by the university's Committee on Student Discipline; the reprimands were not to be included in the students' official transcripts. None of the 213 students were dismissed from the university.

West Virginia—In the wake of racial disturbances at Bluefield State College, the West Virginia State Board of Education voted Nov. 26 to close the dormitories and reopen the school Dec. 2 as a commuter college. Policemen had patrolled the campus Nov. 16 following rock-throwing attacks on the student union building and the president's home. The school had been closed indefinitely Nov. 22 after a bomb had damaged the physical education building. Black students had submitted demands that included: more cultural events on campus; resignation of the president, academic dean and other administrators; longer library hours; black history and culture courses; additional financial aid for black students. (About 450 of the school's 1,400 students were black.)

Racial Disorders in Schools

Demonstrations and turmoil flared in schoolrooms across the U.S. during 1968 as black students and parents demanded educational reform and greater emphasis on black culture. Among the numerous reports of school violence:

Black and white students clashed for more than 30 minutes at Hillhouse High School in New Haven Feb. 5 and about 20 minutes at Lee High School Feb. 6. 5 students at Lee High were arrested, and several others suffered minor injuries. New Haven Mayor Richard C. Lee Feb. 6 ordered "police patrols on a saturation basis" at the schools to prevent further outbreaks.

Helmeted policemen and black youths scuffled Sept. 25-28 in the streets of Boston's Roxbury section. The violence followed a "black-power" rally that grew out of demonstrations by high school students who demanded the right to wear African dress to classes and to organize black student unions. Negroes looted several stores after the rally Sept. 25 and pelted policemen from rooftops with rocks, cans and pieces of asphalt. City Council member Thomas I. Atkins, a Negro, said Sept. 28 that the dispute "went into the streets because the school system was too rigid to respond" to student unrest. Mayor Kevin H. White Sept. 26 announced the formation of a biracial committee to study tensions in the school system and school decentralization proposals.

Roxbury's Martin Luther King Jr. middle school was closed indefinitely Dec. 5 after student rioting in which a black teacher, Emery Miller, was attacked by black pupils. This was the 3d time since September that the school had been closed because of student disorders. The school had been the center of a conflict between the black community and the predominantly white school department. The Dec. 5 outbreak followed the appointment of a white principal, John J. Bradley, to replace John A. Joyce, a Negro who had resigned because he could not control disorders at the school.

After 9 days of clashes between white and black students in 7 Philadelphia high schools, Mayor James H. J. Tate denounced the Board of Education Oct. 16 as "inept" and promised to end the confrontations, which had temporarily closed several of the schools. An emergency "hot line" phone system was established so that Philadelphia high school principals could communicate with one another in case of trouble.

Arrests Follow Detroit Bombings

Following a series of 8 bombings in the Detroit area, 11 young men and women described as "hippie types" were arrested Nov. 11, 1968 on conspiracy charges in what Detroit police called an "anti-establishment, anti-government" bombing plot. Lt. William McCoy of the city's Special Investigation Bureau said that there was no indication that the defendants were members of any formal organization. The bombing targets included a recruiting office of the Central Intelligence Agency, cars belonging to 3 policemen and an Army recruiter, a draft board office, a suburban school administration building and the University of Michigan Institute of Science & Technology.

CAMPUS ANARCHY & GHETTO VIOLENCE (1969)

Black and other minority college students demonstrated with varying degrees of violence during 1969 in demands for minority study programs, for the admission of more educationally deprived students to colleges and often for a voice in curriculum preparation and faculty hiring. Colleges announced reforms and state legislatures acted to bar further campus disruptions.

Small-scale violent disturbances took place in urban areas in 1969, and Justice Department officials said they believed that the era of large-scale urban rioting had come to an end. A wave of minor racial disturbances spread across Wisconsin, Illinois, New Jersey and parts of the South.

Members of the militant Black Panther Party were involved in violent clashes with police in cities across the country. 21 Panthers were indicted in New York on bomb-plot charges. 8 Black Panthers were arrested in New Haven on murder and conspiracy charges after the body of a tortured Panther member was discovered.

Anti-war protests in 1969 began with a "counter-inaugural" by youthful demonstrators in Washington, D.C. Militant members of the Weatherman faction of SDS rampaged through the streets in Chicago in October.

Film actress Sharon Tate and 3 friends were murdered in her home near Bel Air, Calif. Charles Manson, leader of a nomadic clan of drifters, was indicted with 4 followers for the murders.

Action to Combat Campus Turmoil

Gov. Ronald Reagan asked the California legislature Jan. 7, 1969 to help him drive "criminal anarchists and latter-day Fascists" off California campuses. Delivering his state-of-the-state message, Reagan declared that it was "time to make it completely clear: higher education in our state colleges and universities is not a right, it is a privilege." He promised to submit legislative proposals "for the expulsion of students or the dismissal of teachers who interfere with the educational process and [to] strengthen the trespass laws to keep troublemakers off the campus." "It is a matter of making sure that no group is ever permitted to unjustly force its will upon the people," Reagan said.

The *N.Y. Times* Jan. 26 reported a movement by the Co-ordinating Center for Democratic Opinion, based in New York, to organize faculty groups across the nation to combat campus disorder. Murray Baron, a member of the group's national council, said that the center had received responses from more than 100 campuses. Prof. Sidney Hook, chairman of the center and retired head of the NYU philosophy department, had gone to West Coast colleges to organize faculty there. Hook asserted that "where-ever there has been student 'resistance' or irresponsibility, it was always with the support, covert or overt, of a few members of the faculty." The *Times* article also reported that 350 faculty members at the N. Y. State University center at Buffalo had signed a petition urging that students or faculty members who resort to violence be suspended and that 581 University of Connecticut teachers had signed a statement pledging support to the administration in controlling disorders.

The National Collegiate Athletic Association, at its 63d annual convention in Los Angeles, had voted 167-79 Jan. 8 to permit any of its 706 member colleges to withdraw scholarships and grants from student athletes guilty of violating campus or athletic department rules. In the past the NCAA had barred member colleges from withdrawing such financial assistance once it had been granted.

The University of Illinois trustees agreed Jan. 15 to new procedures under which court action would be taken to bring about the dismissal of any student found guilty of knowingly participating in a coercive or disruptive demonstration on the campus. The trustees' decision endorsed the recommendations of a report compiled after a disorderly 2-day sit-in by black students in Sept. 1968. The trustees Feb. 19, on the recommendation of the university's president, David Dodds Henry, authorized university authorities to cooperate with state law enforcers in prosecuting some of the 244 students arrested in September.

At Harvard, however, the faculty of arts and sciences voted Jan. 14 to overrule disciplinary recommendations made by the university's administrative board. The board had called for the expulsion of 5 students who had taken part Dec. 12, 1968 in a sit-in against the ROTC unit on campus. All 5 had been disciplined for a previous demonstration. The faculty voted to approve the board's suggested penalty but to suspend the sentences and thus put on probation some 60 students involved in the December sit-in. Teachers and students had petitioned for amnesty for the sit-in participants.

More than 100 black students crowded Feb. 7 into the first meeting of a Harvard class on the control and elimination of slum riots and denounced the course as racist. The course's syllabus was cancelled after the sit-in. In a letter to Harvard President Nathan M. Pusey, 108 Harvard professors protested against the student intrusion and the cancellation as an "infringement upon . . . academic rights." Signers of the letter included Henry Rosovsky, chairman of a faculty committee that had recommended a degree program in Afro-American studies, and Martin Kilson, the only Negro in Harvard's Arts & Sciences faculty. Pusey Feb. 18 responded to the letter in a statement that emphasized the need for "sufficient understanding, historical sense, reason and self-control to insist that coercive methods have no place in this university community." The chief threats to academic freedom in the past had come from outside the university, Pusey said. "The irony and tragedy of the present is that now the threats to academic liberty and integrity often come from within."

A Columbia University committee of faculty, students and administrative officers recommended Feb. 7 that the university waive punishment of 367 students involved in campus disorders in Apr. 1968 and permit 16 suspended students to seek readmission to the university. Dr. Andrew W. Cordier, Columbia's acting president, endorsed the committee's recommendations Feb. 11. He issued a statement calling for swifter disciplinary action against students involved in future campus disorders and for "conscious and articulate participation" by faculty and students in restructuring the university. 12 Columbia students had filed suit in N.Y. State Supreme Court Jan. 10 in a demand that the university's trustees be dismissed for failing to maintain a "state of tranquility" required for study and teaching. They charged that there was a "serious and imminent danger of renewed outbreaks" due to the university's leniency and vacillation in dealing with campus radicals and its bias in favor of hiring faculty members with leftist tendencies. The students called on the court "to safeguard the interests of nonradical and conservative students."

A "get-tough" policy for dealing with campus disorders was announced Feb. 17 by the Rev. Theodore M. Hesburgh, president of the University of Notre Dame at South Bend, Ind. Hesburgh pledged prompt expulsion of students who disrupted the operation of the university. Hesburgh's statement was endorsed by Pres. Nixon in a letter of praise written to the priest and released by the White House Feb. 24. The President told Hesburgh that he shared his concern over campus disorders and wanted to "applaud the forthright stand you have taken." Nixon said: "If the integrity of our universities is to be preserved, then certain principles must be re-established and certain basic rules enforced. Intimidation and threats remain outlaw weapons in a free society. A fundamental governing principle of any great university is that the rule of reason and not the rule of force prevails. Whoever rejects that principle forfeits his right to be a member of the academic community. The university administrator who fails to uphold the principle jeopardizes one of the central pillars of his institution and weakens the very foundation of American education."

Hesburgh said in his policy letter that his stand was a result of a "clear mandate from his university community" to see that legitimate means of dissent were assured but that "obstruction of the life of the university" was outlawed as an illegitimate means of dissent. According to new rules Hesburgh outlined, "anyone or any group that substitutes force for rational persuasion, be it violent or non-violent, will be given 15 minutes of meditation to . . . desist." Then, if they refused to stop their use of force, they would be suspended from the university. Those who refused to identify themselves as members of the university would be dealt with by the law as trespassers or disturbers of the peace. If students continued disruptive activities after being notified of suspension, they would be expelled after 5 minutes and the law would "deal with them as nonstudents." Hesburgh said that the university would tolerate disruption from neither students nor faculty.

In his letter to Hesburgh, Pres. Nixon suggested that federal and state action be considered "to cope with the growing lawlessness and violence on our campuses." He said he had directed Vice Pres. Spiro T. Agnew to discuss such action, "consistent with the traditional independence of American universities," at the National Governors Conference, which later met in Washington, D.C. Feb. 26-27. The executive committee of the conference Feb. 26 issued a statement extending "full support" to the President "relative to the preservation and advancement of higher education." It pledged to take steps to insure educational opportunities for "the vast number of students" threatened by "lawless acts" of relatively few students.

At the Washington conference Feb. 27, the governors adopted the executive committee statement but rejected a resolution by Gov. Ronald Reagan (R., Calif.) that the Justice Department make a "full and complete investigation into the instigators, the causes and the effects of [campus] violence." The Reagan proposal was rejected after Agnew told the governors that the Justice Department "routinely" kept an eye on campus disruption and that Atty. Gen. John N. Mitchell had said that the call for an investigation "really was superfluous." The governors were given copies of a letter from Hesburgh to Agnew, and Agnew asked the governors to study the letter and give him their thoughts on it. In the letter, Hesburgh emphasized that universities could best solve their own problems of student disruption and that when outside help was needed, "let it be understood that the university, and only the university, public or private, makes this determination."

Martin Meyerson, president of the State University of New York at Buffalo, commenting Feb. 25 on Hesburgh's statement, said that he opposed the substitution of force for "rational persuasion" but that he was equally concerned "by the adult backlash which seeks to punish the young for the same kind of activities that in a union, for example, would be a part of normal behavior." He added that "what is constitutionally protected off the campus ... [should be] constitutionally protected on the campus." Gaylord P. Harnwell, president of the University of Pennsylvania, said that he agreed with the President and that actions would have to be taken against disruptive students "with the concurrence of all elements of the university community." Fred H. Harrington, president of the University of Wisconsin, said that he expected more expulsions and arrests on campus but that in order to keep universities open, "it's no less important that we introduce the reforms that are needed and keep the lines open to students to maintain the dialogue."

A petition deploring violence on campus was signed by 12,000 Michigan State University students by Feb. 26. (The university had an enrollment of 40,000.) An organizer of the drive said its purpose was to show "that a majority of students are against violence and disruptive behavior." The university's student governing board had asserted Feb. 19 that student participants in recent demonstrations at the university had been dupes of outside agitators. The student board called for the expulsion of anybody found guilty of "this violence."

Pres. Nixon, commenting Mar. 22 on "the present turmoil" on college campuses, held that the universities should handle the situation themselves. "The federal government cannot, should not, must not enforce" the "first principles" of academic freedom, the Presidential statement declared. "That is fundamentally the task and responsibility of the university community." The "first principles," as defined by Nixon, were: (1) "Universities and colleges are places of excellence in which men are judged by achievement and merit in defined areas," and (2) "violence or the threat of violence may never be permitted to influence the actions or judgments of the university community." "Once it does," he said, "the community, almost by definition, ceases to be a university." Campus violence was endangering intellectual freedom in America, the President said, because it "seemingly" was becoming an "accepted" characteristic of "the clash of opinion within university confines." The objective of the violence was becoming "increasingly" clear—"to politicize" the student bodies and "the institutions as well." Nixon, however, warned against reassertion of first principles in a student-protest situation "while ignoring the issues that are foremost in the minds of these students." This would be "slothful and dishonest" and "in the end futile," he said. "Students today point to many wrongs which must be made right," such as a "depersonalization of the educational experience," "a deep and growing social unrest," reflected by the student unrest, and lack of university reform.

Nixon said he had directed the Health, Education & Welfare (HEW) Department "to launch new initiatives toward easing tensions in our educational community." He also referred in his statement to a letter sent that week by HEW Secy. Robert H. Finch to the presidents of colleges and universities to call their attention to recently enacted provisions "which provide for the withdrawal of various forms of federal support to students found guilty of violation of criminal statutes in connection with campus disorders." Pointing out that "the burden of administration" of applying the aid-withdrawal provisions "falls upon the institutions," Finch urged administrators "to review university policy and regulations with regard to student participation in campus affairs in order to guarantee that in maintaining order on the campus the right of legitimate and responsible dissent is fully protected." The provisions referred to by Finch, neither of which had ever been invoked, called for the withholding of federal educational aid from (a) students convicted of crimes or deemed by the institution to be guilty of "serious" violation of regulations and from (b) students convicted of crimes related to campus disorder.

Finch told a House Education subcommittee Apr. 18 that colleges and universities beset with student disturbances "have brought much of it on themselves." They had been, possibly, "the least responsive to massive changes" taking place in American society, he said, and had failed to react to a "clear need" for "constant self-examination and self-renewal." "In attempting to serve many masters—government and industry among them—they have tended to serve none of them well," Finch said. In many instances the student disruptions were "solidly based in legitimate grievances," he declared. Testifying on legislation for controlling campus violence, Finch opposed a proposal to bar federal aid to universities plagued by protest. This would "penalize a great majority of students for the conduct of a few," he warned. Such legislation should be aimed at the "hard-core extremists, not the vast majority of hardworking students," he said.

A position paper issued Apr. 17 by the board of directors of the American Council on Education stated that the "academic community has the responsibility to deal promptly and directly with disruptions" and that campus dissidents "should not be encouraged to expect amnesty from the effects of the law." The paper approved by the council, which represented 1,500 member institutions and associations, had been drafted in Chicago 2 weeks earlier at a meeting of 28 university presidents and foundation officials. The statement blamed the disorders on "a minute group of destroyers who have abandoned hope in today's society." It said the "great majority" of U.S. campuses had remained peaceful "despite the nationwide publicity given to student disorders." It reported that "on the undisturbed campuses and among the majority of orderly students, however, there are widely shared discontents which extremists are at times able to manipulate to destructive ends." It warned that "reform and self-renewal in higher education are on-going imperatives." Dr. Logan Wilson, president of the council, reported that the Chicago conference and the position paper were attempts to develop a consensus on the appropriate university response "to this crisis in public confidence." Among educators who attended the Chicago drafting session were Harvard Pres. Pusey and University of Notre Dame Pres. Hesburgh.

Dr. Calvin H. Plimpton, president of Amherst College (Massachusetts), warned Pres. Nixon in a letter dated Apr. 29 that campus unrest would continue "until you and the other political leaders of our country address more effectively, massively, and persistently the major social and foreign problems of our society." The message was sent "in behalf of an overwhelming majority of Amherst students, faculty and administration." The letter took issue with the Administration view that campus turmoil was caused by a small minority of students. The statement said that it was not a "conspiracy by a few" that caused unrest but "a shared sense that the nation has no adequate plans for meeting the crises of our society." The decision to draft the letter was made after two days of discussion at Amherst. Classes had been suspended Apr. 24-25, according to the letter, to permit an examination of "our beliefs about the nature of higher education and the governance of educational institutions."

Students Seize Campus Buildings

Members of the Afro-American Society at Brandeis University (Waltham, Mass.) had seized the campus communications center Jan. 8, 1969 and held it for 11 days in demands for an autonomous black studies department, amnesty for demonstrators and more recognition of Negroes on campus. The building was seized by about 15 black students, but the number of the occupants swelled. About 65 students ended their occupation Jan. 18 after the amnesty demand had been met. (The students had been suspended Jan. 11 after failing to meet the administration's deadline for evacuating the building.) Morris Berthold Abram, 50, who had become president of the university Sept. 1, 1968, had insisted that force was not necessary to remove the students from the building. The faculty voted to establish an Afro-American studies department, but Abrams rejected the demonstrators' demand for student control over appointing the new department's head and faculty. The building had been seized one day after 2 of the dissidents at strife-torn San Francisco State College—Dr. Arlene Daniels, a sociology professor, and Bill Middleton, a graduate student and Black Student Union member—had visited Brandeis and urged support for militancy. Brandeis operated normally during the seige for most of its 2,600 enrolled students. (Brandeis had more than 100 black students and faculty members.) Some 200 students held a sit-in at the campus administration building Jan. 9 in support of the amnesty demand.

More than 20 black students took over the administration building at Swarthmore College (Pa.) Jan. 9 in a demand for the admission of more black students and the hiring of more black faculty and administration members. The occupation, conducted by the Swarthmore Afro-American Student Society (SASS), was ended Jan. 16 after Dr. Courtney C. Smith, 52, president of the college, was stricken fatally with a heart attack while preparing for a meeting with the demonstrators. A SASS spokesman said they had abandoned the sit-in out of respect for Smith but would press their demands later. The protesters demanded amnesty for demonstrators and a greater voice in policy-making. Swarthmore, a

Quaker-affiliated school outside Philadelphia, had 47 black students out of an enrollment of 1,024.

About 70 Negroes and about 75 white members of the Students for a Democratic Society seized the administration building at the University of Minnesota in Minneapolis Jan. 14-15. They ended their occupation after reaching a settlement with university authorities. A degree program in Afro-American studies was among their demands. The demonstrators were confronted by some 200 white students who gathered outside the building and raised a "white power" sign in protest against the occupation.

About 30 black students ended a sit-in at the University of Pittsburgh's computer center Jan. 16 after the administration agreed to speed action on demands that included the creation of an Institute for Black Studies.

About 400 students occupied the administration building of the University of Chicago Jan. 30, and varying numbers of them held the building until Feb. 14 in protest against the ouster of Mrs. Marlene Dixon, 32, a faculty member with New Left political leanings. The demonstration ended in failure. Protest leaders contended that Mrs. Dixon, an assistant professor of sociology who described herself as a Marxist, was being dismissed because she was a woman, because of her political views and because in her career she emphasized classroom teaching rather than publication of research and used unorthodox methods of instruction. The sociology department's tenured members had made the decision not to rehire Mrs. Dixon after the expiration of her contract in Sept. 1969. The university, which had refrained from the threat of force to remove the students, suspended 61 protesters Feb. 6. Dallin Oaks, chairman of the disciplinary committee, said that the suspensions had been ordered because the students persisted in "disruptive conduct." The 61 offenders had failed to respond to summonses to appear before the committee. The summonses had been issued to students who had occupied the building for 4 days. 2 students who had appeared before the committee were not punished. (22 more demonstrators were suspended Feb. 13.)

Mrs. Dixon's dismissal remained the main issue of the University of Chicago protest, but demonstrators disagreed over secondary demands. They agreed on a demand for amnesty for all demonstrators. Some protesters demanded an equal voice for students in the hiring and dismissal of faculty, but a Students for a Democratic Society faction proposed Feb. 2 that "student power" demands should be dropped in favor of pressure on the university to aid neighboring slum residents and to recruit students from poor families.

10 young men, reportedly armed with literature issued by the Minutemen, a militant rightwing organization, broke past student guards of the occupied University of Chicago building Feb. 8 and began fighting with protesters. A student and a campus policeman were injured, and 3 of the new invaders were arrested.

The Chicago student occupation ended Feb. 14 with an admission of failure. Protest leader Jeff Blum told his fellow demonstrators as they decided to capitulate: "We must admit to ourselves that we lost. There was no campus uproar over the failure to rehire Mrs. Dixon, nor was there any campus demand for amnesty for the sit-inners. . . . Perhaps our movement is too radical for the campus at this time."

The faculty council of the University of Chicago senate called Feb. 26 for the expulsion of disruptive students and the use of police on campus if necessary to control disorder. Dr. Bruno Bettelheim, psychiatrist and professor of psychology at the university, had told reporters Jan. 31 that "many of these kids [the demonstrators] are very sick . . ., paranoid." He said their actions were like those of the German students who had supported Hitler.

After reaching agreement with a faculty committee at the predominantly black North Carolina Agricultural & Technical College (Greensboro), 125 protesting students Feb. 6 ended a brief occupation of the administration building. A university official said that some of the student demands, which included academic policy concessions and a black studies program, had been met.

Black and white students clashed with policemen on the Duke University campus (Durham, N.C.) Feb. 13, 9 hours after some 60 black students had seized the campus administration building in a demand for a non-graded, special black education program, a black studies program, money for black student union facilities and an end to "racist" policies at the university. (There were about 100 Negroes among the 8,000 students at Duke.) The police had been called by Duke's president, Dr. Douglas M. Knight, and by the chairman of the board of trustees, Charles B. Wade (vice president of the R. J. Reynolds Tobacco Co.). The police arrived as the occupiers filed out of the seized building, but about 1,000 students, mostly white, had gathered in front of the building in support of the Negroes. Policemen, using tear gas and clubs, battled with the demonstrators after protesters began pounding a police car. 26 persons were injured, including 5 policemen apparently hit by rocks or tear gas canisters that the students hurled back at them. 2 hours after the police arrived, they withdrew from the area of the demonstration, with students screaming jeers and insults after them. The university Feb. 16 announced a compromise settlement. The school agreed to a new black studies program, believed to be the first accepted at a major Southern university. The university also agreed to let black students have their own dormitory and to hire an adviser to the Negroes who would be acceptable to students and administration.

Students at the predominantly black Wiley College in Marshall Tex. barricaded and padlocked several buildings Feb. 18 in a demand for academic reform, academic freedom and the resignation of the college president, Dr. T. W. Cole. Cole, who had received a report of an arms cache on the campus, ordered the students off the campus Feb. 25 and closed the school until further notice. A dormitory search turned up no arms.

800 students at State University of New York's Stony Brook campus seized the library building temporarily Feb. 20 in a demand for the retention of Assistant Dean John De Francesco, whom the university had decided not to reappoint, and for the creation of a joint student-faculty committee on university staff appointments. Dr. John S. Toll, president of the university, met with student demonstration leaders to work out an agreement on their demands, but protest leaders said that they viewed Toll's response as "unacceptable." About 150 Stony Brook students barred an Army recruiter from holding interviews on campus Feb. 24 and held a 4-hour sit-in at the university administration offices in a protest against campus recruitment by the armed services and by corporations with defense contracts.

Some 200 black and white students at Eastern Michigan University attempted to seize the administration building at Ypsilanti Feb. 20 but were blocked by deputy sheriffs posted inside the building. Twelve demonstrators were arrested. The students were pressing for an expanded black studies department.

Black students at the Newark, N.J. campus of Rutgers University (Rutgers-Newark) Feb. 24 seized Conklin Hall, which contained classrooms, faculty offices and the university switchboard. They demanded the dismissal of 2 admissions officers and a voice in admissions and administration policy. The Black Organization of Students, which claimed some 100 members among the 130 Negroes at Rutgers-Newark, had organized the demonstration.

After students at Pennsylvania State University (University Park) had occupied the administration building for several hours

Feb. 24, university officials Feb. 25 obtained a court injunction that banned sit-ins. The students, who were demanding equal rights for women students and an end to military recruiting on campus, filed peacefully out of the building after the injunction was read to them. Dr. Eric A. Walker, the university president, said in a statement to the university's 38,000 students that any student found guilty of disrupting the operation of the university would be expelled.

Student Disruptions in California

A state of emergency was declared at San Fernando Valley (Calif.) State College Jan. 9, 1969 by the acting president, Dr. Delmar T. Oviatt. He had received a report that a "conspiracy," which involved bringing arms onto the campus, had been planned at a meeting held outside the campus the night of Jan. 8. More than 235 demonstrators were arrested during an unauthorized rally on the campus Jan. 9 in defiance of Oviatt's order. A series of secret meetings of faculty members and representatives of the Black Student Union and the United Mexican-American Students was then arranged by Herbert L. Carter, head of the Los Angeles County Committee on Human Relations. The *N.Y. Times* reported Feb. 16 that an agreement reached at the meetings called for separate Negro and Mexican-American studies departments, the admission of 700 new minority-group students, the hiring of staff members from minority groups and a procedure for airing student grievances against faculty members.

Violence broke out at San Jose (Calif.) State College Jan. 17 when some 50 students ran through campus buildings, broke windows, splashed paint and set off sprinkler systems. A policeman's car windshield was shattered by a bullet during the disruption. The rioting students had been at a student-faculty rally in support of a strike called by the American Federation of Teachers to reverse the ouster of 26 teachers who had been dropped after 5 consecutive unexplained absences. (The strike ended Feb. 14.)

Striking teachers and students continued to disrupt activities at San Francisco State College with often-violent demonstrations. The college's acting president, S.I. Hayakawa, sought to dismiss striking teachers and restore order on the campus. A rally held Jan. 23, by striking student members of the Third World Liberation Front in defiance of new campus restrictions on demonstrations resulted in 483 arrests. The 3d World Liberation Front, an organization of minority-group students, among them members of the Black Student Union, held the rally in support of 15 "non-negotiable" demands, which included the creation of an autonomous ethnic studies department and the admission of more students from minority groups. The arrests came after students clashed with police who were trying to break up the demonstration. Before the rally there had been only 189 arrests since the students began their strike Nov. 6, 1968.

Emergency Declared in Berkeley Student Strike

Clashes between police and striking students of the 3d World Liberation Front resulted in 20 arrests Feb. 4, 1969 at the University of California at Berkeley. Gov. Ronald Reagan Feb. 5 declared "a state of extreme emergency" at Berkeley and authorized the California Highway Patrol to provide all necessary aid to help local police maintain order. The strike had been called Jan. 22 in a demand for an ethnic studies program relevant to other minority-group students as well as Negroes. The Feb. 4 disorders erupted when some 300 demonstrators refused police orders to clear the main gate of the 28,000-student campus. The police used nightsticks against demonstrators, and the students fought with sticks, stones, bottles and cans.

At a news conference announcing the declared state of emergency, Reagan said Feb. 5 that students attending classes had been "assaulted and severely beaten" and that "arson and firebombings" had occurred. A fire Jan. 22 had caused $400,000 worth of damage to Wheeler Hall, a 50-year-old campus building; 3d World leaders said that they "deplored" the fire and that arsonists might have been trying to discredit their strike. At a Feb. 6 news conference, 3d World leaders Fernando Garcia and Jeffrey Leong denounced Reagan's declaration as "an attempt to mobilize the reactionary forces in the state."

University authorities had announced Jan. 1 that 7 students had been dismissed, 31 suspended and 133 placed on probation for their actions in a sit-in and seizure of a campus building in October.

More than 150 policemen arrived on campus Feb. 17 to supervise a picket line of students and teaching assistants. The police were met with a barrage of rocks, bottles and stench bombs thrown by the demonstrators. In the clash that followed, 5 persons were injured, including a policeman and a black photographer for a campus newspaper.

Queens College in Turmoil

Black and Puerto Rican participants in a special program for poverty-area students at Queens College (N.Y. City) had conducted a series of demonstrations and invasions of offices at the college beginning Jan. 3, 1969. The demonstrators demanded that the program, dubbed SEEK (for Search for Education, Elevation & Knowledge), be made autonomous at the college and that SEEK's white director, Joseph P. Mulholland, 40, resign or be dismissed. They demanded the right to hire and fire personnel, determine courses and course content, allocate money and admit students. The protest group, the Black & Puerto Rican Student-Faculty-Counselor Coalition, feared, despite administration assertions to the contrary, that the college planned to phase out SEEK or fragment authority for the program among various academic departments. Under SEEK, slum youths received stipends, remedial aid, tutoring and counseling in small classes taught by teachers specifically hired for the program. Of Queens' 26,000 students, some 700 (80% of them black, 15% Puerto Rican) were in SEEK.

Youths believed to be SEEK participants invaded the Queens College faculty dining room, the registrar's office and the library Jan. 6. They smashed dishes and scattered records and cards. The college president, Dr. Joseph P. McMurray, 56, Jan. 7 ordered the campus closed for 2 days "to avoid possible physical violence." He rejected proposals for police or disciplinary action. The college reopened Jan. 10 for exams.

About 15 Negroes ransacked Mulholland's office Jan. 13, shortly before a SEEK student, Shirley Williams, announced the formation of a group in his support. Mulholland, who was supported by a large group of faculty members, asserted that a majority of SEEK participants would back him if they were given a secret vote.

An advisory group appointed by the chancellor of City University recommended Feb. 3 that Mulholland be replaced by a Negro or Puerto Rican in September. It rejected autonomy for the program but said that SEEK students should get a greater voice in the administration of the program. Mulholland resigned Feb. 4, but the militants expressed their disapproval of the college's choice of a temporary successor, Dean of Faculty Robert W. Hartle, 48, also white. 8 demonstrators ransacked Hartle's office Feb. 5, overturned furniture, scattered books and ripped out phones. About 50 other protesters occupied the SEEK administration offices. McMurray announced Feb. 6 that he would submit for appointment as director and assistant director of SEEK names "recommended" to him by the coalition that led the demonstrations. 2 men were appointed, Lloyd Delany, a black professor in the education department, and Rafael Rodriguez, a lecturer in the romance and Slavic languages department. A statement from the student/faculty coalition said that the group had "unanimously selected" the 2 men.

New sit-ins and disruptions at Queens College led to 39 arrests Apr. 1 when 500 policemen cleared demonstrators from the Social Science building. After the police action, members of the Ad Hoc Committee to End Political Supression immediately reoccupied the Social Science building and continued sit-in activity at various campus buildings until police were called in again May 2, and the college was closed until May 6. The sit-in that led to the 39 arrests Apr. 1 was unrelated to the January protests.

The spring disorders began at the Social Science building Mar. 27 in a demand for (a) the reinstatement of 3 students who had been suspended after leading a protest against General Electric Co. recruiters March 11 and (b) the retention of Dr. Sheila Delany, an assistant English professor who had been notified that she would not be rehired. After the police action, the protesters added demands that the college reinstate Dr. Henry Lesnick, the sole faculty member arrested Apr. 1, and drop administrative and criminal charges against all who were arrested.

The dissidents "escalated" their activity by a day-long occupation of 4 floors of 13-story Lefrak Hall (the administration building) Apr. 16 and a 4-day student strike Apr. 21-24. Angered by college Pres. McMurray's response to their demands, members of the Ad Hoc Committee reoccupied the administration building Apr. 28. A conservative group calling itself the Student Coalition sat in at the college registrar's office May 1 in protest against the administration's failure to call in police to end the occupation. The faculty voted 286-248 May 1 to request that charges be dropped against the 39 who were arrested Apr. 1 but only if the building occupation were ended.

Following a May 1 meeting of SEEK students, black students smashed windows in the faculty dining room and overturned card catalogues and smashed display cases in the main library in a demand for curriculum changes and control of faculty hiring in the SEEK program. After additional violence May 2, the police were called and the college closed until May 7. McMurray said that he had decided to call police after members of the Black & Puerto Rican Coalition had said they would use "any means necessary" to achieve their demands. Students occupying the adminstration building left on hearing that policemen were coming.

Queens College Prof. Henry Lesnick and 31 men students were sentenced to 15 days in jail June 19 for criminal trespass on charges arising from the Apr. 1 demonstration. 7 women students were fined $250 each.

Disorders at CCNY

About 100 to 200 black and Puerto Rican students occupied the administration building of the City College of New York for nearly 4 hours Feb. 13. The demonstrators, who called themselves the Black & Puerto Rican Community, complained that Buell G. Gallagher, the college president, had not met demands they had submitted Feb. 6. Among the demands were the creation of a separate School of Black & Puerto Rican Studies, a student voice in policies of the college's SEEK program, separate orientation for minority-group freshman, a numerical reflection of the racial composition of the city's high schools in incoming freshmen classes and a requirement that education majors study black and Puerto Rican history and the Spanish language. Gallagher had described his written reply to the students as "affirmative answers to all their demands." He said Feb. 14: "I have refused to say no on each point, and I have found it difficult to say yes." (A college spokesman said that 12% 15% of CCNY's 11,000 students were black or Puerto Rican and that half of these were SEEK participants.) Small groups of Negroes and Puerto Ricans raced through CCNY buildings Feb. 17, and several dozen incidents of minor vandalism were reported. College officials said that city police had been consulted but not summoned. Dean of Students Nicholas Paster said that "the kind of action the police might bring would be an escalation of the type of thing we want to avoid."

CCNY Pres. Gallagher ordered the college closed Apr. 22 after some 150 black and Pueto Rican students locked themselves inside the gates of the college's south campus. Gallagher May 9 announced his immediate resignation after the city Board of Higher Education and a number of court orders forced the college to reopen against the judgment of the administration and faculty.

The college had been closed for a 2d day Apr. 23 after Gallagher and the protesters barricaded inside the south campus had agreed to discuss their demand that CCNY's enrollment reflect the student population of the city's high schools, which was more than 50% black and Puerto Rican. The demonstrators also made demands about ethnic-studies programs, and they demanded a voice for students in the administration of the college's SEEK program. Gallagher had indicated Apr. 22 that the protesters' demands would be hard to meet because of city and state budget cuts for education. (Gallagher had submitted his resignation in protest against the cuts, which, he said, would cripple the operation of the school, one of the senior colleges of the City University of New York [CUNY].)

Gallagher Apr. 24 ordered the college closed until Apr. 29. He was backed by a faculty resolution passed by 117-94 vote. The faculty voted 221-1 to "oppose the employment of force or the resort to injunctive procedures in order to resolve this dispute as long as negotiations are going forward." Gallagher promised Apr. 28 that CCNY would remain closed as long as negotiations continued with the dissidents, and the faculty supported his promise. 3 court orders, however, were obtained to force the reopening of CCNY. 2 writs, obtained May 1 by Rep. Mario Biaggi (D.,N.Y.) and by the Jewish Defense League, required that Gallagher, the Board of Higher Education and City University Chancellor Albert H. Bowker show in court why CCNY should not be reopened. City Controller Mario A. Procaccino, a CCNY alumnus and a Democratic candidate for mayor of New York, got the 3d court order May 2.

Faced with the court orders, the Board of Higher Education May 4 directed that the college reopen.

After a city official had served a restraining order prohibiting the occupation, about 250 black and Puerto Rican students, joined by about 50 white SDS supporters, marched out of the south campus May 5. CCNY opened in its entirety May 6 for the first time in 2 weeks, but disruptive incidents continued.

Gallagher closed the college again May 7 after racial battles between black dissidents and white counter-demonstrators. The violence reportedly began when black students and supporters roamed the campus and ordered white students from classrooms and college buildings. Many white students and faculty members were attacked and beaten. But supporters of the black and Puerto Rican students charged that threats by whites had started the fighting. Police restored quiet only after about 7 white students were injured by club-swinging black students. College officials then announced to a crowd of 500 cheering white students that CCNY would be opened the next day "with adequate police protection." The college reopened May 8, although some professors cancelled classes or met with students off campus.

Gallagher announced May 9 that he had asked the Board of Higher Education "to relieve me of my duties and responsibilities" as CCNY president "at the earliest possible moment and certainly not later" than Monday morning May 12. At the insistence of the Board of Higher Education, the campus remained open May 9. The faculty senate, in a resolution, deplored the opening of the college "against the advice of the faculty senate" and deplored the "political interference that forced the resignation of Dr. Gallagher."

The board May 10 appointed as acting president Dr. Joseph Copeland, 61, a botanist on the CCNY faculty for 41 years. Copeland said that he was "basically sympathetic" to the dissidents' demands and that he would try to resume negotiations.

Arson, Vandalism & Strife at CUNY Colleges

Fires and acts of vandalism Apr. 18, 1969 disrupted classes at Brooklyn College, a 10,000-student unit of CUNY, after black and Puerto Rican students warned that "all hell" would break loose unless the college met their demands by 1 p.m. The demands— designed to end the college's alleged "racism and genocide"— included "open admission" of black and Puerto Rican applicants regardless of grades, the addition of 25 Negroes and 25 Puerto Ricans to the faculty and the ouster of all white teachers who had shown "racist tendencies." Acting Pres. George A. Peck Apr. 17 issued a statement "sympathizing" with the students' "needs." But Peck said some of the demands were beyond his jurisdiction and depended on CUNY finances and laws.

Peck cancelled all classes the morning of Apr. 29 so that the demands could be discussed. A meeting of the college's Faculty Council Apr. 22 to discuss the dispute had broken up when 6 black students seized the podium from Peck. Students representing the 3d World Coalition had conducted a 6-hour sit-in at one of the campus buildings Apr. 22, but classes had not been disrupted.

About 150 to 200 dissident students vandalized Peck's office Apr. 30 but left when it was rumored that police were about to arrive on the campus. They lit a small fire in the office, smashed a table and ripped phone wires out of the walls. Disruption continued May 2 with SDS members taking part in some incidents. Peck obtained a court injunction against further demonstrations or vandalism; he named 20 students and "100 John and Jane Does." Peck had ordered the campus cleared after several small fires had broken out. The college faculty May 5 adopted a resolution supporting the administration and urging that "all legal means" be used to prevent further disruption.

Firemen called to fight a blaze at the college's administration building May 6 were blocked by about 100 students, most of them black and Puerto Rican. A policeman was hit by a thrown flowerpot as the militants and some 2,000 students who had gathered hurled stones and clods of earth at each other. Classes continued for the rest of the day after 20 policemen dispersed the militants, but incidents of vandalism continued as black students pelted windows with stones. At Peck's request, 75 policemen patrolled the campus May 9 because of the "reign of vandalism, property damage and psychological terror" at the college.

At Queensborough Community College, an 8,500-student 2-year college of CUNY, members of the Student-Faculty Coalition to End Political Suppression clashed with the college president, Dr. Kurt R. Schmeller, 31, over the dismissal of an assistant English professor, Dr. Donald J. Silberman. 50 coalition members staged an eight-hour sit-in at the administration building Apr. 17, 1969 in protest against the firing of Silberman, a member of the leftist Progressive Labor Party, who had been informed that his contract would not be renewed. The sit-in ended when 100 helmeted policemen arrived at Schmeller's request. The protesters left the administration building before the police took any action.

The coalition renewed the administration building sit-in Apr. 21 after overpowering campus security guards at the door. The administration obtained a court order against the protesters, and Dean of Students John J. Prior warned other students gathered in support of the sit-in that no permit had been issued for their rally and that, therefore, they were subject to suspension. As the sit-in continued Apr. 22, Schmeller announced the "summary dismissal" of Silberman and 2 other faculty members for what he called "outrageously unprofessional conduct" by participating in the sit-in. The other 2 professors were Dr. Robert MacDonald of the social science department and Dr. Steven Faigelman of the English department. Schmeller Apr. 22 also obtained a court order requiring the demonstrators to show cause why they should not be held in contempt for violating the restraining order.

13 members of the college department of student personnel Apr. 24 publicly dissociated themselves from Schmeller's actions against what they claimed was a "peaceful, orderly and nonobstructive" demonstration. They said they were convinced that Schmeller's orders "to suspend students, to summon the police and to serve court injunctions were a clear violation of students'

rights." The faculty Apr. 25 voted to reinstate their 3 dismissed colleagues and adopted a resolution criticizing Schmeller's actions. Schmeller said later: "I'm going ahead with the court action on the basis that people are to be held accountable for their actions." With the sit-in in its 3d week, Schmeller May 6 sent letters to the 3 faculty members and offered to submit their dismissals to binding arbitration if they would "leave and no longer take part in the sit-in" and would urge others to discontinue the protest. Silberman rejected the offer even before he received it.

The protesters in the administration building seized the 4th floor of the building May 7 and held it for 3 hours. They refused to leave when Schmeller warned that he would call the police and that they would be subject to criminal trespass charges. Schmeller then summoned the police, but minutes before they arrived, the demonstrators burst out of the building and merged with the crowd.

Silberman, MacDonald, Faigelman, Faigelman's wife and 25 students were arrested May 8 and charged with criminal trespass as a result of the May 7 seizure. MacDonald was also charged with assaulting a school carpenter. The 3 professors were sentenced to 15 days in jail and fined $250 each June 19 for violating the injunction against sit-ins. Steven Auerback, SDS chairman at the school, was sentenced to 5 days in jail and fined $250 for his part in the sit-in.

The N.Y. City Board of Higher Education June 23 adopted a new behavior code to govern CUNY's 9 senior colleges and 6 community colleges. The board declared that the university "has the right, and indeed the obligation, to defend itself" against disorders. The code was filed with the state Board of Regents June 24 in compliance with a new state law. The code forbade unauthorized occupancy of university facilities, obstruction of the rights of members of the university or interference with educational processes, theft or damage of university or personal property and the possession of firearms.

Students Clash with Police & Administrators

A demonstration in support of student demands at Mississippi Valley State College in Itta Bena was broken up Feb. 9, 1969 by 150 Mississippi highway patrolmen, who arrested 15 students. The university then "sent home" 198 other demonstrators. Negro leader Charles Evers appeared at a rally Feb. 10 and urged students to boycott classes and "close this campus down" as a protest against the suspensions. Faced with a class boycott by 90% of the 2,500 students, the college canceled classes Feb. 12. Agreement was finally reached Feb. 14 on student demands for more political speakers on campus and for a course in black history.

About 30 students at Roosevelt University in Chicago took over classes and conducted lessons in black studies Feb. 10-12. A dean who had met with the students said Feb. 12 that he thought that the situation was under control. But 6 students were expelled after another class was disrupted Feb. 17. 100 black and white students at Roosevelt University forced their way Feb. 20 into the office of Rolf A. Weil, the university president, and tried to make him sign a declaration of amnesty for protesters. He refused. The invaders ripped out phones, set off fire alarms and attacked reporters.

Gov. Warren P. Knowles ordered 900 Wisconsin National Guard troops rushed to Madison Feb. 12 to control some 1,000 to 2,000 striking students at the University of Wisconsin. An additional 1,000 troops arrived Feb. 14. The strike had been called Feb. 7 by the Black People's Alliance to support demands for an autonomous black studies department, controlled by black students and faculty, the admission of more black students and other reforms. The strike was preceded by a weeklong symposium on "the black revolution." The symposium, sponsored by 24 campus organizations, drew militant black speakers from Chicago. Among the speakers was Nathan Hare, head of the new black studies department at strife-torn San Francisco State College. Hare asserted that revolution was needed at the University of Wisconsin.

In calling out the Guard, Knowles acted on the request of Madison authorities after the weary local police had patrolled the campus around the clock for 2 days. When the Guard troops first arrived at the campus Feb. 13, they met a dramatically escalated force of student strikers, estimated at 5,000 to 10,000. Demonstrating students clashed with local police armed with riot sticks and tear gas. The troops, with fixed bayonets, prevented mass picketing so that classes could continue. But students blocked traffic on the campus and city streets, pulled fire alarms and turned on fire hoses in campus buildings. As the intensity of the disorders diminished, authorities began withdrawing troops from the campus late Feb. 14. Students agreed to recess the strike Feb. 18. (The university's Afro-American & Race Relations Center, occupying the 3d floor of the 3-story building, was nearly destroyed by fire Feb. 19. The center had been used by strike leaders for strategy meetings.)

Turmoil at Howard University

Howard University law students seized the law school building Feb. 18 in a demand for student participation in implementing academic policies recently agreed on by a student-faculty committee. The student action evidently was not directed against Howard's new law school dean, Mrs. Patricia Roberts Harris. The students chained shut the doors and said they would not leave "without a voice in the operation of this . . . school." Mrs. Harris then said that she would seek a court injunction ordering the students out. Confronted with the order Feb. 19, the students relinquished the building but continued to boycott classes. Mrs. Harris resigned as dean Feb. 27. She charged that Howard's president, James M. Nabrit, and other university officials had placed her in an "untenable position" by negotiating with student protesters behind her back.

Students occupied the Fine Arts Building Mar. 11, and the action spread to the liberal arts and administration buildings, but the buildings were reopened later under a temporary court order. The student actions were based on various complaints. At the School of Social Work first-year graduate students began a boycott of classes Apr. 21 in protest against "unqualified" professors and Dean May Ella Robertson's alleged lack of cooperation in handling student complaints. 2d-year graduate students joined in the boycott Apr. 23. The boycott was the 4th of the year at Howard. Sociology and anthropology students began to boycott classes Apr. 28, and they occupied the office of the head of the department, G. Franklin Edwards. The dissidents demanded student power within the department and teaching that was more relevant to the black community. U.S. marshals served on the dissidents May 6 a temporary restraining order that the administration had sought after students occupied the university computer center for the 2d time.

After the number of seized buildings had risen to 8, Howard Pres. Nabrit accepted faculty advice and closed the university May 7. Incidents of vandalism accompanied the seizures as students and non-students smashed the university snack bar and looted the juke box and cigarette machine. The dissidents later consolidated their holdings to 6 buildings.

The faculty had adopted a resolution calling on Nabrit to close the university, to confer with student leaders and to give the dissidents 24 hours to evacuate the buildings before U.S. marshals would be called in to evict, but not arrest, the protesters.

Students May 8 called a news conference to "demonstrate unity" between the community and campus. At the conference the Rev. Douglas E. Moore, chairman of the Black United Front, said: "No longer do we conceive of Howard University as an educational community separate and distinct from the total black community." The protesters demanded that the black community have a voice in the administration of the university.

Nabrit, in a televised ultimatum May 8, warned the students that they faced forcible eviction. Later that night, after fires had broken out on campus and cars had been stoned, Mayor Walter E. Washington of the District of Columbia mobilized units of the National Guard as a "precautionary measure." It was reported that at least 5 local policemen, 3 federal marshals and 3 civilian passersby had suffered minor injuries during the disruption.

In an early-morning operation May 9, 100 U.S. marshals and 23 campus security guards broke into the occupied buildings and removed the students. 20 protesters were arrested and arraigned on charges of criminal contempt of court. 2 of them said they were not enrolled at Howard.

8 divisions at Howard resumed classes May 12. School of Social Work students, however, continued to boycott classes.

(Rep. Adam Clayton Powell [D.,N.Y.] had said in a speech at Howard Apr. 25 that he would personally serve an injunction against the first university president who dismissed a student because of federal laws barring financial aid to disruptive students.)

Students Seize Buildings at Columbia

Students for a Democratic Society (SDS) at Columbia University (N.Y.) delivered what they termed the "first blow" of a spring protest offensive Mar. 25, 1969 with a peaceful one-day strike. About 225 students picketed 8 buildings on the school's Morningside Heights campus. The strikers demanded abolition of the Reserve Officers Training Corps program, an end to military research and recruiting on campus and the reopening of 197 Columbia-owned apartments to the public.

The Student Afro-American Society (SAS), which with SDS had played a major role in the spring 1968 disruption at Columbia, remained aloof from the SDS action. But 20 black students Apr. 14 seized the Columbia College admissions office in Hamilton Hall, the building held by SAS during the Apr. 1968 seizures. SAS charged that "Columbia University has been and still remains systematically racist and oppressive in its relations with black people." The group demanded a special admissions board and staff "nominated and authorized by black students" to determine Columbia's admissions and recruitment policies for black students. Columbia officials warned SAS Apr. 14 that the occupation was illegal, but 16 protesters remained in the building for a 2d day. University lawyers obtained a court order to end the occupation, and the black students vacated the building April 16 before the court order was served. 200 SDS supporters occupied Philosophy Hall April 17, to "win demands for an end to ROTC, war research and racism." Fights broke out between the protesters and members of Students for Columbia University, an anti-SDS group, who tried to prevent SDS members from blocking the doors. The protesters left the building voluntarily after a brief scuffle with officials attempting to serve a court order against the occupation.

A building seizure was attempted Apr. 19 by 32 members of a breakaway radical faction of SDS called the SDS Expansion Committee, a group including members of the Trotskyite Progressive Labor party. The 32 protesters vacated the building 6 hours later saying they felt they lacked campus and community support.

It was announced Apr. 19 that 800 Columbia professors had signed a statement deploring campus violence and asserting that the university had "the obligation to defend itself" against disruption.

Groups of about 150 high school students were brought onto the campus by SDS Apr. 20 and 21 to support demands for open admission of all graduates of neighboring high schools.

Tensions rose Apr. 30 when 160 SDS members seized Mathematics and Fayerweather Halls. During one of the takeovers, James S. Young, a government professor, was clubbed in the face by an unidentified radical student. 8 other professors and a graduate student remained in Fayerweather for a counter sit-in. The SDS group left the building May 1 shortly after warrants had been signed for their arrests on contempt of court charges for refusing to obey earlier court orders. 5 SDS leaders surrendered to law officers May 2 after State Supreme Court Justice Charles Marks had ordered the arrest of any person who could be identified as having participated in the seizures.

In the midst of renewed demonstrations against Columbia's plan to build a gymnasium in city-owned Morningside Park, Acting Pres. Andrew W. Cordier had said Feb. 27 that since "a sizable field of opinion in the community" objected to the gym, he would recommend that the university not proceed with the plan. The Board of Trustees affirmed Cordier's recommendation Mar. 3.

Faced with demonstrations against the university's Naval ROTC, the university trustees voted May 13 to abolish the program at Columbia by June 1971. Military recruiting at Columbia Jan. 20-21 had been marked by SDS demonstrations, scuffles between students and some vandalism.

Harvard Revolt

A student revolt at Harvard University began Apr. 9, 1969 with the seizure of University Hall, the main administration building, by 300 militant students. The revolt grew to a campus-wide student strike Apr. 11. The rebellion escalated after the administration called in 400 policemen Apr. 10 to end University Hall's 17-hour occupation. About 180 persons were arrested and 41 reported injured.

The occupation of University Hall followed a noon rally led by SDS (Students for a Democratic Society). During the rally, SDS presented 6 demands, including the abolition of Reserve Officer Training Corps units on campus, the rollback of rents for Harvard-owned apartments in Cambridge, Mass. to the Jan. 1, 1968 level and the curbing of university expansion into poor neighborhoods in Cambridge and Boston. The ouster of the ROTC units emerged as the main issue of the occupation. Although the administration had agreed to a faculty decision to strip ROTC courses of academic status, Harvard Pres. Nathan M. Pusey had indicated that the university would negotiate with the Pentagon to try to preserve Harvard's 3 ROTC units. SDS demanded that "all existing ROTC contracts" be broken and that ROTC scholarships be replaced with university scholarships.

During the take-over of the building, 9 university deans were ejected from their offices by force. Several deans who refused to leave were roughly shoved, dragged or carried from the building. Despite a 4 p.m. warning by Dean Franklin L. Ford of the Faculty of Arts & Sciences that the students would be subject to criminal trespass charges if they did not clear the building within 15 minutes, more than 200 students remained throughout the night.

400 state and local policemen, summoned by Pusey and his aides, arrived at dawn and cleared the students from University Hall in an action that took less than 20 minutes. As rumors of the impending "bust" had spread through the campus, students had gathered in front of the hall to block the police. Harvard Dean Fred L. Glimp gave the students a final warning, apparently not heard within the building. The police then charged with nightsticks,

cleared students from the steps of the hall, moved into the building and dragged students out. A student inside described the action as "efficient and rough as anything." Another student said the police "made no attempt to cope with the kind of 'non-violence' we were using." Most of the injured students suffered head cuts, and at least 7 policemen received treatment for minor injuries. The education editor of *Life* magazine reportedly was clubbed by the police from behind, thrown to the ground and beaten. According to arrest statistics, 41 of those arrested were Harvard undergraduates, 29 were Radcliffe students, 28 were Harvard graduate students, 8 were students elsewhere and 30 did not present student identification.

Pusey and Ford Apr. 11 defended the decision to call the police. Pusey said that the students "did not intend to bargain" and that "the issue was a direct assault upon the authority of the university and upon rational processes and accepted procedures." Ford conceded that "perhaps a majority" of the university community felt that the police should not have been used, but he called the action unavoidable; he said University Hall contained confidential and irreplaceable records and papers. The *N.Y. Times* Apr. 11 quoted Ford and other Harvard officials as saying they had not been surprised by the uprising because it had been planned and threatened for more than 3 weeks. "We've been given almost an exact date with only the issue left open," Ford said.

"Moderate" students opposed to the use of police at the university joined Apr. 10 in the SDS call for a student strike. 1,500 students voted overwhelmingly for a resolution that said: "We condemn the administration for its unnecessary use of police and condemn the police for their brutality." They demanded that "the police not be brought onto the campus again," called for amnesty for the demonstrators, demanded that the university government be revised to include members of the "entire university community" and called for Pusey's resignation "if these demands are not met."

The Harvard Faculty of Arts & Sciences voted 395-13 Apr. 11 to deplore the student occupation of University Hall, but its resolution said that "we also deplore the entry of police into any university." The faculty refused to condemn the administration for calling the police but asked the university to drop criminal charges against those arrested.

The Harvard Corp. Apr. 13 issued a statement warning that further campus violence could result in the closing of the university.

The publication of a letter, apparently removed by demonstrators from files in University Hall, seemed to make the original ROTC dispute the major issue. The letter, dated Feb. 11, from Ford to Pusey, expressed Ford's displeasure at the faculty decision to remove academic credit from the ROTC and suggested ways of preserving the units on campus. Nearly 6,000 students voted Apr. 14, by a narrow margin, to continue the strike for 3 more days.

The Harvard Board of Overseers Apr. 14 issued a statement "unequivocally" supporting Pusey's decision to call in the police. The board also set up 2 committees—one to review the immediate crisis and to report its findings promptly and a 2d to make a deeper study of the factors underlying the crisis. In its statement, the board expressed regret that the "hostile occupation of University Hall necessitated the use of police" but emphasized that the "fundamental issue" was whether violence could be allowed to interfere with the functioning of the university. The board insisted that "immediate and unconditional abrogation" of the ROTC program "would constitute an indefensible breach of faith with the students now enrolled."

By 385-25 vote Apr. 17, the Arts & Sciences Faculty declared that the university should sever all official connections with the ROTC and should enter no new contractual arrangements with the Defense Department. The ROTC, however, could remain as an extracurricular activity. The Harvard Corp. confirmed the faculty's ROTC decision Apr. 18. The Arts & Sciences Faculty voted 251-158 Apr. 22 to give black students a vote in the selection of professors for a black studies program. This was the first time that students at Harvard had been given such power over faculty appointments.

SDS continued to apply pressure through a series of individual protest actions. A group of 500 students participated in a "mill-in" at University Hall Apr. 21. The protesters did not interfere with people entering or leaving the building, and they evacuated the hall promptly at 5 p.m. when the building closed, but they did block any work there. Other SDS actions included an invasion of the university planning office Apr. 25 in protest against Harvard's expansion policies and a rowdy invasion Apr. 28 of the office of Radcliffe Pres. Mary Ingraham Bunting, 58, in protest against probation action taken against 22 Radcliffe girls for participating in a Dec. 1968 sit-in.

Despite Harvard Administration efforts to drop criminal trespass charges against students who took part in the Apr. 9 occupation of University Hall, District Court Judge M. Edward Viola, 67, refused Apr. 18 to drop the charges. All but 4 of 173 student defendants were found guilty of criminal trespass May 1. Viola imposed on the convicted 169 defendants the maximum penalty allowed for the misdemeanor, a $20 fine. Carl D. Offner, 25, a Harvard graduate student, was given a one-year jail sentence May 16 for assaulting Dean Robert B. Watson during the Apr. 9 University Hall seizure.

(Dr. S. I. Hayakawa, acting president of San Francisco State College, had said in an interview published in the *Washington Post* Apr. 18 that the Harvard faculty had "double-crossed" Harvard Pres. Pusey in failing to support his use of police to end the building seizure. Hayakawa accused some professors of "an unconscious cultural snobbery"—a "deeprooted prejudice" against "those who are not college-educated"—in condoning student violence while "not [being] willing to give the police that much of a break.")

About 150 black Harvard students occupied University Hall for 6 hours Dec. 5 in a protest against hiring policy. The demonstrators, led by a blanket group called the Organization for Black Unity (OBU), left after the university agreed to submit their demands to committees. They had demanded that 20% of all workers on university construction sites be members of minority groups and that the university promote a predominantly black group of painter's helpers to journeymen and raise their pay. About 75 black students were temporarily suspended Dec. 11 after the OBU led another occupation of University Hall. They left the hall after 5 hours when they were served with a court order to end the demonstration. (In an earlier demonstration over the same issue, a smaller group of SDS members had barricaded Dean Ernest R. May in his office for over an hour Nov. 19. 16 of the students were expelled from the university Dec. 15 or ordered to withdraw for varying lengths of time.)

Weapons Carried in Cornell Building Seizure

About 100 black students seized the student union building at Cornell University in Ithaca, N.Y. Apr. 19, 1969. They emerged Apr. 20, 36 hours later, carrying 17 rifles and shotguns. The demonstrators, members of the university Afro-American Society, ended their occupation of Willard Straight Hall after Dean of Faculty Robert D. Miller agreed to recommend that disciplinary proceedings be dropped against 3 Negroes involved in demonstrations in Dec. 1968. The seizure, during Parents Weekend at the university, took place after a cross was burned Apr. 18 in front of Wari House, a co-op residence for 12 black co-eds.

The building was occupied at about 6 a.m. Apr. 19. Black students ran through the halls of the student union yelling "Fire." They ousted some 30 visiting parents and 40 university employes from the building. The demonstrators took over the campus radio station WVBR; Edward L. Whitfield, 19, a sophomore from Little Rock, Ark. and chairman of Cornell's Afro-American Society, announced over WVBR that the black students had taken the building in protest against the "racist attitudes" of the university. Student operators of the station then shut off the transmitter controlled by the Negroes and resumed broadcasting from an apartment in Ithaca. The black students said that they would not leave the building until disciplinary proceedings instituted against 3 of their members were declared "null and void" and an investigation into the cross-burning incident was begun. The cross had been burned hours after a student-faculty disciplinary board had given reprimands—considered a light punishment—to 3 black students for actions during Dec. 1968 agitation for a separate "black college" within Cornell.

The firearms were taken into the occupied hall after a group of about 15 white students, led by members of the Delta Upsilon fraternity, attempted a counter-invasion of the building. 4 students were hurt when the Negroes repulsed the white invaders.

After the black students ended their occupation Apr. 20, 15 armed Negroes stood guard as university officials signed the amnesty agreement that Miller had negotiated. Miller had agreed to ask the faculty to nullify disciplinary proceedings against the three black students. The agreement also granted demands that the university: (a) press no civil or criminal charges against those involved in the occupation and supply legal assistance against any civil charges that might arise out of the demonstration; (b) supply 24-hour protection for the Afro-American center and black co-op residences and begin an investigation into the cross burning and the counter-invasion attempt by the fraternity men; (c) consider a new campus judicial system, to be devised with the help of black students.

At a news conference later Apr. 20, Miller said that the agreement was "not capitulation to the blacks" and that the students were fully aware that it would have to be approved by the faculty. He said the black students had been allowed to retain their guns because of "a very real fear that they were subject to reprisal."

After Miller promised the black students that he would resign if the agreement were repudiated, the Cornell faculty voted overwhelmingly Apr. 21 to reject the demand for nullification of the reprimands against the 3 students. The faculty said that it sympathized with the problems of black students trying to adjust to life at Cornell, and it approved a resolution condemning the burning of the cross.

Before the faculty vote, Cornell Pres. James Alfred Perkins, 57, had announced an "emergency action" to deal with the crisis. He said no more guns would be permitted on campus and no more occupations would be tolerated.

After some 8,000 white students gathered at the university's Barton Hall in support of the black students, the faculty voted Apr. 23 to rescind its Apr. 21 decision, and it nullified disciplinary proceedings against the 3 students. About 3,000 students had stayed overnight on an enormous basketball court in Barton Hall; some called their action a peaceful "sit-in," others insisted that they were engaging in a "seizure."

3 faculty members Apr. 24 announced their resignations in protest against what they termed their colleagues' "abject capitulation" to "intimidation," and several other professors signed a pledge to stop teaching until all guns and rifles on campus were surrendered. Allan Bloom, who resigned as a government professor, warned that "those who make the revolution do not cease their demands with the accession to power." Myron Rusk, a government professor, said: "An atmosphere of menace has now been established so that it has become difficult for a professor to profess what he really believes. If this trend continues, students will hear in the classrooms not what the professors truly believe but what the professors believe the class will accept. That's not what students come to a university for." Allen P. Sindler, resigning as chairman of the government department, said the faculty had bowed to "a latent and almost manifest show of coercion."

Perkins announced Apr. 27 that the black students had assured him that all their guns had been removed from the campus. He said that he had lifted the emergency measures of Apr. 21. Perkins conceded in a statement Apr. 27 that Cornell had paid a high price to end the occupation. But he insisted that it was necessary to make the concessions to the black students to end "much too great a risk of bloodshed." He denounced instances of "intimidation" on the campus by blacks as well as whites.

The university trustees instructed Perkins May 1 to implement a 10-point declaration to insure that "tactics of terror" on the campus would be met by "firm and appropriate response." The declaration would guarantee the right of free speech and the freedom to teach and learn at the university. "Bigotry and racial discrimination" were condemned and "orderly change" was declared essential to the life of the university. But the trustees declared that "the university is not a sanctuary from the law" and that "violence and the threat of violence" were "unacceptable as expressions of dissent."

Following the occupation, Perkins was criticized for pressing criminal trespass charges against 8 SDS members who had broken into a restricted area during an ROTC drill May 2. The SDS students had painted anti-ROTC slogans on a Navy deck gun in the enclosed area. Prof. Sindler, 41, said May 4 that the SDS protest clearly was not a "very serious breach of the law." Sindler, leader of Duke University's civil rights movement in the 1950s, said that the discipline of the SDS students should have been handled within the university but that Cornell had "denied the validity of the present adjudicative system" when dealing with the black occupation. At the arraignment of the 8 SDS members May 5, Prof. Harrop A. Freeman of the Cornell Law School said that the university would be charged with discriminatory enforcement of its regulations in the arrest of the SDS students.

A special investigating committee of Cornell's trustees said Sept. 10 that the university's failure to enforce disciplinary procedures "over the last 2 or 3 years" had led to the disorders. The panel condemned the administration for lack of planning and warned the campus that order must be maintained.

The N.Y. State Assembly Apr. 28 had overwhelmingly adopted a bill to outlaw guns on school and college property in the state. The bill had been drafted by Gov. Nelson A. Rockefeller's office during the heat of the Cornell crisis. Rockefeller Apr. 21 had signed a measure to require colleges and universities in the state to adopt regulations for the "maintenance of public order" or lose state financial aid. Rockefeller had said then that the "intolerable situation on the Cornell University campus dramatizes the urgent need for adequate plans for student-university relations and clear rules governing conduct on the campus."

Cornell University July 21 announced revised campus regulations against disruptions. The new rules included bans on the possession or use of firearms and on forceful interference with or obstruction of campus activities. (The firearms ban had been adopted May 1.)

Armed Students Seize Voorhees Buildings

A group of 30 to 75 students armed with guns and knives took over the library-administration building at the predominantly black

Voorhees College (Denmark, S.C.) Apr. 28, 1969 and the adjacent science building Apr. 29. Sympathizing students looted the cafeteria to get food for them. 30 of the protesters, including 5 women, were arrested Apr. 29, moments after reaching an agreement with the administration, which had guaranteed amnesty for the dissidents. The arrests were made by state troopers after the students had marched out peacefully. The state police had been called to the campus along with National Guardsmen against the wishes of Voorhees' president, Dr. John F. Potts.

The protesters Apr. 28 had named the occupied buildings "the liberated Malcolm X University" and had presented 14 demands, including the establishment of a degree program in Afro-American studies. Leaflets thrown from the seized buildings read: "These students have secured guns for self-defense purposes only and they have refused to leave the building. We aren't going to allow another Orangeburg."

Gov. Robert E. McNair Apr. 29 declared a state of emergency at the college and sent in 300 National Guardsmen at the request of the trustees of the 710-student, Episcopal Church-supported school.

After the arrests, Potts said: "We had it all worked out. . . . The whole thing was settled, and now this." Potts' accord with the dissidents included a promise that a black-studies program would begin Sept. 1 and an agreement to give passing marks to students of a white professor who had failed many students.

Nixon & Mitchell Urge Firmness on Campus

Controversy over the appropriate national approach to campus disruption intensified after Pres. Nixon and Atty. Gen. John N. Mitchell made strong statements on the subject.

Nixon called on college officials Apr. 29, 1969 to "have the backbone to stand up against" violence and terrorist tactics of campus revolutionaries. In an impromptu speech before the U.S. Chamber of Commerce, meeting in Washington, the President said educational leaders "must recognize that there can be no compromise with lawlessness and no surrender to force if free education is to survive in the United States." While upholding reform, peaceful dissent and the right of students to a voice in determining courses and regulations, Nixon said that "under no circumstances should they be given control of the colleges and universities." The President said that in situations "where students, in the name of dissent and . . . change, terrorize other students and faculty members, when they rifle files, when they engage in violence, when they carry guns and knives in the classrooms, then I say it is time for the faculties, boards of trustees and school administrators to have the backbone to stand up against this kind of situation."

In a Law Day speech in Detroit May 1, Mitchell called for "an end to minority tyranny on the nation's campuses and for the immediate establishment of civil peace and the protection of individual rights." "The time has come for an end to patience," he said. "The time has come for us to demand ... that university officials, local law enforcement agencies and local courts apply the law. ... If arrests must be made, then arrests there should be. If violators must be prosecuted, then prosecutions there should be. It is no admission of defeat, as some may claim, to use reasonable physical force to eliminate physical force. The price of civil tranquility cannot be paid by submission to violence and terror." "Seizures of university buildings and imprisonment of university officials" were not "legitimate acts of civil disobedience," Mitchell declared. "Students do not enjoy any special prerogative to interfere with the rights of other students. Demonstrators do not have a constitutional right to cordon off a street, or to block entrance to a building or to refuse to allow anyone to pass who will not listen to their exhortations." "When a violent outbreak occurs," college officials "should not take it upon themselves to decide how long the violence should endure and what rights should be trampled upon until local government is called in," Mitchell insisted. "When people may be injured, when personal property may be destroyed and when chaos begins, the university official only aids lawlessness by procrastination and negotiation."

A resolution approved by some 800 delegates at the 55th annual convention of the American Association of University Professors (AAUP) in Minneapolis, Minn. May 3 charged that the policy set forth in Mitchell's speech was "a direct threat to academic freedom and autonomy." The resolution was passed despite a telegrammed appeal from the Justice Department that the AAUP delay the statement until delegates could be provided with "an authoritative text" of Mitchell's speech. In the AAUP resolution, Mitchell was quoted as referring to campus militants as "ideological criminals" and "new barbarians." It charged that Mitchell had used "indiscriminate" and "dangerous" language in his attack. The association voted to "unreservedly condemn any forcible interference with teaching, learning and research" but said that "the current crisis can only be compounded by vengeful [government] reprisals."

A panel of 5 members of the Nixon Administration had agreed before the Chamber of Commerce delegates in Washington Apr. 28 that campus disruption was the work of a militant few. Health, Education & Welfare Secy. Robert H. Finch said that militants traveling from campus to campus fomented trouble but that it was difficult to enforce laws against such activity. Labor Secy. George P. Shultz traced the disorders to "an effort by a few to force their views on others." Agriculture Secy. Clifford M. Hardin said he was in "full agreement" with Shultz and added that college students were being "stirred up by professionals." Stephen Hess, 35, an assistant to President Nixon's urban affairs expert Daniel Patrick Moynihan, reported that student-body presidents had assured him that "the radicals are small in number."

James E. Allen Jr., 58, at a Washington news conference May 8 following his swearing in as U.S. education commissioner, called for "positive approaches" to the problem of campus disorder. He said that it "isn't enough to talk about punitive measures or to chastise the institutions." HEW Secy. Finch, who appeared with Allen at the news conference, called legislation to cut off aid from universities that fail to curb unrest a "meat ax approach." Finch, however, denied that he and Allen differed with Atty. Gen. Mitchell and others in the Administration who had advocated a hard-line approach.

In testimony May 8 before the House Special Education Subcommittee, Harvard Pres. Nathan M. Pusey urged Congress to give universities time to solve the problem of student unrest. He asked the public to recognize the depth of the problems on campuses and to "entreat their legislators not to seek to effect correction by hasty enactments which cannot reach to the root of the difficulty and will in all probability only spread the discontent." Rep. William D. Hathaway (D., Me.) of the subcommittee agreed that Congress should not interfere with the universities but said "it would be difficult to persuade more than 40 or 50 members of the House to agree to place a moratorium" on legislation to deal with disruption. (The group's parent committee, the House Education & Labor Committee, was considering legislation to withhold federal aid from universities whose administrations failed to act forcefully against disruption.) University of Michigan Pres. Robben W. Fleming joined in Pusey's plea and told the subcommittee that restrictive legislation would "do more harm than good." He warned that legislators should not "succumb" to the "illusion" that a militant few were the cause of disruption. He contended that campus unrest resulted from "the widespread discontent among our young people" about "our present national priorities."

Police Battle Rioters at Berkeley 'People's Park'

About 70 rioters and bystanders were injured by gunfire and about 20 arrested as police and National Guardsmen battled 2,000 demonstrators near the Berkeley campus of the University of California May 15, 1969. A non-student, James Rector, 25, died May 19 as a result of wounds. The rioting began after Berkeley Chancellor Roger W. Heyns announced that he would evict hundreds of "street people" who had taken over a university-owned vacant field and established a "people's park" on the site.

Work on the "people's park" had begun Apr. 20 when 500 students, faculty members and hippies planted flowers and laid sod with the help of a rented bulldozer on the $1 million site the university had planned eventually to use for student housing. The group began to turn the muddy 445-by-275 foot plot into a park with swings, benches and pieces of sculpture. Heyns then announced that a fence would be put up "to re-establish the conveniently forgotten fact that the field is indeed the university's and to exclude unauthorized persons from the site."

Several hundred policemen removed a group from the park early May 15, and work began on the fence. During a rally held at Berkeley's Sproul Hall Plaza later in the day, Dan Siegel, the campus' student president-elect, shouted: "Let's go down and take over the park." The protesters were met by a platoon of Alameda County sheriff's deputies. Tear gas failed to disperse the demonstrators, who were hurling rocks at the police. The deputies then fired into the crowd with birdshot-loaded riot guns. Gov. Ronald Reagan ordered an undisclosed number of Guardsmen to active duty to help local police, imposed a 10-p.m.-to-6-a.m. curfew on the city and outlawed assemblies and parades. (Reagan had not yet lifted the state of extreme emergency declared in Berkeley Feb. 5.)

There were more arrests during the next 3 days as protests continued. About 100 members of the Berkeley faculty took part in a "protest vigil" May 19 to condemn "the bloodshed and the continued threat of bloodshed that was consequent upon university action" in closing the park.

Violence broke out again May 20 after the disclosure that Rector, a San Jose carpenter who was in Berkeley to visit a friend, had died May 19 following surgery to treat buckshot wounds suffered May 15. According to witnesses, a police officer had fired on Rector as he took refuge on a roof when the trouble started. Some 2,000 demonstrators, led by 25 to 30 faculty members, took part in a silent "funeral march" that was met by policemen and Guard troops at the edge of the campus. Police used tear gas to disperse the crowd and break up a group of 500 demonstrators who began to advance on Heyns' house shouting "Murderer! Murderer!" 30 minutes later a National Guard helicopter dropped on the campus a white, skin-stinging and tear-producing powder later identified as a substance used against the Viet Cong in Vietnam. A Berkeley policeman said the helicopter action had been ordered by Sheriff Frank I. Madigan, field commander of the campus operation. A group of faculty members May 21 denounced the heilcopter gassing and charged that the campus had been turned into "an experimental lab for the National Guard."

More than 500 demonstrators were arrested when they tried to march through downtown Berkeley May 22. The university's Academic Senate voted May 23 to request a Justice Department investigation of "police and military lawlessness" on the campus but rejected a resolution calling for Heyns' resignation. The senate also voted 642 to 95 to support the continuation of the "people's park." About 85% of 19,969 students who voted in a campus referendum also supported the continuation of the park.

Acting on charges of police brutality leveled by demonstrators arrested May 22, U.S. District Court Judge Robert H. Peckham May 24 issued a temporary restraining order on Sheriff Madigan to prohibit mistreatment of prisoners arrested in the disorders. Prisoners interviewed after their release said they had been forced to lie on their stomachs for 2 to 5 hours and had been beaten by police.

Over the objections of Berkeley Mayor Wallace Johnson, the city council, by 5-4 vote May 23, passed a resolution urging that the state of emergency be lifted and troops withdrawn. Most of the Guard troops were removed from Berkeley May 24, but Reagan said that the state of extreme emergency would continue "until such time as we are sure the danger of violence is over with." The governor, however, lifted restrictions against assemblies and parades and voided a 10-p.m.-to-6 a.m. no-loitering law. About 300 of the original 2,000 Guard troops remained on duty in Berkeley.

Gunfire & Death on Greensboro (N.C.) Campus

One student was killed and at least 5 policemen injured when police and 300 National Guardsmen exchanged fire with snipers

May 21-23, 1969 at predominantly black North Carolina Agricultural & Technical State University in Greensboro. The trouble had begun at the all-black Dudley High School, and it spilled over onto the 4,100-student A & T campus.

Police used tear gas to disperse Dudley High students who began throwing rocks May 21 in anger at a school election in which a student militant had been barred from the ballot. A & T students then took up the cause. There were reports of sniper fire directed at police and rocks thrown at cars driven by whites near the university.

Willie Ernest Grimes, 20, an A & T honor student, was found shot to death on the campus May 22. The students blamed police, but an autopsy report showed that the fatal bullet had been shot from a smaller-caliber gun than weapons used by police. L. C. Dowdy, president of the university, ordered the campus closed "in the interest of the safety of our students and members of the university community." An 8-p.m.-to-5-a.m. curfew was ordered by Greensboro Mayor Jack Elam.

Guardsmen moved onto the campus May 23 after police had been pinned down by sniper fire from a university dormitory. Using tear gas and rifle fire, the troops cleared the campus. A National Guard plane and police helicopter were used to spray tear gas and smoke over the besieged dormitory. About 200 students were taken into custody but were later released. Police confiscated 8 weapons from the building.

Elam lifted the state of emergency and curfew May 24. At a news conference, the A & T student body's president-elect, Vince McCullough, said Grimes had pleaded with police not to shoot before he had been killed. McCullough said 50 white youths armed with chains and guns were harassing Negroes in the area, and he asserted that A & T students were attempting to protect the community when the gunfire began. Police reported that car-loads of white youths were in the area but claimed that Grimes had been killed in crossfire between police and snipers.

Campus Building Seizures Continue

Police arrested 105 University of Michigan students and one professor in Ann Arbor Sept. 26, 1969 while evicting protesters who had occupied a campus building for 12 hours in an attempt to force the board of regents to establish a student-run discount book store. Among those arrested were the president and vice president of the university's Student Government Council. About

600 students had marched on a meeting of the regents Sept. 19 and forced them to adjourn.

About 35 black students occupied part of the administration building at Vassar College in Poughkeepsie, N.Y. before dawn Oct. 30 in a demand for the reform and expansion of the school's black-studies program and for a dormitory for black students. The demonstration was organized by the school's Afro-American Society. The sit-in ended Nov. 1 after the college agreed to provide "contiguous residential space" for interested black students and endorsed a "significant expansion" and a reformed grading system for Vassar's experimental black studies program.

60 Yale students led by the Students for a Democratic Society (SDS) occupied the university's personnel offices for 4 hours Nov. 3 and held 4 business office officials captive during the demonstration. The university suspended 47 of the students who refused to leave the building after a warning. The students were protesting the firing of a black dining hall worker, who was reinstated Nov. 4 after a fact-finding meeting.

Legislation Against Campus Disruption

Rep. Edith Green (D., Ore.) June 9, 1969 had introduced a bill to deal with campus disorders. The legislation had the support of 12 Republican and 2 Democratic committee members of the House Education & Labor Committee but was strongly opposed by U.S. Education Commissioner James E. Allen. The bill would cut off federal funds to colleges that failed to enact codes of conduct and discipline and would strengthen existing laws that withheld aid from students or teachers convicted of engaging in disorders. Student and faculty members applying for federal aid would be required to file an affidavit on any convictions in the past 24 months for a crime involving forceful disruption on a campus.

The Senate Permanent Subcommittee on Investigations May 9 had opened hearings on campus violence, and Sen. John L. McClellan (D., Ark.), the committee chairman, introduced July 22 legislation that would make it a federal offense to disrupt operations of a federally aided college. In testimony before the Mc-Clellan committee July 1, Kenneth S. Pitzer, president of Stanford University (Palo Alto, Calif.), had argued against legislation that would deny federal aid to institutions or students involved in disorders. He said such legislation would "do more harm than good" and contended that universities should have the right to handle disruptions without federal interference. In April and

May Stanford had been the site of 2 sit-ins by students protesting chemical and biological warfare studies at the university.

Gov. Ronald Reagan of California Sept. 3 signed into law 2 bills designed to curb campus disruption in the state. The new laws made it a misdemeanor to willfully disturb the peace of a campus or to refuse to leave a campus or return without permission if suspended. The legislation also denied financial aid to students convicted of participating in disorders.

The Wisconsin Assembly Nov. 4 gave final legislative approval to a bill requested by Gov. Warren P. Knowles to deny state financial support to students convicted of participating in campus disruption and to declare such students ineligible for admission and employment at state universities for periods of up to two years. (In what was considered the first application of a federal law denying aid to student disrupters, Wisconsin Atty. Gen. Robert W. Warren had ruled in August that 25 students seeking readmission to Oshkosh State University after suspensions were ineligible for federal aid. Warren said, however, that the students must first be given a hearing to determine whether they had been convicted of a criminal offense or found guilty in a school disciplinary hearing.)

Violence Commission Statement on Campus Turmoil

The National Commission on the Causes & Prevention of Violence had warned June 9, 1969 that new legislation intended to punish students or colleges for campus disorders is "likely to spread, not reduce, the difficulty." The statement, prepared during a 2-day meeting of the commission the previous week, was the first to carry the commission's policy seal. Other studies commissioned by the panel had been released without comment. The statement was released at a Washington news conference by Commission Chairman Milton S. Eisenhower. The statement explained that the campus situation was so threatening and the need for "calm appraisal" so essential, "that his commission feels compelled to speak now rather than to remain silent until publication of its final report next fall."

The statement dealt with the multiple causes of student discontent and the methods of a "small but determined minority" bent on "destruction of existing institutions" or convinced that "violence and disruption may be the only effective way of achieving societal and university reform." It condemned as a "misconception" the belief of some college officials that "civil law should not apply to internal campus affairs." The panel asserted that college administrations were loathe to apply sanctions of expulsion or suspension because of "exposure of dismissed students to the draft and what students call the 'death sentence' of Vietnam."

The commission urged colleges to seek a "broad consensus" on permissible methods of dissent and manners of dealing with disruption that exceeded legitimate bounds. It cited the declaration of the American Council on Education as a starting point of such a consensus. Specifically, the panel suggested that campuses should agree on and adopt student conduct codes and discipline procedures and should review such policies where they already existed. Universities, the commission said, should also prepare contingency plans for dealing with campus disorders and should decide and publicize the conditions under which they would use "(I) campus disciplinary procedures, (II) campus police, (III) court injunctions, (IV) other court sanctions and (V) the civil police." The panel warned that although officials had agreed civil force was necessary in some situations, "the degree of force actually employed has frequently been perceived as excessive by the majority of the campus community, whose sympathies then turned against the university authorities."

The commission said that universities should address themselves to campus government reform and that professors should assume the responsibility to "deal appropriately and effectively" with issues raised in student demands. It emphasized the importance of improved "communications both on the campus and with alumni and the general public."

While recognizing that American citizens "are justifiably angry" at rebellious students, the commission deplored the public's support of legislation that would withhold financial aid from students engaged in disruption and from colleges that failed to deal effectively with unrest. It said that the result of such legislation "may be to radicalize a much larger number by convincing them that existing governmental institutions are as inhumane as the revolutionaries claim." The panel supported legislation that would help universities "deal more effectively with the tactics of obstruction." It suggested that local trespass laws might be reviewed and made effective against "forcible interference with the First Amendment rights of others."

The commission June 24 released a report in which a study group warned that universities across the country would become "screened and guarded camps" if state legislatures enacted politically popular measures intended to suppress disorders. The study group made the report after investigating the events that led to a student strike and violence at San Francisco State College. The study was released without comment by the commission.

The June 24 report, written under the direction of San Francisco attorney William H. Orrick Jr., said the violence at San Francisco State "mirrors the turmoil, the sharply divergent outlook and economic and social imbalances which bitterly divide the American people today." James Brann, one of the authors of the study, issued an independent statement June 24 complaining that the investigators had found that police over-reaction had intensified the violence but that this had been deleted from the final report. The report acknowledged that "instances of police over-reaction" had occurred at San Francisco State but said that this was inevitable in view of the many student-police confrontation there. Orrick explained that the report's purpose was to focus on the causes and prevention of campus conflicts and not to evaluate police behavior.

Commission Reports Analyze Aspects of Violence

The National Commission on the Causes & Prevention of Violence analyzed the various aspects of U.S. violence in the reports it continued to issue during 1969. A scholarly report traced the history of violence in the U.S. A study group reported that excessive police militancy had contributed to violence against demonstrators. The commission urged nationwide confiscation of private citizens' handguns to reduce the level of violence. It said that an increased risk of assassination called for changes in Presidential campaign practices. The panel reported on the rise in urban crime and recommended reforms to curtail frustration in the nation's youth. The commission urged reform of the justice system and warned that unless group violence was made unrewarding, extremist tactics might replace legal processes. Commission members were divided over the issue of civil disobedience. In its final report the commission urged a reordering of the country's national priorities. Among details of the various reports:

Tradition of violence—A group of scholars appointed by the commission reported June 5 that in America, the "grievances and satisfactions of violence have so reinforced one another that we have become a rather bloody-minded people in both action and reaction." The 350,000-word report, "Violence in America: Historical and Comparative Perspectives," was prepared under the direction of Dr. Hugh Davis Graham, associate professor of history at Johns

Hopkins University, and Dr. Ted Robert Gurr, assistant professor of politics at Princeton. The report's general conclusion, written by Graham and Gurr, asserted that Americans had always been a violent people but that they "have been given to a kind of historical amnesia that masks much of their turbulent past."

Although the study cited 19th Century periods in which there was "greater relative turbulence" in America, it said that the 1960s "rank as one of our most violent eras." It held that the scope and magnitude of antiwar protest, urban unrest and black violence, university disorders and political assassinations were "essentially unprecedented in our history." The scholars said that the U.S. was "among the half-dozen most tumultuous nations in the world" in the post-1948 era.

The scholars examined labor violence in the U.S. to analyze the effects of governmental use of force for social control and the success of collective violence "as an instrument for accomplishing group objectives." They said that the effectiveness of governmental force depended on its legitimacy and consistency and on the success of "remedial action" for the causes of discontent. They found that peaceful protest had been more effective than violence in achieving objectives.

Police militancy—A report released by the commission June 10 said that the militancy and political activism of police in America threatened to undermine public confidence in the nation's legal system. Police militancy, the report said, "seems to have exceeded reasonable bounds" and contributed to "police violence" against demonstrators. The 276-page report, entitled "The Politics of Protest: Violent Aspects of Protest and Confrontations," was prepared under the direction of Jerome H. Skolnick, 38, a member of the Center for the Study of Law & Society at the University of California at Berkeley.

According to the study, police in the U.S. had developed into "a self-conscious, independent political power," which sometimes "rivals even duly elected officials in influence." The researchers blamed FBI Director J. Edgar Hoover for much of alleged police misconception about protesters. The report said Hoover had encouraged the view that mass protest was the result of conspiracy, often directed by Communist agitators. As a result, said the study group, police were often unable to distinguish "dissent" from "subversion." "No government institution appears so deficient in its understanding of the constructive role of dissent in a constitutional democracy as the police," the panel said. It warned that the nation had a choice between commitment to social reform or the emergence of a police state, "a society of garrison cities where order is enforced without due process of law and without the consent of the governed."

The researchers found that U.S. policemen were "overworked, undertrained, underpaid and undereducated." They recommended that the federal government review its role "in the development of the current police view of protest and protesters."

Handgun curbs—The commission July 28 urged the nationwide confiscation of handguns owned by private citizens as a step toward curbing violence. In a statement adopted by 9 of 13 commission members, the panel recommended legislation to set up federal minimum standards of firearm control that would restrict ownership of handguns to those who could demonstrate reasonable need for them.

The commission said it had found that the "availability of guns contributes substantially to violence in American society." It emphasized that handguns rather than long firearms were associated with crime and that firearms "generally facilitate rather than cause violence." The commission reported a sharp increase in the ownership of firearms over the past 5 years and estimated that 90 million firearms were in private hands in the U.S. About half of the nation's households had at least one gun. The panel attributed increased gun sales to a rising fear of violence and to the "exhortations of extremist groups, both black and white." Although the commission cited statistics to show that violent crimes increasingly were committed by persons using handguns, it warned that guns in the home were dangerous and rarely could effectively protect a household.

The commission said the nation lacked an effective firearms policy because of "our culture's casual attitude toward firearms and its heritage of the armed, self-reliant citizen." But it said that a national policy aimed at "reducing the availability of the handgun" would reduce firearms violence. It recommended that states be given the first opportunity to develop effective firearms legislation in conformity with minimum national standards but that federal handgun licensing apply in states that fail to enact appropriate state laws within four years. Recommended legislation would restrict ownership of handguns to police and private guards, small businesses in high crime areas, and "others with a special need for self-protection." The panel said federal regulations should not include normal household protection as a sufficient reason for handgun ownership. Recommended long-gun regulations included a system of indentification for long-gun owners but not registration of the guns.

The 4 panel members who dissented argued that "each state should be permitted to determine for itself without additional restrictions from the federal government the system which best meets its needs." The dissenters were Sen. Roman L. Hruska (R., Neb.), Rep. Hale Boggs (D., La.), Judge Ernest W. McFarland, presiding member of the Arizona Supreme Court, and Leon Jaworski, Houston lawyer. The commission also released without comment a 268-page staff report on firearms prepared for the panel.

TV violence unabated—The commission July 5 released a preliminary statistical study of TV violence based on a comparison of a sample week of viewing in early October in 1967 and 1968. The study, prepared by a research team from the University of Pennsylvania's Annenberg School of Communications, concluded that there was "no evidence of over-all decline in the prevalence of violence from 1967 to 1968." The study also found that TV's "good guys" and "bad guys" were equally likely to commit acts of violence.

Assassination risks grow—The commission warned Nov. 2 that conditions that might lead to an increased risk of conspiratorial assassination appeared to be developing in the U.S. The commission recommended basic changes in Presidential campaign practices, including increased Secret Service protection, avoidance of massive outdoor political rallies and more reliance on TV for national exposure.

Although recent assassinations in the U.S. had not been the products of conspiracies, the commission said, "many of the conditions associated with conspiratorial assassination in other countries appear to be developing in this country." Among such conditions cited by the panel were more intense political violence, talk and incidents of urban guerrilla warfare such as occurred in Cleveland in July 1968, "constant excoriation of America's institutions and leaders" resulting from the "rhetoric of revolution," a high level of racial tensions and "rapid socio-economic change."

"Present trends," the panel noted, "warn of an escalating risk of assassination, not only for Presidents, but for other office holders at every level of government, as well as leaders of civil rights and political-interest groups." The commission specifically warned that the increased number of Negroes in political office could become targets for both black and white extremists.

The commission recommended that "Congress enact a law that would grant free television time to Presidential candidates during the final weeks" of a campaign in order to "establish a new pattern in Presidential campaigning and to reduce significantly the

pressure toward personal appearances in all parts of the country."
The panel also urged that the Secret Service be empowered to
protect public officials and candidates whose lives might be "imper-
iled as a result of threat, vilification, deep controversy, or other
hazarding circumstances." It recommended that state and local
governments review procedures for offering protection to local
officials and candidates.

Urban crime—The commission warned Nov. 23 that the fear
of violent crime "is gnawing at the vitals of urban America." In
an 8,000-word report, the panel said that in a few more years,
"lacking effective public action," cities would be divided into
"fortified" high-rise residential compounds and ghetto neighborhoods, which would be "places of terror." At a news conference
in Washington Nov. 23, Milton S. Eisenhower, chairman of the
commission, said that the report—"Violent Crime: Homicide,
Assault, Rape and Robbery"—was "by all odds the most important" of those released by the panel.

According to the report, FBI statistics showed that between
1960 and 1968, the rate of criminal homicide reported in the U.S.
had increased by 36%, forcible rape by 65%, aggravated assault
by 67% and robbery by 119%. The panel said the U.S. had the
highest reported rate of violent crime of any of the modern, stable
nations in the world. "The 26 cities with 500,000 or more residents
and containing about 17% of our total population contribute about
45% of the total reported major violent crimes," the commission
said.

The commission cited urban arrest statistics indicating that
violence was concentrated among youths between the ages of 15
and 20. Between 1958 and 1967, arrest rates of the 10-14 age group
for assault and robbery had increased 200% to 300%. The panel
found that violent crime in cities was committed "primarily by
individuals at the lower end of the occupational scale" and that
urban arrest rates for violent crime were disproportionately high
for urban Negroes. "These differences," the commission contended,
"are not, in fact, racial; they are primarily a result of conditions
of life in the ghetto slum." Victim-offender studies showed that
assaultive violence, as opposed to robbery, "is primarily between
white offenders and white victims and black offenders and black
victims."

The panel suggested that high-rise apartment dwellings might
become "fortified cells for upper-middle and high-income populations living at prime locations in the city"; that suburban neighborhoods would be protected from excessive violence mainly by

"economic homogeneity" and distance from the central city; that "ownership of guns will be almost universal in the suburbs," and that "armed citizens in cars" would patrol neighborhoods closer to the city. The commission warned that radical right- and left-wing groups "will have tremendous armories of weapons which could be brought into play with or without provocation." Safe urban areas, said the panel, would be interconnected by "sanitized" expressways. Slum neighborhoods would be scenes of widespread crime, "perhaps entirely out of police control during nighttime hours." The commission predicted "intensifying hatred and deepening division" between residents of safe areas and ghettos.

Reforms for youth—The commission called Nov. 25 for draft reforms and a constitutional amendment to lower the minimum voting age to 18. The report, "Challenge to Youth," also recommended that state and federal laws be relaxed to make use and incidental possession of marijuana no more than a misdemeanor. Commission Chairman Eisenhower, introducing the report at a Washington news conference, said many youths turned to violence in frustration at not being able to influence policy by voting. It said young people "face the prospect of having to fight in a war most of them believe is unjustified, or futile or both" and "see a society built on the principle of human equality that has not assured equal opportunity in life." It said that for persons under 21, "the anachronistic voting age limitations [in all but 4 states] tend to alienate them from systematic political processes" and drive them towards sometimes violent alternatives. The commission contended that harsh marijuana penalties had "become a principal source of frustration and alienation among the young."

Group violence—The commission said Dec. 3 that unless ways were found to make group violence "both unnecessary and unrewarding" as a political tactic, the danger existed in America that "extreme, unlawful tactics will replace legal processes as the usual way of pressing demands." The statement also said that the "widely held belief that protesting groups usually behave violently is not supported by fact." The panel contended that group violence occurred when "expectations about rights and status are continually frustrated," when "peaceful efforts to press these claims yield inadequate results" or when "the claims of groups who feel disadvantaged are viewed as threats by other groups occupying a higher status in society."

To lessen the danger of group violence, the commission recommended legislation that would empower federal courts to grant injunctions, sought by private citizens or the attorney general, against threatened interference with freedoms of speech, press or assembly. Such injunctions might be used against campus disrupters or against police or local officials who refused to grant demonstration permits. Finding that few of 16 major city governments studied had established "formal, dependable links with dissident groups" or adequate plans for dealing with disorders," the commission urged police departments to improve preparations for handling large-scale protests.

Civil disobedience—The commission Dec. 8 issued a statement condemning massive civil disobedience, including nonviolent action. By a bare 7-6 majority, the panel said that even nonviolent civil disobedience could lead to "nationwide disobedience of many laws and thus anarchy." The 6 dissenters, who included Chairman Eisenhower, endorsed a longer staff report condemning "violent or coercive" tactics of civil disobedience.

The majority said that since segregationist governors, civil-rights leaders and striking teachers had ignored court orders in recent years, "it was not surprising that college students destroyed scientific equipment and research data, interfered with the rights of others ... and in several instances temporarily closed their colleges." As an alternative to massive civil disobedience, the majority urged that the constitutionality of laws to be tested by individuals or small groups. They said the majority of dissenters should abide by a questionable law until it was invalidated by the courts.

Several of the dissenters, including the panel's two black members—Judge A. Leon Higginbotham Jr. and Howard University Law Prof. Patricia Roberts Harris—wrote separate dissents. Mrs. Harris said that civil disobedience, when there was a willing acceptance of the penalty, "can represent the highest loyalty and respect for a democratic society. Such respect and self-sacrifice may well prevent, rather than cause, violence." Higginbotham said that if the majority's doctrine of waiting for court decisions had been adhered to in the 1960s, "probably not one present major civil-rights statute would have been enacted." Another dissenter, Terence Cardinal Cooke, archbishop of New York, said that peaceful civil disobedience was justified only as a last resort and only when a civil law "is conscientiously regarded as being clearly in conflict with a higher law—namely our Constitution, the natural law or divine law." Other dissenters were Sen. Philip A. Hart (D., Mich.) and Dr. W. Walter Menninger.

Final report—The commission, in its final report, issued Dec. 12, 1969, called on the nation to commit at least $20 billion a year to solving social problems. The report, entitled "To Establish Justice, To Insure Domestic Tranquility," said the nation could divert $19 billion from defense to domestic spending after the conclusion of the Vietnam war. In the summary of its 338-page report, the commission called for a reordering of national priorities. "Our most serious challenges to date," the panel contended, "have been external—the kind this strong and resourceful country could unite against. While serious external dangers remain, the graver threats today are internal: haphazard urbanization, racial discrimination, disfiguring of the environment, the dislocation of human identity and motivation created by an affluent society—all resulting in a rising tide of individual violence."

The commission said that although necessary funds might not be available until the conclusion of the nation's involvement in Vietnam, an immediate commitment to domestic programs should be made: "We believe the time has come to question whether expenditures for the general welfare should continue to be subordinated to those for national defense."

Commission Chairman Milton S. Eisenhower said he had presented the final report, which included nine statements and recommendations previously made public by the commission, to President Nixon. Eisenhower said "the President authorized me to say he is gravely concerned about the problems we studied . . . and that he will study with care every part of this report."

Urban Study Warn on Black/White Split

A study by 2 private urban groups had warned Feb. 27, 1969 that the nation was "a year closer to 2 societies—black and white, increasingly separate and scarcely less unequal." The report, entitled "One Year Later," recalled the 1968 findings of the President's National Advisory (Kerner) Commission on Civil Disorders that America was "moving toward 2 societies, one black, one white—separate and unequal." 2 former members of the Kerner commission, N.Y. Mayor John V. Lindsay and Sen. Fred R. Harris (D., Okla.), and the commission's staff director, Washington lawyer David Ginsburg, served on the review board for the new study, a joint effort of the Urban Coalition and Urban America, Inc. Lindsay and Harris had led an unsuccessful effort to reconvene the Kerner commission; they had argued that without follow-up, the Kerner report would have little effect. Donald Canty, director of Urban America's information center, headed the staff that made the 3-month study and wrote the report.

John W. Gardner, ex-secretary of health, education and welfare and chairman of the Urban Coalition, released the study at a news conference Feb. 27. He emphasized that the report "makes it clear that the nation's response to the crisis of the cities has been perilously inadequate."

A major finding of "One Year Later" was that the "most recent trend" in population movement had not diminished the "physical distance" between black and white Americans. The trend showed a "virtual stoppage" of black immigration from the South and a "sharp increase" in the rate of white departure from central city areas; while city ghettos were increasing in area and declining in population density, there were also indications of growth in suburban ghettos. The study noted an increased division between blacks and whites in the "perceptions and experiences of American society." The deepening concern of some white Americans over ghetto problems, which had grown with the publication of the Kerner report and the death of Martin Luther King Jr., had been "counterbalanced—perhaps overbalanced—by a deepening of aversion and resistance on the part of others." As a reason for this growing aversion and "outright resistance to slum-ghetto needs and demands," the report cited an increasing concern for law and order that followed the assassination of Sen. Robert F. Kennedy. The report warned that the mood of Negroes, standing somewhere "in the spectrum between militancy and submission," was "not moving in the direction of patience."

The report said that Kerner commission predictions about the consequences of U.S. policies dealing with the urban crisis had proved correct: There was some change in ghetto conditions but not enough and an increase in number but a decline in intensity of civil disorders "due primarily to more sophisticated response by police and the military." If the Kerner commission proved to be "equally correct about the long run," the report warned, "the nation in its neglect may be sowing the seeds of unprecedented future disorders and division."

President Releases Funds to Aid Riot-Stricken Cities

Pres. Nixon Apr. 8 ordered that $9 million of emergency funds of the Housing & Urban Development (HUD) Department be made available immediately to rehabilitate riot-damaged areas in 20 cities. At least $200 million more was to be channeled for the same purpose through accelerated processing of funds appropriated for fiscal 1969 urban renewal, beautification and other HUD programs. HUD also was directed to plan to spend an "appropriate" amount of fiscal 1970 funds on the program.

The effort stemmed from Nixon's visit Jan. 27 to a riot-damaged area of Washington and his subsequent request for a survey of riot-torn areas across the country. "There could be no more searing symbol of governmental inability to act than those rubble-strewn lots and desolate, decaying buildings, once a vital part of a community's life and now left to rot," the President said in a statement released Apr. 8. "Little rehabilitation or reconstruction has taken place." The riot scars were evidence of "impotence of modern government at all levels," he declared. "No wonder our citizens are beginning to question government's ability to perform."

HUD Secy. George W. Romney, in an accompanying statement, pledged to seek "maximum cooperation with the cities involved" in the rehabilitation effort, which would focus first on playgrounds, parks, cleanup services and repairs to public buildings and streets. Romney also pledged to respond to requests for similar help from other areas.

The 20 cities selected for the special effort were Akron, Baltimore, Boston, Cleveland, Chicago, Detroit, Kansas City, Mo., Los Angeles, Louisville, Ky., Memphis, Nashville, Newark, New Haven, New York, Pittsburgh, Providence, R.I., Rochester, Tampa, Washington and Wilmington, Del.

Scattered Violence Marks King Assassination Anniversary

Demonstrators rallied in major cities across the nation Apr. 4-6, 1969 to commemorate the first anniversary of the death of Dr. Martin Luther King Jr. and to protest against the war in Vietnam. Violence broke out in some cities but was quickly brought under control. *Among developments reported:*

Chicago—Gov. Richard Ogilvie orderd the 4,800-member Illinois National Guard to duty April 3 at the request of Chicago Mayor Richard J. Daley as disturbances in the city's black neighborhoods resulted in the arrest of more than 200 persons. Police were able to control the disturbances, caused mostly by black youth, before the troops arrived. Ogilvie said that Daley had requested the troops "to head off any worse trouble by activating the Guard early."

The disturbances had apparently begun near high schools in the city, in some cases after memorial services for King. The violence was limited mostly to rock and bottle throwing, although some looting was reported. Passing motorists were harrassed, and windows were broken. Some 90 persons were reported injured, including 4 policemen, but only 2 were hospitalized. Police controlling the disorders were restrained; they fired only once, into the air, to break up a crowd menacing police cars. A reporter at police headquarters said that youths arrested appeared to be unhurt and were reminded of their rights.

Memphis—Scattered violence and looting was brought quickly under control by Memphis policemen Apr. 4 while some 10,000 persons gathered in tribute to King. Mayor Henry Loeb imposed a dawn-to-dusk curfew after black youths ran through the city streets breaking windows and looting stores as the memorial parade passed. Cut off from the violence by the police, the demonstrators waited quietly while the disorder was quelled. Riot police and National Guardsmen were on hand but were kept out of sight while traffic officers wearing regular equipment controlled the crowd.

Urban Racial Violence

Racial unrest with sporadic violence, looting, sniping and firebombing was reported during 1969 in cities from Hartford to Tacoma and in the South.

There was firebombing and rock-throwing in Jacksonville Fla. Jan. 23 after a white man was acquitted of murder in the 1968 death of Rudolph Homer Hargett, 18, a Negro. Police said that the incidents apparently were related to the trial. Lee Charles Bradley, 24, had admitted firing one rifle shot at black youths while driving through an area where stone throwing had been reported following the death of Martin Luther King Jr. Hargett, who had been home from the Air Force on leave, had been hit with a bullet between the eyes. 2 Negroes were on the six-man jury that found Bradley innocent of 2d-degree murder. (Scores of Negroes roamed through Jacksonville Oct. 31, smashing store windows, setting fires, looting and overturning parked cars after a report that a white truck driver had shot a Negro. Police riot squads and a heavy rain quelled the disorder after a black security guard was shot and a service station operator had died of a heart attack.)

Edwin T. Pratt, 38, executive director of the Seattle Urban League, was shot to death Jan. 26 in front of his home in suburban Richmond Heights. Urban League officials said that Pratt had received numerous threats on his life.

Assistant Police Chief Jesse L. Wolf, 44, of Port Gibson, Miss. was arrested Apr. 18 for the fatal shooting that day of Roosevelt Jackson, 24, a Negro. Wolf's release Apr. 19 on $5,000 bail touched off a brick-throwing demonstration the next day. Charles Evers charged that the release had violated the law, and he claimed that protesting Negroes had been beaten by state highway patrolmen. At his hearing April 21, Wolf was ordered held for grand jury action on a manslaughter charge. District Attorney John Ellis confirmed May 23 that the grand jury had refused to indict Wolf. Police claimed that Jackson had been shot while resisting arrest at his home.

3 nights of racial unrest in Cairo, Ill. Apr. 26-28 were marked by firebombings and sniping. Bombs were used Apr. 28 to set fire to a health department building adjacent to Pyramid Courts, a black housing project, and fireman and police were met with sniper fire when they responded to the fire. 200 National Guardsmen and 60 state policemen were sent into Cairo Apr. 29, and a curfew was imposed. The curfew was not lifted until May 2; half of the Guard force left Cairo May 4. Lt. Gov. Paul Simon had recommended Apr. 22 that Cairo Police Chief Carl J. Clutts be fired as the first step towards easing racial tension and improving law enforcement in the city. (Clutts was replaced in the summer by William H. Petersen.) Simon had charged that the Pyramid Courts project had been left without law enforcement and had warned that "there is real danger there will be additional bloodshed."

Gov. Richard B. Ogilvie ordered state troopers to Cairo June 19 to quell disturbances after 4 fires erupted in the city. One of the fires razed the Cairo Wood Products, Inc. plant, which employed many of Cairo's Negroes. The plant was located near Pyramid Courts. The state troopers replaced an all-white vigilante committee that had been accused of terrorizing Cairo's black population. The committee, called the White Hats, had been organized after Cairo's 1967 racial disturbances. Under pressure from the Illinois attorney general's office, the White Hats were disbanded June 23 when the state legislature ordered Cairo Sheriff Chesley Willis to terminate all existing deputies' commissions. Willis had designated many White Hat members as deputy sheriffs and deputy coroners.

A 22-year-old black woman was wounded Sept. 16 as gunfire erupted in Pyramid Courts, which had been the scene of racial disorders throughout the summer. Spokesmen for the Black United Front, which was launched to lead protests against racial discrimination in Cairo, said the gunfire had begun when "white racists" started shooting at the housing project with rifles and machineguns. The front's chairman, the Rev. Charles Koen, said the residents of Pyramid Courts "returned the fire." Koen said that the shooting came from members of the United Citizens for Community Action, a militant white group led by Cairo lumber dealer Robert Cunningham. Cunningham denied Koen's charge, claiming that militant Negroes had started the shooting. (Mayor Lee P. Stenzel and Police Chief Petersen had resigned Sept 15, warning that more racial bloodshed was imminent.)

Gov. Robert W. Scott of North Carolina had ordered 150 to 200 National Guardsmen into Winston-Salem Apr. 29 to enforce a curfew that had been imposed after 2 nights of racial unrest. The trouble had begun Apr. 27 when a black policeman critically wounded an escaped black convict. Black youths hurled rocks at police, and several fires were set. Firemen were driven from a fire near a public housing development Apr. 28 by gunfire.

Violence erupted in Burlington, N.C. May 16 after police had arrested 17 black youths who had tried to march on the administration building of Walter Williams High School to protest failure of the integrated high school to elect a black cheerleader. Black youths threw firebombs at 2 stores and began looting. Police were met with sniper fire when they attempted to restore order. One youth, Leon Mebane, 16, was killed by police crossfire, and 29 persons were arrested. Mayor W. L. Beamon ordered a curfew May 17, and Gov. Scott ordered 400 National Guard troops into the city.

The fatal shooting of a black youth, Dexter Johnson, 17, by a black policeman, Charles Knox, 28, in Newark, N.J. May 19, touched off sporadic violence and looting. A police spokesman said dozens of stores were looted and several merchants were "dragged from their stores and their stores cleaned out," while crowds of black youths hurled rocks and bottles at passing police cars. The city's entire 1,400-man police force was called to quell the disturbances, and police were ordered to spray tear gas into looted stores that did not hold food. (Knox was suspended from the force following the shooting.) Black community leaders and youth workers patrolled the streets of the South and Central Wards May 20 in an effort to maintain calm. A curfew was imposed, but scattered instances of rock-throwing and looting continued during the night. Following a meeting with black and white community leaders May 21, Mayor Hugh J. Addonizio lifted the curfew. The violence was the worst in the city since the July 1967 riots.

Police patrolled Hartford, Conn. streets June 5 in an effort to halt widespread looting and vandalism by Negroes. About 22 stores in the city's predominantly black and Puerto Rican North End were looted. At least 2 persons were wounded in the battle between police and looters. Police patrolled the streets for a night June 6, enforcing a city-wide curfew ordered by Hartford City Manager Elisha C. Freedman. Mayor Anne Uccello said that the disorders were "unprovoked criminal acts and may be the result of a conspiracy designed to foment trouble in this area."

The slaying of a 14-year-old black girl by a policeman ignited a wave of looting and fire bombing on Omaha's North Side June 24-25. Bands of youths roamed city streets, tossing molotov cocktails into smashed windows. Police patrols were unable to curb the widespread looting as firemen battled blazes started by firebombs. The violence had begun when Patrolman James Loder fatally shot a young girl while investigating a burglary report. Loder was charged with manslaughter and released on bond. Sporadic sniper fire marked the city's 3d night of violence June 26, but Mayor Eugene Leahy, after meeting with black and white leaders, said the "situation is under control."

Snipers fired on National Guard troops July 17 during racial violence in Youngstown, O. The troops had been ordered into the city July 16 on the 2nd night of looting, firebombing and rock throwing. The violence followed a demonstration by 100 young Negroes in support of a boycott against an East Side dairy store. The store's owner had been charged with assault and battery a few weeks earlier after a black woman complained that he had kicked her. 12 injuries and 25 arrests had been reported by July 17 when a special curfew was ordered. The curfew was lifted July 19, and the troops began withdrawing July 20 after 2 nights of relative calm.

Firebombing, looting and sniper fire erupted in Columbus, O. July 21, and Gov. James A. Rhodes ordered 1,350 National Guardsmen into the city. The trouble had started in an integrated section on the East Side following a neighborbood quarrel in which a Negro was shot to death by a white man. Dave E. Chestnut, 69, operator of a dry cleaning store, was charged with 2d-degree murder in the death of Roy Beasley, 27, a city public works employe. They reportedly had argued about the Beasley children playing in Chestnut's backyard. During the violence that followed, George M. Stulz, 47, a white man who had offered to direct traffic, was killed by sniper fire. Within the next 3 days, 434 persons were arrested, many for curfew violations, 36 persons were injured and 4 major fires were reported.

Gov. Raymond P. Shafer of Pennsylvania called out National Guard troops July 22 to help state and local police quell racial violence and sniping that had plagued York since July 17. Mayor John L. Snyder proclaimed an 8-p.m.-to-6-a.m. curfew as shooting spread from a predominantly black section in southwest York to other parts of the city. The mayor had ordered a less stringent curfew July 19. Police said that the violence had been touched off July 17 when a black youth accidentally set fire to his own clothing and blamed the injury on a white gang. Mrs. Lillie B. Allen, 27, a black woman visiting the city, was killed by sniper fire July 21, and an exchange of gunfire described by police as a "shootout" took place between black and white gangs. Patrolman Henry C. Shaad, 23, who had been critically injured by sniper fire July 18, died Aug. 1 from his wounds. Guardsmen were withdrawn into armories and the curfew was relaxed July 25 after order had been restored. The National Guard and state police left the city July 28. Black community leaders were critical of police handling of the violence. Lionel Bailey, staff member of a city antipoverty agency, the Community Progress Council, said July 21 that police curbed Negroes during the violence to the exclusion of "motorcycle gangs and carloads of whites with guns." Elmer C. Woodyard, 27, a black policeman, resigned from the force July 22, alleging police "bigotry" and a "senseless use of firepower."

Gov. John McKeithen of Louisiana called up 500 National Guard troops July 31 after groups of Negroes broke store windows and assaulted 4 whites in downtown Baton Rouge. Mayor W. W. Dumas imposed a dusk-to-dawn curfew as state troopers, local police and Guardsmen patrolled the streets after incidents of fire-bombing and sniper fire were reported. The violence began after a peaceful rally of 400 Negroes who were protesting the fatal shooting of two black youths by a white policeman earlier in July. Dumas extended the curfew for a night Aug. 1.

Street violence and firebombings erupted in the Puerto Rican neighborhoods of Passaic, N.J., Aug. 3-8 following a demonstration by more than 200 Puerto Ricans Aug. 3 to protest poor housing conditions. After the rally, bands of youths roamed downtown streets, smashing windows and tossing firebombs. The City Council imposed a limited curfew Aug. 4 after police used tear gas to disperse crowds in the Puerto Rican section. During the disorders a firebomb was thrown onto the roof of Passaic's city hall, but there was no serious damage. Passaic Mayor Bernard Pinck ordered a dusk-to-dawn curfew Aug. 5. A school was firebombed and bottles were hurled at policemen in the Dundee section. Aug 6. The curfew was lifted Aug. 10 as disorders in the Dundee section subsided. More than 131 persons were arrested during the 6 nights of disorder.

Sporadic and sometimes violent confrontations between Negroes and whites erupted in Somerville, Tenn., after a white father and son allegedly bludgeoned two black women Aug. 12. That assault led to mass civil rights demonstrations, mass arrests of Negroes, a black boycott of Somerville's merchants and much litigation. The tensions began when a sheriff's deputy told the injured women that they would have to come to the courthouse to swear out warrants for their assailants' arrests 3 days later the father and son were arrested. The youth pleaded guilty and was placed on probation as a juvenile offender. The father was bound over to the grand jury. The delay in the man's trial further incensed black community leaders. A boycott of Somerville merchants was started. After several days of non-violent picketing, Somerville police confiscated the demonstrators' placards as illegal.   The following day about 500 demonstrators converged on the Somerville courthouse, but special deputies dispersed them after warning them that the protest was illegal. Police reported 141 arrests during the confrontation.

Somerville merchants obtained a Circuit Court injunction forbidding picketing, marching and intimidation of area merchants, but demonstrators ignored the order and marched through the downtown area Sept. 6. Police repelled the marchers by turning high-pressure water hoses on them and swinging riot clubs. Mayor I. P. Yancey then imposed a dusk-to-dawn curfew. The injunction was overturned by a federal court, but U.S. District Court Judge Bailey Brown reversed that counter-injunction when 500 black students attempted to enroll in the predominantly white Fayette County High School and were turned back by policemen using riot clubs. Brown then appealed to Tennessee Gov. Buford Ellington to send in state patrolmen to maintain order. Ellington agreed, and armed state patrolmen curbed further violence.

Widespread vandalism and looting erupted in Niagara Falls, N.Y. Aug. 17 after a fight between black and white youths in a movie theater spilled out into the street. The fracas continued as 300 youths smashed windows and snarled downtown traffic. The police also reported minor looting. New trouble erupted later Aug. 17 when a crowd of black youths reportedly assaulted 3 black Canadian men in a car in the city's predominantly black East Falls Street area. City Manager Donald J. O'Hara placed Niagara Falls' policemen on double shifts Aug. 18 to contain widespread vandalism and prevent racial clashes. O'Hara declared a state of emergency Aug. 18 but lifted it several hours later. He called in 130 policemen Aug. 19 to combat vandalism, but looting continued through Aug. 20.

Widespread sniper fire broke out in Tacoma's predominantly black Hilltop district Aug. 18, but police reported nobody wounded. Tacoma police said the shooting, which took place in a half-mile-wide area, was not triggered by one incident. 20 people were arrested and charged with assault in connection with the sniper fire. The gunfire took place during the 2d consecutive night of unrest in Tacoma. Black and white gangs roamed the city streets Aug. 17 after police dispersed a crowd watching a fight between a black and a white family over auto parking spaces.

The Lakewood, N.J. Township Council imposed a rigid curfew Aug. 19 after a weekend of violence and firebombings culminated in a confrontation between Negroes and Lakewood police. Police used tear gas to disperse a crowd of 200 youths after being pelted with rocks, bottles and firebombs. More than 25 persons were arrested. The disorders had started Aug. 16 after 2 black policemen arrested 3 black youths for fighting in the street. Bands of youths converged on the predominantly black East Side, refusing to obey an order from Lakewood Mayor John Franklin to withdraw.

Arkansas National Guardsmen and state troopers moved into Forrest City, Ark. Aug. 27 to disperse crowds of whites who were demanding the lynching of 3 young Negroes accused of raping a 15-year-old white girl Aug. 23. The Guardsmen and troopers cleared the city's downtown streets after 100 whites swarmed around the St. Francis County Jail, where the suspects were held. Gov. Winthrop Rockefeller had sent the Guardsmen to Forrest City Aug. 26 after whites had refused to obey a curfew ordered by the town's mayor, Robert L. Cope.

Youthful gangs roamed the black section of Grand Rapids, Mich. Aug. 29, hurling rocks and bottles at passing police cars. 6 persons, including 4 policemen, were injured. One white man was pulled from his car and beaten before police rescued him.

200 National Guardsmen moved into Fort Lauderdale, Fla. Sept. 2 after lootings, firebombings and sniper fire erupted in the city's predominantly black northwest section. The outbreak began Aug. 30 after a report that a black woman had been shot by a sheriff's deputy while he was chasing a speeding motorist. Sniper fire and rock throwing began as area residents poured out of housing developments to jeer police. Police maintained that the woman was wounded by a sniper. The disorders continued Sept. 1 as police and firemen battled looters in the city's northwest section. Firemen used high-pressure water hoses to disperse crowds while police patrolled the streets arresting looters. Gov. Claude R.

Kirk Jr.'s office ordered the National Guard on alert but did not order the Guardsmen into the city until Sept. 2, after a state of emergency was declared by the Fort Lauderdale City Council. The council declared the emergency as sniper fire and lootings increased in the northwest area. The council also ordered an 8-p.m.-to-6-a.m. curfew for the 200-block northwest section. Gunfire continued Sept. 3, but Guardsmen and police reduced the disorders.

Racial disorders swept the black and Puerto Rican neighborhoods of Hartford, Conn. Sept. 1-5 as armed state and local policemen battled looters and snipers. Police reported more than 500 arrests and scores injured, including 2 persons wounded by snipers. More than 70 stores were demolished. The disorders had begun Sept. 1 when youths attacksd a North End fire station, smashing windows and attempting to destroy the apparatus inside. The youths were driven off by policemen who fired tear gas into the crowd. North End community leaders said the crowd was angered by an Aug. 31 news article in which the *Hartford Times* quoted a fireman in a North End firehouse as saying: Puerto Ricans were "pigs, that's all, pigs." A dusk-to-dawn curfew was ordered Sept. 2 as looting, firebombings and sporadic sniper fire continued in a 40-block area of the North End. State troopers used tear gas to disperse crowds and stop looting, which continued in the North End. City officials reported that Albany Avenue, where most of the looting and firebombings had taken place, was a "shambles." Relative calm returned Sept. 4. The curfew was lifted Sept. 5 as tensions subsided. Police maintained heavy patrols, but the 100 state troopers, called in Sept 2, were withdrawn.

Disorder spread through black neighborhoods of Camden, N.J. Sept. 2-5 after shotgun fire had killed a rookie white policeman and a 15-year-old black girl Sept. 2. The two victims were shot during skirmishes between police and snipers in the predominantly black South Side section of Camden. At least 2 other persons were wounded by shotgun blasts. Policemen clashed with South Side residents and arrested 4 on assault charges. Negroes charged that during the fight, policemen had beaten 2 teen-age black girls. Relative calm was restored Sept. 5, but the full 405-man Camden police force remained on alert to prevent further disorders. Camden city officials said that rain had help end the violence.

One Negro was killed and 8 others wounded by members of a white motorcycle club in Parkesburg, Pa. Sept. 2. 4 men, 3 of them members of the club, were arrested and charged with murder. The slain man, Harry Dickinson, was a spokesman for the

Parkesburg Laymen's Action Council, which had been founded 2 months previously in an effort to keep racial peace in the town. News of the shooting spread to Coatsville, an industrial town 7 miles away, and Negroes swarmed into the streets, breaking windows, before police dispersed the crowds.

Dale Watson of Tupelo, Miss., a member of a branch organization of the Ku Klux Klan, was arrested in Fayette, Miss. Sept. 9 as he drove a car filled with weapons into the parking lot of a store owned by Fayette Mayor Charles Evers. Several hours earlier, Evers, the first black mayor in Mississippi, had received phone calls warning that an attempt would be made on his life. Fayette Police Chief Robert Vanderson and his men arrested Watson after uncovering 5 guns in his car. Federal Treasury Department agents Sept. 10 arrested 2 more white men—Pat Massengale and Bobby D. Haywood—suspected of conspiring to assassinate Evers.

Bands of black youths roamed through the predominantly black West Side of Las Vegas, Nev. Oct. 5-8, setting parked cars afire and looting stores. At least 2 people were killed. The disorders began Oct. 5 when policemen stopped a black taxi driver for what the police called a routine traffic check. Later, black youths began smashing windows at a shopping center about a mile from the city's downtown area. Police used tear gas to disperse the rioters. Mayor Oran Gragson declared a state of emergency Oct. 6, asked Gov. Paul Laxalt to place the National Guard on stand-by alert and imposed a dusk-to-dawn curfew on the 40-block riot area. Firemen were pelted with rocks and bottles as they answered alarms in the riot area; police indicated that most of the blazes were sparked by firebombs. A black youth and a white salesman were shot and killed Oct. 7 during the 3d consecutive night of disorders. The youth was killed when he and several other youths attempted to hold up a liquor store. Police said the salesman was shot by a black gunman while the salesman was making a delivery in the West Side. The violence subsided Oct. 8 when National Guardsmen were placed on a stand-by alert at local armories. Mayor Gragson lifted the curfew Oct. 8.

A black youth was shot and killed and 9 policemen were wounded Oct. 10 as police and snipers exchanged gunfire in the predominantly black West Side of Chicago. The gunfire began when sniper fire broke out as 4 policemen chased 3 black youths past the Horner Housing Project. Police said the fleeing youths had been seen committing a robbery. According to the patrolmen, the dead youth had opened fire on his pursuers before he was slain. But black residents of the Horner project said the shooting began when the police attempted to block the youths as they were walking down the street.

Roving bands of Negroes battled police with rocks and bottles in Springfield, Mass. Oct. 14-18 after police arrested 19 persons following a demonstration at the city's welfare office Oct. 14. About 300 welfare recipients had marched on the welfare office in Springfield's black area to demand winter clothing allowances. Police arrested a handful of the demonstrators after they entered the office, and the disorders began several hours after the arrests. Negroes in the predominantly black Chestnut Hill area smashed windows, looted stores and fought police with rocks and bottles. Mayor Frank H. Freedman ordered a dusk-to-dawn curfew Oct. 15. The curfew was lifted Oct. 18 after the violence had subsided.

(Justice Department officials reported Aug. 23 that they believed the era of large-scale urban rioting had come to an end. Authorities said rioting in urban areas in 1969 was reduced at least 50% from 1968, in both the number of people involved and the severity of the disorders. Justice Department officials said, however, that they did not believe tensions between the races had lessened. In some large metropolitan areas, according to the officials, militant whites and Negroes appeared to be observing an uneasy armed truce.)

SNCC Drops 'Nonviolent' From Name

The Student Nonviolent Coordinating Committee (SNCC) announced July 22, 1969 that it had dropped the word 'nonviolent' from its title. It also announced that H. Rap Brown, 25, had been renamed chairman of the militant organization. (Brown had stepped down from the post in 1968, and Philip Hutchings had been named director.)

Brown said at a news conference at SNCC's new national headquarters in New York that "if a situation demands that you retaliate violently, you're no longer hindered or pampered by the 'nonviolent' in your name." He said the organization, renamed the Student National Coordinating Committee, did not "accept unconditional nonviolence as a tactic. All tactics must be considered. Violence must be considered."

(A Senate subcommittee had heard June 25 that SNCC had passed through its first, "nonviolent" period and since 1966, had been in a "black power phase." In testimony before the investigations subcommittee of the Senate Government Operations

Committee, Philip R. Manuel, the subcommittee's chief investigator, said SNCC had closed its ranks to whites and had shifted its emphasis to the "need for violence" to achieve black power. Manuel said SNCC advocated the stockpiling of weapons for use in armed conflict.)

Racial Clashes at Marine Bases

Racial problems at the U.S. Marine Corps' Camp Lejeune, N.C. flared July 20, 1969 into a battle between whites and blacks. Cpl. Edward Bankston, 20, died July 27 from a skull fracture suffered during the July 20 fighting between about 30 black and Puerto Rican Marines and about 14 white Marines. Bankston, of Picayune, Miss., had been one of 3 white Marines hospitalized after the clash. 3 black and 2 Puerto Rican Marines were charged Aug. 7 with Bankston's murder, rioting and assault.

Maj. Gen. Michael P. Ryan, commander of the 2d Marine Division, said July 28 that there had been a large number of racial fights on the base but probably fewer than in any city with 35,000 young men, the number of Marines stationed at Camp Lejeune. A Marine officer said Aug. 9, however, that a report submitted Apr. 22, 3 months before the fighting, had warned the camp's commanding officer of a "racial problem of considerable magnitude" at Camp Lejeune. The report was made by a group of officers called the Ad Hoc Committee on Equal Treatment & Opportunity at Camp Lejeune, N.C. The report said that "many white officers and noncommissioned officers retain prejudices and deliberately practice them" and that they failed to comply with Marine policies against discrimination.

A clash between black and white Marines at the Kaneohe Marine Corps Air Station near Honolulu Aug. 10 resulted in injuries to 16 Marines. A base spokesman said all the injuries were minor. He said "preliminary investigation disclosed that racial overtones were involved."

(A clash involving 200 soldiers took place Aug. 10 at Fort Bragg, N.C. A spokesman said Aug. 11 that the fight began at an enlisted men's club. He added: "This was not a racial riot and it was not a racial fight.")

Marine Pfc. Sylvester T. Hundley, 18, was sentenced in Apr. 1970 to 9 years at hard labor for involuntary manslaughter in Bankston's death. Hundley, a Negro, was also convicted of rioting and aggravated assault. 4 other Marines had previously been convicted and jailed on riot charges in the Camp Lejune clash.

Pittsburgh Job-Bias Clashes

A coalition of black civil rights groups joined several hundred black construction workers and white supporters in demonstrations that shut down $200 million worth of construction projects in Pittsburgh, Pa., Aug. 25-Aug. 29, 1969 after trade unions refused to increase black employment on construction jobs. The Black Construction Coalition (BCC), a loosely organized alliance of several black groups, called for the work stoppage in protest against what it called discriminatory hiring practices for construction jobs. The BCC said Negroes had been denied the jobs because they were not admitted to white-controlled labor unions. The BCC pledged to continue the shutdown at 10 construction sites unless the pace of job integration was "substantially increased."

5 of the sites were shut down Aug. 25 after more than 1,000 demonstrators surged into downtown Pittsburgh, snarled traffic and caused massive tie-ups throughout the city. The project sites were closed on the recommendation of Pittsburgh police, who sought to avert violence between the demonstrators and white construction workers. Work was halted at the other 5 sites by the presence of a 5-block line of protesters, about half of them white.

Police and demonstrators clashed Aug. 26 near the $31.9 million Three Rivers Stadium, being built near downtown Pittsburgh. 180 persons were arrested during the skirmish. 45, including 12 policemen, were injured. The stadium had been the focal point of BCC demands. Police Superintendent James W. Slusser said the stadium scuffle began after some of the demonstrators disrupted traffic. The police moved in with riot clubs, and the demonstrators retreated into downtown Pittsburgh, tying up traffic. The police then cordoned off the marchers and moved in to make the arrests. Byrd Brown, chairman of the NAACP'S Pittsburgh chapter, told the demonstrators to disperse but asked them to return to the stadium site Aug. 27.

About 700 black and white protesters gathered Aug. 27 across the street from the site of the $100 million, 64-story building scheduled to become the headquarters of the U.S. Steel Co. White construction workers on the steel structure dropped objects on demonstrators, and demonstrators hurled bottles at the workers. The police reported 45 arrests and 5 injuries, none serious. The protesters had gone to the construction site after meeting with U.S. Steel officials at the company's temporary headquarters. A spokesman for U.S. Steel said that the company "sympathized completely with their position that all persons should have the same privilege of union membership." But the company rejected the demonstrators' demand that work on the building be halted until more jobs were made available to Negroes.

Mayor Joseph M. Barr announced Aug. 27 that the owners of the 10 halted projects had agreed to stop operations to permit negotiations. The demonstrators responded by announcing that they would suspend demonstrations. The demonstrators sought a black-controlled job-training program, for 500 Negroes, that would guarantee graduates journeyman status in Pittsburgh's trade unions. The Master Builders Association, representing the contractors, had refused to accept a black-run program.

Black Panthers & Other Black Militants

2 members of the militant Black Panther Party had been shot to death Jan. 17, 1969 during a student meeting called at the University of California at Los Angeles (UCLA) to discuss the choice of a director for a proposed Afro-American Studies Center. The victims, both considered major contenders for the center leadership, were John Jerome Huggins, 23, area captain of the Panthers, and Alprentice (Bunchy) Carter, 26, a Panther deputy minister of defense. Acting on what was said to be a lead supplied by Panther members, the police sought 2 brothers, members of a rival black organization, US, as suspects, and both surrendered. George Phillip Stiner, 21, gave himself up in Los Angeles Jan. 20, and his brother Larry Joseph Stiner, 21, surrendered in San Diego Jan. 21. The police said that Larry Stiner was suffering from a gunshot wound that "looked 3 days old." The Stiner brothers were arraigned on murder charges Jan. 23.* The victims and suspects were members of a special UCLA program that permitted persons with "high potential" but low grades or felony convictions to enroll at the university.

One policeman was killed and another policeman and 4 Negroes wounded Mar. 29 in a gun battle following a meeting of a black separatist group, the Republic of New Africa, at a church in a Detroit ghetto. According to the police, Patrolmen Michael Czapski, 22, and Richard Worobec, 28, were shot shortly before midnight as they approached to question about 12 armed black men outside the New Bethel Baptist Church. Czapski was killed. Worobec, wounded, crawled into his patrol car and radioed for

---

*The two Stiners were then free on bail on charges of armed robbery, attempted murder, assault with a deadly weapon and kidnaping stemming from the holdup of a Santa Ana bar in Mar. 1968.

help. The police asserted that reinforcements who rushed to the scene were met by gunfire from inside of the church, where the attackers retreated. 4 Negroes were wounded as the shooting continued inside the church. Negroes inside the church asserted that the police had entered the building "with guns blazing" and that the firing lasted about 10 minutes. The Rev. C. L. Franklin, father of singer Aretha Franklin and pastor at the church, said that if leaders of the separatist organization "hadn't hollered to the people in the church to fall to the benches, [the police] might have killed several people." (Franklin said that he had rented the church to the New Africa group as a meeting hall.) Among 138 persons arrested and released within a day were Herman B. Ferguson and Arthur Harris, New York Negroes who had been convicted in 1968 of conspiracy to murder moderate black leaders. (Both were free on bail pending appeals.)

21 Black Panthers were indicted in New York Apr. 2 on charges of plotting to set off bombs Apr. 3 in 5 mid-town department stores, to dynamite the tracks of the Penn Central Railroad and to bomb a Bronx (N.Y. City) police station. District Attorney Frank S. Hogan, announcing the indictment, said that the militants had intended to destroy what they considered to be part of "the power structure." In early morning raids, the police seized 12 of the defendants at their homes or at the homes of friends. The police said they had confiscated firearms and explosives in making the arrests. 2 defendants were already in jail in Newark, N.J. on robbery charges, and a 3d gave himself up to the police Apr. 3. Those arrested pleaded not guilty to the charges, and bail was set at $100,000 for each.

One of those arrested Apr. 2 was Robert S. Collier, 32, who had served 21 months in jail after a 1965 conviction on charges of conspiring to blow up national monuments. Another was Joan Victoria Bird, 19, a student nurse who had been indicted Feb. 7 on a charge of attempting to murder 2 policemen in New York in January. Similar charges had been dropped against 2 other Panthers named in the Apr. 2 indictment: Lumumba Abdul Shakur, 27, described as a Panther captain, and Clark Squares, 32. Also arrested were Michael Tabor (known also as Cetewayo), 23, described as a Panther captain; Shakur's wife, Afeni, 23; Walter Johnson (also known as Baba Odinga), 24, John J. Casson (Ali Hassan), 28, Alex McKiever (Catarra), 19, Eddie Joseph (Jamal Baltimore), 17, Richard Moore (Analye Dahruba), 25, and Curtis Powell, 33. Lonni Epps, 18, surrendered to the police April 3. Donald Weems (Kwesi Balagoon), 22, and Nathaniel Burns

(Nathaniel Williams and Sekou Odinga), 25, were being held in Newark. Defendants being sought by the police were William King (Kinshasa), 31, Larry Mack, 23, Thomas Berry (Mshina), 26, Lee Roper (Shaba-Um), 22, and Lee Berry (Mkuba).

According to the police, the proposed targets of the conspiracy included the midtown stores of Macy's, Alexander's, Bloomingdale's, Korvette's and Abercrombie & Fitch; the tracks of the New Haven branch of Penn Central at 6 locations in Harlem; and, as a diversionary action, a police station in the Bronx.

3 Black Panthers were charged Apr. 18 with the shooting of 2 policemen in the Crown Heights section of Brooklyn, N.Y., Aug. 2, 1968. One defendant, Joudon Ford, 20, was arrested in Brooklyn; a 2d defendant, Ronald B. Hill, 20, was awaiting trial on a weapons charge in New Haven; and the 3d, William Hampton, 28, was at large.

8 Black Panthers—6 women and 2 men—were arrested in New Haven, Conn., on murder and conspiracy charges May 22 after the body of a Negro identified as Alex Rackley, 24, had been discovered in the Coginchaug River in Middlefield the previous day. Rackley, a member of the New York Panther party, allegedly had been tried and tortured by Black Panthers at a kangaroo court in New Haven, reportedly because he was suspected of disloyalty to the party. New Haven Police Chief James F. Ahern said "there is a direct link between the murder and the recent arrests of 21 Black Panthers in New York City for planning to blow up public buildings." Among the Panthers arrested was Erika Huggins, 21, of New Haven, whose husband, John, had been killed Jan. 17 at UCLA.

The FBI staged a series of raids against Black Panther party field offices June 4-25 in what the bureau described as a hunt for Black Panther suspects in the Rackley murder. Party chairman Bobby Seale rejected the FBI explanation for the raids. Seale charged the bureau June 17 with harassment in an effort "to destroy the Black Panther Party leadership." FBI agents, supported by Colorado state troopers, had used tear gas to rout and arrest 2 Black Panther fugitives from the offices of the Denver Panthers June 5. A raid on the Chicago office June 4 had failed to yield the fugitive sought. FBI agents in Salt Lake City June 6 arrested party member Lonnie McLucas of New Haven, Conn. on charges of unlawful flight to avoid prosecution for rackley's Murder.

Bobby Seale was arrested by FBI agents in San Francisco Aug. 19 on a murder charge in the Rackley case. According to Police Chief Ahern, Seale had spoken at Yale University in New

Haven May 19 and was in New Haven at the time of the slaying. George Sams Jr., sought in connection with the slaying, was turned over to FBI agents in Buffalo, N.Y. Aug. 21 by Canadian authorities.

Sams Dec. 1 pleaded guilty to 2d-degree murder charges in Rackley's death. Sams, in a statement to police, said he had been ordered from Berkeley, Calif. to take part in the purge of Black Panther Party chapters in the East. According to Sams, Rackley was slain on Seale's direct orders. Sams named Lonnie McLucas and Warren Kimbro as Rackley's murderers. Sams admitted torturing Rackley with scalding hot water. After Sams entered his plea, a 2d defendant, Loretta Luckes, changed her plea to guilty on charges of conspiring to kidnap resulting in death. Kimbro Jan. 16, 1970 pleaded guilty to 2d-degree murder. McLucas was convicted Aug. 31, 1970 of conspiracy to murder Rackley. Charges against Seale and Mrs. Huggins were dismissed by Judge Harold H. Mulvey May 25, 1971 after the jury deadlocked. Mulvey June 23, 1971 imposed life sentences on Sams and Kimbro.

13 Sacramento policemen were wounded and 37 persons were arrested after more than 6 hours of sniper fire June 16 in the city's Oak Park district. Black Panther Party leaders charged that police had stormed their offices after tossing tear gas canisters into the building. After viewing the damage to Black Panther headquarters, Sacramento Mayor Richard Marriott said June 17 that he was "shocked and horrified" at the police's action. James Mott, a Black Panther officer, charged that the police had invaded the building because they were seeking to destroy the organization. The police retorted they had ordered parked cars off the lawn of an adjacent park and had been greeted by a fusillade of rifle fire.

FBI Director J. Edgar Hoover claimed July 15 that among black extremist groups, the Black Panther Party represented "the greatest threat to the internal security of the country." Hoover, in the bureau's annual report for fiscal 1969, accused the party of assaulting policemen and staging violent confrontations with federal authorities throughout the nation.

5 Chicago policemen were wounded July 31 in a gun battle with Black Panther Party members at the party's Illinois headquarters. Both sides accused the other of firing the initial shot. Police said the firing began when 2 policemen attempted to stop 2 men carrying what police said appeared to be sawed-off shotguns in front of the party's offices. The police said that when the patrolmen left their car to investigate, the 2 men fled into the Panthers' headquarters and began firing. Bobby Rush, Panther deputy

minister of defense, denied the provocation and said that the police had "pulled up in front of the office, jumped out of the car and started shooting."

A Chicago policeman was wounded Oct. 4 in a gun battle on the roof of Black Panther Party headquarters. 7 party members were arrested and charged with attempted murder and resisting arrest.

2 Chicago policemen were killed and 6 wounded Nov. 13 during a gun battle between the police and Black Panther members. A 19-year old youth associated with the party was killed by the police after he allegedly shot a patrolman. According to the police, the battle began when a police cruiser moved into Chicago's South Side to answer a distress call and was fired upon by snipers. A patrolman, Francis Rappaport, was killed by a youth a block from the police cruiser. Rappaport's alleged killer, Spurgeon J. Winters, was shot and killed by other policemen. The original distress call had been telephoned by Winters' sister, who told police that the Panthers had come into the area with guns. Patrolman John Gilhooley, who was wounded during the fracas, died later in a Chicago hospital.

Police in Chicago staged a pre-dawn raid on an apartment near the Panthers' headquarters Dec. 4 and killed Fred Hampton, Illinois party chairman. The police also shot and killed Mark Clark, described by police as a Panthers leader in Peoria, Ill. 4 others, 2 of them women, were wounded. According to police reports, the raid was carried out on a warrant on the basis of information that Hampton's apartment was being used to stockpile weapons. The police asserted that when they knocked on the door a woman opend fire with a shotgun. Police said that at least 200 shots were fired during a "shootout" that lasted 10 or 12 minutes. Spokesmen for the Panthers Dec. 5 denied this. They claimed that Hampton was "murdered in his bed" by police who opened fire as they burst through the door. The Panthers took newsmen through Hampton's apartment to support their argument that the only shooting was done by the police. A black Chicago alderman and attorneys for the Black Panthers claimed Dec. 6 that an independent autopsy performed on Hampton's body "confirms our theory that he was murdered while he was asleep." The autopsy, performed by 3 white doctors, was held at the funeral home owned by Alderman A. A. Rayner, who had called for an investigation of the affair. (Rayner later confirmed that he had co-signed the lease for the Panthers' headquarters.) A coroner's jury ruled Jan. 21, 1970 that the killing of Hampton and Clark was justifiable.

The 7 Black Panthers who survived the Dec. 1969 Chicago raid were indicted by a Chicago grand jury Jan. 30, 1970 on charges of attempted murder and armed violence. Those indicted were Brenda Harris, Verlina Brewer, Blair Anderson, Ronald Satchell, Harold Bell, Deborah Johnson and Louis Truelock.

A special federal grand jury, impaneled in Chicago by the Justice Department to investigate the Dec. 1969 raid, reported May 15, 1970 that the police had grossly exaggerated the Panthers' resistance during the shooting incident. The jury reported that the police had sprayed the Panthers' apartment with at least 82 bullets, while only one shot was apparently fired by the Panthers inside. But the jury concluded that it could find no evidence on which to indict members of the raiding party for violations of the slain Panthers' civil rights. The jury said it had speculated that the policemen could have been returning one another's gunfire as one possible explanation for the 82-shot fusillade. The jury conceded that its probe might have led to prosecution of the policemen if the Black Panthers who survived the raid had agreed to testify before the panel. (The 7 had asserted that they would talk only to a "peer group.") Less than 10 hours before the grand jury released its report, 3 high ranking Chicago police officers were demoted. All had been connected with the raid.

Cook County Criminal Court Judge Philip J. Romiti acquitted State's Attorney Edward V. Hanrahan and 13 co-defendants Oct. 25, 1972 of charges of conspiring to obstruct justice in the shootout slaying of Hampton and Clark. Romiti said the evidence presented by the special county prosecutor amounted to "not much more than conjecture and speculation." The defendants had waived a jury trial. The prosecution's case had been damaged by the discovery during the trial of written statements made to their lawyer by 4 Panthers who had survived the 1969 incident. The statements contradicted their testimony before a grand jury that they had not fired shots at the police.

Police in Los Angeles, armed with tear-gas rifles, fought a 4-hour battle with members of the Black Panther Party Dec. 8, 1969 following a raid on party headquarters. 3 policemen and 3 Panthers were wounded. The police said they had moved on the Panthers' office in search of a cache of illegal weapons and 2 party members wanted in connection with an assault charge. The police said they had arrested 11 Panthers, including 3 women, at the party's headquarters, and 13 others at 2 other sites. According to police reports, the raiding parties had seized 2 machineguns, 3 shotguns, several rifles and several hundred rounds of ammunition.

A total of 300 policemen exchanged shots with those inside the headquarters, who surrendered after tear gas was lobbed into the building. California State Sen. Mervyn Dymally denounced the raid as "part of a national plan of political repression against the Panthers." Dymally, whose constituency was the Los Angeles area in which the police raids took place, said the gun battle was not an isolated incident.

The American Civil Liberties Union (ACLU) Dec. 28 released a report of a survey of 9 metropolitan centers that had led the organization to conclude that law enforcement agencies across the country were "waging a drive against the Black Panther Party resulting in serious civil liberties violations." The survey was prepared for submission to an independent commission headed by former Supreme Court Justice Arthur J. Goldberg and Roy Wilkens, head of the NAACP. The survey, covering police operations against the Panthers, was conducted by ACLU affiliates in New York, Los Angeles, Chicago, San Francisco, Philadelphia, and major metropolitan areas in Connecticut, Wisconsin, Indiana and Michigan. The data included alleged "repeated arrests" of members of the Black Panthers while they were circulating political literature and police raids on allegedly "specious charges."

Demonstrators Protest Vietnam War

Activities, some of them violent, to protest the continuation of the Vietnam war were reported from Washington to San Francisco in 1969.

A group of 300 to 400 youthful antiwar demonstrators hurled rocks, bottles and obscenities at Richard M. Nixon's limousine Jan. 20 as it took the President to his inauguration. It was the first time a group of this size had attempted to disrupt a Presidential inauguration. The youths were part of a larger group, numbering up to 6,000, which had been assembled in Washington by the National Mobilization Committee to End the War in Vietnam for an orderly, nonviolent, 3-day "counter-inaugural." The smaller group of ultramilitants had decided Jan. 19 to ignore the nonviolent aims of the committee's leaders. The disruption reportedly was led by members of Students for a Democratic Society (SDS) and Co-Aim, the Committee for an Anti-Imperialist Movement. The mobilization committee, called "the Mobe" by the demonstrators, had staged a symbolic counter-inaugural parade Jan. 19, in which thousands of youths marched the reverse of the official inaugural parade route. At least 22 demonstrators were arrested during the day, most of them for scuffles that erupted at the end of the parade.

(A study of the protests staged in Washington during the Jan. 20 inauguration, released May 31, said that protesters and police had been generally restrained and well-behaved. A study group of the National Commission on the Causes & Prevention of Violence found that close cooperation among protest leaders and government officials had assured that the counter-inaugural demonstrations would result in little violence and few injuries. The report was prepared under the direction of Joseph R. Sahid, a co-director of the commission's law and law-enforcement study group. The report said that the counter-inaugural episode proved that large-scale demonstrations could be organized and controlled, even with the presence of "numbers of unruly participants.")

12 members of the so-called 'Milwaukee 14' group of draft protesters were convicted of burglary, theft and arson May 26 in Milwaukee Circuit Court. The defendants were members of a group of Catholics, including 7 clergymen, charged with entering a Milwaukee Selective Service office Sept. 24, 1968, and seizing and burning thousands of draft files. Judge Charles L. Larson, 61, sentenced 11 of the 12 defendants June 6 to concurrent 2-year jail terms and 4 years' probation. The defendants, who conducted their own defense, attempted to turn the trial into a forum for attacking the draft system and the Vietnam war. The 11 defendants sentenced June 6 were: The Rev. Robert Cunnane, Stoughton, Mass.; the Rev. Anthony J. Mullanoy, Boston; Brother Basil K. O'Leary, Wilnona, Minn.; James H. Forest, New York; Robert E. Graf, Milwaukee; the Rev. Lawrence E. Rosenbaugh, Milwaukee; Donald J. Cotton, Milwaukee; the Rev. Alfred L. Janicke, Minneapolis; Fred J. Ojile, Minneapolis; the Rev. James W. Harney, North Weymouth, Mass.; and Douglas Marvey, Minneapolis. The 12th defendant, the Rev. John Higginbotham, 28, of St. Cloud, Minn., was sentenced to 2 years in prison June 20.

The federal trial of 12 of the Milwaukee protesters began June 10. Cunnane and Higginbotham pleaded guilty to charges of interfering with the Selective Service System, and Federal Judge Myron L. Gordon dismissed 2 other charges against them—conspiracy and destruction of draft files. Gordon dismissed all charges against the other 10 defendants June 11. He said that pretrail publicity had made it impossible to select an impartial jury.

18 persons had been arrested in Chicago May 25 for destroying draft records. The Chicago group included 2 Catholic priests and a Jesuit seminarian. 8 of those arrested came from Milwaukee;

3 had worked with Father Rosenbaugh, one of the Milwaukee defendants, in a community center for alcoholics and poor people. 10 of those arrested were sentenced in federal district court to prison terms ranging from 5 to 10 years June 9, 1970. The 10-year terms—2 5-year sentences to be served consecutively—were dealt to 3 defendants who disappeared during the last week of the trial. Arrest warrants were issued for the Rev. Nicholas J. Riddell, 40, Milwaukee, a Carmelite priest, and Linda J. Quint, 22, of Chicago, both of whom walked out of the trial June 3, and for Charles Muse, 21, of Roxbury, Mass., who disappeared June 5 when the defendants were convicted. Riddell, Miss Quint and 2 other defendants—Edward Gargan, 19, and William Durkin, 20, both of Milwaukee—based their defense on insanity. Their attorney had argued May 8 that "insanity is a culturally determined aspect" and the defendants "have a delusion that our cherished institutions are being perverted." Gargan, Durkin and the following 5 defendants were sentenced to 2 5-year terms to be served concurrently: Frederick Chase, 25, of Detroit; Joseph E. Mulligan, 27, a Jesuit seminarian from North Aurora, Ill.; William Sweeney, 20, of Milwaukee; Margaret Katroscik, 23, of Detroit; and Charles Fullenkamp, 21, of Burbank, S.D. 4 fugitives who failed to appear at the beginning of the trial were the Rev. John Pietra, a Carmelite priest from Canada; John Phillips of Boston; John Loll of New York, and Charles Smith of Wabasha, Minn.

9 Roman Catholics were convicted June 6, 1969 in Baltimore County Circuit Court of state charges of robbery and assault for the burning of draft records in a Catonsville, Md. selective service office in May 1968. The defendants, including 2 priests, 2 former priests and a former nun, were sentenced to 2 to $3\frac{1}{2}$ years in prison. They had received similar sentences in Oct. 1968 after conviction on federal charges for their attack on the Catonsville office. Circuit Court Judge Kenneth C. Proctor decided the state trail without a jury on the basis of the transcript of the federal trial. The state and federal sentences were to be served concurrently. The defendants were: The Rev. Philip Berrigan and Thomas Lewis, who were serving 6-year terms for destroying Selective Service files in Baltimore Oct. 27, 1967 and who had received $3\frac{1}{2}$-year jail terms in 1968; the Rev. Daniel Berrigan, brother of Father Philip, Thomas Melville, a former Maryknoll priest, and George Miscne, 3-year terms; Marjorie Melville, a former Maryknoll nun and wife of Melville, Mary Moylan, 32, John Hogan, 33, a former Maryknoll brother, and David Darst, 26, a Christian brother, 2-year sentences.

Hundreds of SDS members staged a series of demonstrations and radical actions in Chicago Oct. 8-11 to coincide with the conspiracy trial of 8 protest leaders charged with fomenting disorders during the 1968 Democratic National Convention. Gov. Richard B. Ogilvie ordered 2,500 National Guardsmen to duty Oct. 9 after helmeted demonstrators clashed with local police the night before following a rally at Chicago's Lincoln Park. 60 persons were arrested and 3 radicals were shot, one by a policeman who said he shot a demonstrator who had been clubbing him. The demonstrators, members of the Weatherman SDS faction that had dominated the organization since the group had split at a convention earlier in the year, chose the slogan "Bring the War Home" for their 4-day campaign. (The faction took their name from a line in Bob Dylan's song "Subterranean Homesick Blues": "You don't need a weatherman to tell which way the wind blows.") Police arrested 12 demonstrators Oct. 9 when 60 members of the Weatherman "women's militia" charged police lines after announcing that they would "destroy" a military induction center. Other arrests came during a police raid on a church in suburban Evanston early Oct. 11. Later that day, 103 demonstrators were arrested as they charged police lines in the heart of the Chicago business district. The resulting violence injured 24 policemen and scores of demonstrators. The police said Oct. 13 that 290 demonstrators had been arrested; 2 Weatherman leaders, Mark Rudd and Bernardine Dohrn, were among those arrested. Richard Elrod, one of Chicago's assistant city attorneys, was injured during the Oct. 11 violence. He was reported in "very serious" condition in a hospital and paralyzed from the neck down. Brian Flanagan, 22, New York, a National Merit Scholarship finalist, was charged with attempted murder in the incident.

More than 250,000 protesters gathered in Washington Nov. 15 to participate in the largest antiwar demonstration in U.S. history. The march was sponsored by the New Mobilization Committee to End the War in Vietnam (the "New Mobe"), which also sponsored a parallel San Francisco protest drawing, according to varying estimates, 60,000 to 175,000 demonstrators and a Nov. 13-15 March Against Death in Washington involving more than 40,000 persons. In anticipation of possible violence during the Nov. 15 mass demonstration in the capital, the Pentagon had announced Nov. 12 that 9,000 troops had been moved to special posts in the Washington area. However the only incidents of violence came not during the New Mobe marches but during 2 demonstrations Nov. 14 and 15 by a splinter minority of militant protesters.

In order to control the crowd, the New Mobe had organized
thousands of parade marshals to give advice to the demonstrators
and to help the 3,000-man District of Columbia police force keep
the peace. During the March Against Death, which began Nov. 13
and lasted for about 40 hours, each of the 46,000 participants
carried the name of an American soldier killed in Vietnam
or of a Vietnamese village allegedly destroyed by American
troops.

While the March Against Death continued, 1,000 to 2,000
militant radicals clashed with Washington policemen Nov. 14 near
the South Vietnamese embassy. The trouble grew out of a rally held
at Washington's Dupont Circle by SDS factions, the Mad Dogs, the
Crazies and the Youth International Party (Yippies). As police
threw tear gas to stop the marchers on the way to the embassy,
the militants hurled rocks which broke some 50 store windows
and damaged about 40 police cruisers. A number of policemen received minor injuries, and at least 20 demonstrators were arrested.
The radicals had split off from the main rally to march on the
Justice Department in a demonstration led by Yippies and supporters of defendants in the Chicago conspiracy trial. The crowd,
numbering about 6,000, carried banners reading "Stop the Trial"
and "Free [Panther leader] Bobby Seale." Several young demonstrators ran up a Vietcong flag on the main flagpole of the Justice
Department building, but police replaced it with a U.S. flag. The
police began using tear gas when demonstrators started throwing
rocks and bottles at the building. Most of the demonstrators began
to retreat, but radicals urged them on to a confrontation. Parade
marshals placed themselves between police and the crowd, pushing
the protesters back and urging calm as police released wave after
wave of tear gas. One policeman told reporters Nov. 16: "Those
marshals tried real hard. . . . I'm sorry some of them got caught
in the gas." At about 7 p.m. police and National Guardsmen dispersed the remaining youths. Windows in some 50 buildings were
broken during the melee. The police reported Nov. 16 that 135
arrests had been made.

More than 1,000 military policemen repelled 4,000 civilian
demonstrators Oct. 12 at the Fort Dix Army base in New Jersey.
About 20 antiwar and militant groups participated in the protest
to demand the release of "The Fort Dix 38"—soldiers charged
with a variety of offenses growing out of a June 1969 riot at the
base stockade. No arrests or injuries were reported. The protest
began with a rally at a Wrightstown coffeehouse, the center of
radical activities at the base. The demonstrators marched toward

the base entrance where they met a line of MPs. The protesters were dispersed by tear gas.

Extremists Arrested in Bombing & Sniping Attacks

The FBI Nov. 14, 1969 arrested 3 men and a woman as alleged radical-terrorists who had set off 8 bombings in major corporate and government structures in New York since July.

The suspects included Samuel Melville, the alleged ringleader, who, the FBI said, had fashioned the bombs from stolen dynamite. The others were George Demmerle, John D. Hughey 3d and Jane Lauren Alpert. Being sought was a 5th suspect, Pat Swinton, who, the FBI said, had formerly worked for the North American Congress of Latin America. The FBI said the organization "correlates research" on what the group calls "U.S. imperialism in Latin America." (An FBI agent testified at a pretrial hearing Dec. 30 that Demmerle was an FBI informant who had tipped off the FBI about the group's activities. According to the FBI, Demmerle had volunteered his services to the government in 1966.)

The 5 suspects were charged with setting off or planting bombs in the following places: July 27—a United Fruit Co. pier on the Hudson River; Aug. 20—the Marine Midland Grace Trust Co. building on Broadway; Sept. 19—the Federal Office Building at Federal Plaza; Oct. 7—the U.S. Armed Forces Examining & Entrance Station at Whitehall Street; Nov. 11—RCA Building at Rockefeller Plaza; General Motors Corp. Building on 5th Avenue, and the Chase Manhattan Building at Chase Manhattan Plaza; and Nov. 12—the Criminal Courts Building and an Army truck parked near the 69th Regiment Armory.

23 members of the militant Weatherman faction of the Students for a Democratic Society were arrested Nov. 18 and charged with conspiring to commit murder and other offenses in connection with a Nov. 8 sniper attack on the Cambridge, Mass. police headquarters. Eric Mann, 28, leader of the local Weatherman faction, was also arrested and charged with assault with intent to commit murder. But Judge M. Edward Viola Nov. 29 dismissed the charges against Mann and 20 of the group after a young prosecution witness testified that he had signed a statement implicating some of the Weathermen under threats from police. 5 Weathermen were fined a total of $700 in district court in Boston Dec. 16 on charges arising from the incident. 2 of the defendants received jail sentences.

'Manson Family' Murders Actress Sharon Tate & 3 Friends

Film actress Sharon Tate, 26, wife of film director Roman Polanski, 36, was found murdered Aug. 9, 1969 in her house in Benedict Canyon, near Bel Air, Calif. She was 8 months pregnant. Also slain in and around the house were 3 of her friends, Hollywood hair stylist Thomas John (Jay) Sebring, 35; Voyteck Frykowski, 37, a Polish refugee friend of Polanski; and his girl friend, coffee heiress Abigail (Gibby) Folger, 26. Steven Parent, 18, a friend of caretaker William Garretson, 19, was found shot to death in his car near the house. Polanski was in London at the time.

A Los Angeles County grand jury Dec. 8 handed down indictments against Charles M. Manson, a leader of a nomadic group of young drifters who roamed the California wastelands near Death Valley, and 4 of his followers for the murder of Miss Tate and the others. The 5, who described themselves as a "family," were also indicted with a 6th person for the slayings Aug. 10 of Leno and Rosemary LaBianca in their home near Beverly Hills, Calif. The chief prosecution witness during the Dec. 6-8 hearings in Los Angeles was Susan Denise Atkins, who was herself indicted. Miss Atkins testified that she was under a "hypnotic spell" imposed by Manson during the slayings. In addition to Miss Atkins and Manson, those indicted were Linda Louise Kasabian, who was arrested in New Hampshire; Patricia Krenwinkel, who was arrested in Mobile, Ala.; and Charles (Tex.) Watson, who was arrested in Texas. The 6th defendant, Leslie Van Houten (Sankston), was indicted for conspiracy, but only 2 murder counts were handed down against her. They were in connection with the LaBianca slayings.

Manson, Miss Atkins and Miss Krenwinkel were convicted Jan. 26, 1971 on 7 counts of first-degree murder. Miss Van Houten was convicted on 2 counts of murder. All 4 were also convicted of conspiracy to commit murder. The key prosecution witness was Mrs. Kasabian, who said that she had accompanied the killers to the Tate home on the night of the murders. Mrs. Kasabian testified that Manson had ordered the Tate murders as well at the slayings the next day of the LaBiancas. Other state witnesses said Manson had ordered the murders in the hope of triggering a race war between whites and blacks. Several of the witnesses said Manson believed that the blacks would be the victors in a race war, that they would turn to him and that he would assume a leadership role.

The jury Mar. 21, 1971 recommended that Manson and the 3 girls convicted with him be executed in the gas chamber. During the penalty hearings, the 3 girls admitted that they had participated in the murders under the influence of LSD. The 3 insisted, however, that Manson had nothing to do with the killings. Miss Atkins said Feb. 9 that she had personally killed Miss Tate on the orders of Linda Kasabian.

Charles Watson admitted at his trial in Los Angeles Sept. 2, 1971 that he had killed Sharon Tate and the 6 other victims. Watson said he had participated in the murders on Manson's orders. Describing the LaBianca slayings, Watson said Manson had ordered the group "to go in and do like last night and make sure everyone is dead." Watson, 25, was convicted Oct. 12 and sentenced to death Oct. 21.

Manson, 37, was sentenced in Los Angeles Dec. 13, 1971 to life in prison on his conviction of murder in 2 more 1969 slayings, the killings of Gary Hinman, a musician, and Donald Shea, a ranch hand.

WAR, RACE & EXTREMISM (1970)

Nationwide Disturbances

Campus turmoil, antiwar protests, terrorist bombings, urban disturbances and racial violence continued to trouble the nation in 1970. Dissidents from the University of California's Santa Barbara campus burned a Bank of America branch. Riot-equipped police dispersed firebombing and rock-throwing students in Buffalo, N.Y. Fire damaged the Berkeley campus library, and Berkeley police battled radicals. Police dispersed demonstrators at San Francisco State College. 20 students were wounded by shotgun fire in violence at Ohio State University. Violence followed a Yale rally in support of the Black Panthers.

Violent demonstrations swept the campuses in May after Pres. Nixon announced that he was sending U.S. troops into Cambodia. Ohio National Guardsmen fired into a crowd at Kent State University, killing 4 students. Firebombings, protest marches, vandalism and building seizures were reported from New Jersey to California. Antiwar organizations rallied students in a nationwide strike that reached 448 campuses. 2 students were slain by police bullets at Jackson State College in Mississippi. 2 University of Kansas students died in street disorders.

Antiwar protesters demonstrated in U.S. cities. Construction workers fought antiwar demonstrators on Wall Street.

A sharp rise in terrorist bombings was reported in 1970. Bombs injured a West Virginia prosecutor and destroyed Denver school buses. Explosions demolished a bomb factory in a New York townhouse. Bombs were set off in government buildings, industrial property, private homes, schools, colleges, churches and synagogues from New York to Berkeley. An explosion at the University of Wisconsin damaged a mathematics research center and killed a research worker. Congress passed legislation increasing the penalties for terrorist bombings.

Turmoil and racial violence plagued the cities. State troopers routed a white mob attacking school buses bringing black children to a previously all-white school in Lamar, S.C. Police in riot gear maintained order in River Rouge, Mich. after clashes between black and white youths. 6 blacks died in racial violence in Augusta, Ga. Sporadic violence erupted in the South and Northeast. Puerto Rican youths rampaged in Jersey City, N.J. Firemen and

155

police were injured in a clash in New York. Youths battled the police in New Brunswick, N.J. and Chicago. Carloads of armed blacks riddled the Cairo, Ill. police station with gunfire during continued clashes between whites and blacks. Extremists intensified attacks on law officers; policemen were slain in Chicago, Berkeley, Philadelphia and Omaha.

Warning Against 'Political Exploitation of Campus Problems'

A committee of the American Council on Education, appointed in 1969 to study student unrest, released a report Apr. 25, 1970 citing dangerous responses to the problems of campus disruption. The 18-member panel—composed of college presidents and other educators, student leaders and private citizens and headed by former Organization of American States envoy Sol M. Linowitz—warned against "political exploitation of campus problems by some public figures." The report said "repressive and provocative pronouncements" by officials "have the same inflammatory effect that extremist rhetoric has on the campus." Releasing the report in Washington, Linowitz said students cited as inflammatory various remarks by Vice Pres. Spiro T. Agnew and by California Gov. Ronald Reagan. The committee, in its study, also said legislative attempts to deal with unrest were "deeply disturbing" and tended to restrict free inquiry.

Citing the war in Vietnam and student power as the two major sources of campus tension, the study said Vietnam would remain a devisive issue "until the nation ceases to force young men to fight in a war they believe unjust."

To ease other tensions, the committee recommended that attempts be made to establish "effective communications so that policy questions and grievances can be aired by the campus community." The group advocated giving students autonomous power over nonacademic activities and the opportunity to participate in curriculum decisions. University presidents should remain accessible to students and faculty and should "take positive steps to explain their plans and policies" to the community, the panel said. Disciplinary procedures and policies dealing with disruption should be formalized and outdated rules eliminated, it added.

Student Turmoil

Rioting students at the University of California's Santa Barbara campus set fire Feb. 25, 1970 to a Bank of America branch in Isla Vista, a community adjoining the university. Disturbances in the small community, populated mostly by about 9,000 students, had started Feb. 24 when protesters threw rocks and bottles at police who had just arrested 2 youths for obscenity, arson and resisting arrest. The campus, however, had been restless since the spring of 1969, when students had protested the dismissal of instructor William L. Allen.

Gov. Ronald Reagan came to Santa Barbara Feb. 26 and declared a state of "extreme emergency" following the disorders of the previous night when 36 demonstrators were arrested and 25 sheriff's deputies were reported injured. National Guard troops were activated early Feb. 27 after another night of disorders resulted in 16 more arrests. The troops remained in the area until they were withdrawn Mar. 2 after 3 days of relative calm. Reagan blamed the disorders partially on William M. Kunstler, defense lawyer in the Chicago conspiracy trial, who had spoken at a student rally Feb. 25. Greg Knell, vice president of the Associated Students of the University of Santa Barbara, said Feb. 26 that the riots were a spontaneous reaction to police agitation and student frustration over inaction on their grievances.

(Reagan, remarking on the need to end student violence, said Apr. 7 that "if it takes a blood bath, let's get it over with." He explained later that he had not realized he had used the expression, which he called "a figure of speech.")

A University of California student was shot and killed Apr. 18 after new violence broke out in the Isla Vista area near the Santa Barbara campus. Kevin P. Moran, 22, a senior, was slain by what appeared to be a stray police bullet as he emerged from a Bank of America branch after he had helped put out an early morning fire caused by a molotov cocktail. The branch, the same one that had been destroyed Feb. 25 by a firebomb, had reopened Mar. 7.* Police officials at first contended that Moran had been killed by sniper fire directed at the police. Santa Barbara County Sheriff James W. Webster said Apr. 20, however, that a city policeman had acknowledged that his rifle had accidentally discharged at the time of the shooting. He said that the bullet had evidently ricocheted before hitting Moran and that it was "so deformed . . . that positive identification is extremely doubtful."

The renewed disorder at Santa Barbara had begun Apr. 16 after several hours of speeches on the campus, one of them delivered by Mrs. Nancy Rubin, wife of Yippie leader Jerry Rubin. Rubin, invited to speak by a student group, had been barred from

---

*A bomb blew a hole in the roof of the same branch bank Dec. 15.

the campus by university officials and prohibited from speaking in Isla Vista by the county board of supervisors. Police used tear gas in what militants described as a surprise attack on student demonstrators. 4 students, 3 of them women, were wounded by police birdshot. Radical students, angered by the police action, wandered through Isla Vista Apr. 17, lighting small fires and throwing rocks. Moran had been one of several students answering an appeal from the student-body president to help put out trash fires.

(2 firebombs were thrown through the window of a Bank of America branch in Los Angeles Apr. 21.)

Students at the Buffalo campus of the State University of York had seized 4 classroom and administration buildings and called a student strike Feb. 27. This followed 2 nights of violence on the campus that had begun when riot-equipped city police dispersed groups of students who had damaged several buildings with rocks and firebombs. 12 persons, including 2 campus security guards, had been injured and 16 demonstrators arrested Feb. 25. The demonstrators quit the occupied buildings Feb. 28 after being served with a court order. The strike continued, but university officials estimated that only 1,000 students out of a 16,000-student enrollment were involved. Both the moderate Student Association, a student government group, and the more radical War Council, including students associated with the Students for a Democratic Society (SDS), supported the strike. One of various leaflets issued by the strikers called for an end to "institutional violence" on the campus, including the Reserve Officers Training Corps and Defense Department research projects. Another leaflet urged support for black student demands, including open enrollment, athletic scholarships for black athletes and help for Buffalo's ghetto residents. Other leaflets demanded the replacement of the campus police force by a student patrol and the resignation of Dr. Peter F. Regan, acting president of the university, who had succeeded Dr. Martin Mayerson in January. Mayerson had maintained a policy of keeping outside police units off the campus.

Mounted police dispersed 1,200 demonstrators at San Francisco State College Mar. 10 and halted a rampage through a nearby shopping center after arresting 13 persons. It was the first mass demonstration since violent disorders on the campus in 1969. A molotov cocktail that failed to ignite had been thrown earlier into the office of S. I. Hayakawa, the school's president.

Fire caused $320,000 damage to the University of California's Berkeley campus library Mar. 9. The city fire chief said Mar. 12 that arsonists started the blaze.

About 60 persons were arrested during 3 days of disorders Apr. 15-17 on the Berkeley campus. The rioting began with a protest against the Reserve Officers Training Corps. Police armed with tear gas fought to control rampaging groups of radicals who broke windows and threw rocks. Demonstrators tried Apr. 16 to ram through the door of Sproul Hall, the main administration building. Earlier 20 young people forced their way into the faculty club and broke windows and luncheon dishes. A university official said most of the invaders appeared to be high school and junior high school students.

Kansas Gov. Robert B. Docking ordered state troopers and National Guardsmen on standby alert Apr. 20 after a fire, believed to have been set by arsonists, caused $2 million worth of damage to the University of Kansas student building in Lawrence. At the request of Lawrence Mayor Donald E. Metzler, a dusk-to-dawn curfew was imposed. A firebomb had been thrown into Lawrence High School, and there were reports of scattered gunshots from teenagers, both black and white, firing from car windows. 300 Guardsmen and state troopers were called into Lawrence Apr. 21 after a 2d night of violence involving street fires and sporadic sniper attacks. Most of the troops were withdrawn Apr. 24. During the disturbances there had been 60 arrests for curfew violations and disturbing the peace. 3 students were charged Apr. 23 with transporting incendiary devices.

At Stanford University students voted by a slim majority to permit the ROTC program to stay on campus without academic credit. But after results of the referendum were announced Apr. 17, anti-ROTC protests continued, and fires caused $50,000 to $100,000 damage to the Stanford Center for Advanced Studies in the Behavioral Sciences Apr. 24. The university said the work of 10 visiting scholars was destroyed in the blaze, which followed an anti-ROTC sit-in at the campus's old student union building. 42 persons were arrested April 30 after rock-throwing students, whom university officials said were "heated up" by the Cambodian crisis, confronted police. The violence followed a day-long peaceful sit-in at the old Student Union by anti-ROTC protesters.

About 600 students were arrested during 2 days of disorders at Ohio State University in Columbus Apr. 29-30. Gov. James A. Rhodes ordered 1,200 National Guard troops onto the campus Apr. 29. The troops and police used tear gas and pepper gas to break up groups of students protesting the school administration's failure to negotiate their demands for an end to the Reserve Officers Training Corps (ROTC) program on campus and for the admission of 2,500 more black students by the fall. Protesters called for a student strike Apr. 29 after Novice G. Fawcett, president of the university, indicated that he would not negotiate. (Protesters also demanded the establishment of branch campuses in black communities to be run by blacks and the abolition of all war-related campus research.) Fawcett said May 1 that there would be "no amnesty" for those involved in disruptions. More than 50 students had been suspended. Despite reports of about 20 students wounded by shotgun fire, police and Guard units on the Ohio State campus denied firing weapons. Students and faculty members said they saw shooting by the police. Commenting on the publicity over the alleged shooting, Fawcett said, "You'd think they were shot dead." (About 5,000 National Guardsmen were ordered to active duty on the Ohio State campus May 21 after student protesters led by black militants smashed windows and looted shops near the campus. The violence followed a protest rally and reports of interracial violence apparently stemming from disagreements between white and black protesters on whether to resume a student strike that ended May 19.)

More than 13,000 youths crowded the Yale University campus May 1-3 for generally peaceful demonstrations in support of 8 Black Panthers who were awaiting trial in New Haven, Conn. on charges ranging from kidnapping to first-degree murder. 4,000 federal troops, including National Guardsmen and Marine paratroopers, were flown from East Coast bases Apr. 30 to augment New Haven police and Connecticut state troopers. The federal troops, however, remained off the campus as demonstration marshals and campus police succeeded in keeping the demonstrations peaceful. The troopers began leaving New Haven May 3 after most demonstrators had departed.

Yale was selected as the rallying point for the demonstrations because of its proximity to the site of the trial—the New Haven courthouse. Many Yale students were already on strike in support of the Panthers. The strike, which had begun Apr. 21, had received the support of many of the undergraduate faculty. The movement to attract to Yale large numbers of supporters from neighboring universities and colleges gained considerable impetus Apr. 23 when Yale Pres. Kingman Brewster Jr. said he was "skeptical of the ability of black revolutionaries to achieve a fair trial anywhere in the U.S." and that he was "appalled and ashamed" that such a situation had developed. After Vice Pres. Spiro T. Agnew criticized Brewster Apr. 28, more than 3,000 Yale students Apr. 29 signed a petition supporting Brewster and his statement.

The only disruptions during the protest weekend at Yale occurred the night of May 1 when New Haven police fired tear gas on about 1,500 youths who had poured out from the Yale campus and onto the New Haven town green. The police said they used the tear gas only after the youths pelted them with rocks and bottles. The confrontation erupted 3 hours after a demonstration on the campus by 12,000 to 15,000 people had ended peacefully. Police indicated that the group of 1,500 was aroused by a speech delivered by Jerry Rubin, who had told the group that "to free [Panther leader] Bobby Seale, we have to go to the only court left, the court of the streets."

Campuses Violently Protest Cambodia Incursion

A student strike accompanied by both peaceful and violent demonstrations swept U.S. campuses following the announcement Apr. 30, 1970 of U.S. troop movements into Cambodia. The worst outbreaks of violence occurred at Kent State University in Ohio and at Jackson State College in Mississippi, where students were shot and killed in clashes with National Guardsmen and police. 448 colleges and universities were closed by violence or strikes. Student strike leaders joined with antiwar groups to plan massive protest demonstrations. Many student disruptions, however, were caused by issues other than the war.

Maryland Gov. Marvin Mandel declared a state of emergency on the University of Maryland campus in College Park May 4 and called in National Guardsmen after student demonstrators blocked traffic along a major highway for the 2d time in 4 days. The demonstrations had begun May 1 when students ransacked the university's ROTC office. The police used tear gas to disperse the protesters blocking the highway. Some students had thrown rocks at the officers. The confrontation May 1 resulted in 25 arrests and 50 injuries. The demonstrations, in reaction to the Cambodia decision, followed unrest over the arrest of more than 80 students Mar. 24 after a building occupation to protest the school's refusal to grant tenure to 2 assistant professors. Guardsmen carrying unloaded rifles were brought back to College Park May 14 as antiwar students continued demonstrations to block a nearby highway. Martial law was declared May 15, but a midnight-to-6-a.m. curfew was lifted May 19 on condition that no further trouble developed.

Mayor William Dyke of Madison, Wis. declared a state of emergency and Gov. Warren Knowles ordered National Guardsmen to stand by May 5, after about 3,000 University of Wisconsin students tried to raid a Selective Service office. Local police drove back the rock-throwing demonstrators with tear gas. On the troubled Ohio State University campus in Columbus, 2 National Guardsmen suffered injuries as they tried to break up student demonstrations May 5. Students, seeking to seal off the entrances to the university, had thrown bricks at the troops, and the campus was closed May 6. Gov. Louie B. Nunn had sent 250 National Guardsmen "with mounted bayonets and live ammunition" May 5 to the University of Kentucky, where 6 students were arrested and 1,000 protesters dispersed. Illinois Gov. Richard Ogilvy ordered 5,000 Guard troops on duty at various troubled campuses throughout the state May 6. Firebombings were reported on a number of campuses May 6 and 7.

A state of emergency was declared at Southern Illinois University in Carbondale May 8 as National Guard troops hurled tear gas and advanced with fixed bayonets to rout protesters. Troops moved onto the University of New Mexico campus May 8, and a university information officer said there were reports that at least 7 students had been wounded by bayonets. 3 students had been reported stabbed in a flag-raising dispute at the university May 6. 3 more students were injured May 15 when an explosion damaged a house in a predominantly black section of Carbondale, and the university was closed May 18 for the rest of the term.

Michigan Gov. William Milliken declared a state of emergency and a dusk-to-dawn curfew at Eastern Michigan University in Ypsilanti May 13 as police used tear gas to disperse antiwar demonstrators. Assistant Dean George Turner of Illinois State University (Normal) was hospitalized with a head injury received during a battle between about 50 students and an equal number of police May 14. Ohio University (Athens) was closed early May 15, and about 1,500 National Guardsmen with loaded rifles patrolled the campus after a 2d night of disturbances involving rock-throwing students and police armed with tear gas.

A state of emergency was declared May 20, at Fresno State College in California after a firebomb attack the night before had destroyed a $1 million computer center and after about 100 blacks and Mexican-Americans had gone on a window-smashing rampage. The disruptions followed an administrative recommendation that 8 of 12 ethnic study faculty members, including the chairman of the program, not be rehired. After a day's suspension, classes were resumed at the college May 21, but police stood by and the state of emergency continued along with student demonstrations May 22.

Guardsmen Kill 4 Kent State Students

4 students, 2 of them women, were killed at Kent State University in Ohio May 4, as 100 National Guardsmen fired their M-1 rifles into a group of antiwar demonstrators. 11 other students were wounded.

Maj. Gen. Sylvester T. Del. Corso, adjutant general of the Ohio National Guard, said May 4 that the troops, who had run out of tear gas, had fired in reaction to sniper fire "from a nearby rooftop." Corso conceded May 5, however that "there is no evidence" of sniper fire. Reporters and students at the scene of the shooting said demonstrators had thrown rocks and pavement stones at the troops but that there were no shots before the Guardsmen suddenly fired on the students without warning.

The 4 victims were Allison Krause, 19, of Pittsburgh; Sandra Lee Scheuer, 20, of Youngstown; Jeffrey Glenn Miller, 20, of Plainfield, N.Y.; and William K. Schroeder, 19, of Lorain, O. None were described as radicals. Schroeder was 2d in his Reserve Officers Training Corps (ROTC) class at Kent State. The 2 girls, according to friends, were on their way separately to class when struck down.

The shooting occurred 20 minutes after the troops had used tear gas to disperse a student protest against the use of U.S. forces in Cambodia. 600 Guardsmen had been ordered onto the campus the day before after the university's ROTC building had been burned to the ground in the 2d night of disruptions by antiwar students.

A few students began throwing rocks at the Guardsmen as they retreated up a campus hill, and a couple of students threw back a tear gas canister. In all, about 20 rocks allegedly were thrown at the troops, who were about 40 yards from the 500 to 600 students when they turned around, formed a skirmish line and began to fire. Witnesses said many students dropped to the ground but others remained standing, apparently believing the troops were firing into the air. One Guardsman was treated for injuries and released from the hospital.

Maj. Gen. D. E. Manly, commander of the Ohio Highway Patrol unit that was working with the National Guardsmen, May 5 denied earlier reports by the Guards that his men, circling above the campus in a helicopter, had spotted snipers on a rooftop. Brig. Gen. Robert Canterbury, officer in command of the Guards, said May 5: "In my opinion, the fact that there is or is not a sniper is not important. . . . I think the reason the people fired was because they were being assaulted with rocks and concrete." He said that there were no orders to open fire, that the men had made "individual decisions" to shoot when they feared their lives were threatened.

Pres. Nixon, in a statement released by the White House May 4, said the deaths at Kent State "should remind us all once again that when dissent turns to violence it invites tragedy." Nixon said: "It is my hope that this tragic and unfortunate incident will strengthen the determination of all the nation's campuses ... to stand firmly for the right which exists in this country of peaceful dissent and just as strongly against the resort to violence as a means of such expression."

Vice Pres. Agnew said the incident was "predictable and avoidable." He said he had called attention to the "grave dangers which accompany the new politics of violence and confrontation" and that events at Kent State "make the truth of these remarks self-evident."

The President's Commission on Campus Unrest convened in Kent, O. for 3 days of public hearings Aug. 19-21 on the shootings. George Warren, a staff investigator for the commission, testified Aug. 21 that the FBI had "concluded that no other person than a Guardsman fired a weapon" at Kent State. He said ballistics reports indicated that 29 Guardsmen had fired at least 54 shots during the rifle volley that resulted in the death of the students. Commenting on claims that the Guardsmen had fired in response to a sniper attack, Warren said rumors of a sniper might have arisen when a photographer, with a camera mounted on what appeared to be a rifle stock, was sighted on top of a campus building. He said the FBI had described the Guardsmen involved in the shooting as "terribly scared." Corso and Brig. Gen. Robert H. Canterbury, who had commanded the troops at Kent, testified Aug. 19 and 20 that the Guardsmen were given no order to shoot. Kent Mayor Leroy Satrom, testifying Aug. 20, and Kent Police Chief Roy Thompson, appearing Aug. 21, contended that the disturbances had been planned and set off by outside militants. Kent State Pres. Robert T. White said Aug. 19 that Kent had been "targeted" for disruptions by radicals "interested in either doing some burning or shutting us down."

In its report, released Oct. 4, the commission assailed the National Guard shootings. It said, however, that "violent and criminal" actions by students had contributed to the tragedy. The commission emphasized, however, that the event was not unique. The panel said that "only the magnitude of the student disorder and the extent of student deaths and injuries set it apart from the occurrences on numerous other American campuses during the past few years." The "indiscriminate firing" by National Guardsmen at Kent was "unnecessary, unwarranted and inexcusable," the commission declared, but it also asserted that "those who wreaked havoc on the town of Kent, those who burned the ROTC building, those who attacked and stoned National Guardsmen and all those who urged them on and applauded their deeds share the responsibility for the deaths and injuries of May 4."

The report said "no one would have died" in Kent if the Ohio National Guard had followed recommendations of the National Advisory Commission on Civil Disorder and U.S. Army guidelines, both advising against "general issuance of loaded weapons to law enforcement officers engaged in controlling disorders" that fall short of "armed resistance." Repeating what one panel member said was the report's most important conclusion, the commission said: "The Kent State tragedy must surely mark the last time that loaded rifles are issued as a matter of course to Guardsmen confronting student demonstrators."

A special state grand jury in Ravenna, Ohio indicted 25 persons Oct. 16 on charges growing out of the May disturbances at Kent State. No Guardsmen were indicted. The 15-member panel said the Guardsmen were not "subject to criminal prosecution" because they "fired their weapons in the honest and sincere belief ... that they would suffer serious bodily injury had they not done so." The jury said, however, that the weapons used by the troops were "not appropriate in quelling campus disorders." According to the jury report, the "major responsibility" for the disorders "rests clearly with those persons who are charged with the administration of the university." The panel said the Kent administration, "over a period of several years," had "fostered an attitude of laxity, overindulgence, and permissiveness with its students and faculty to the extent that it can no longer regulate the activities of either." The jury also condemned what it called the university's "overemphasis ... on the right to dissent." The jury said that the disorders "constituted a riot" and that the "participants and agitators are guilty of deliberate, criminal conduct." The report added, "Those who were present as cheerleaders and onlookers ... must morally assume a part of the responsibility for what occured." The names of the defendants and charges against them were not made public until police began making arrests Oct. 19. Among the first arrested were Craig Morgan, 21, Kent State's student body president, and Dr. Thomas S. Lough, 42, a sociology professor on the Kent faculty since 1967. Morgan was charged with 2d-degree riot and Lough with inciting to riot.

The state trials of those indicted began in 1971. In the first trial, Jerry Rupe was convicted Nov. 30 of the misdemeanor of interfering with a fireman, but the jury was unable to reach a verdict on 3 felony charges. The state then dismissed charges against Peter Bliek, the 2d defendant. The next 2 defendants, Larry Shub and Thomas G. Fogelsong, pleaded guilty to first-degree riot charges Dec. 1 and Dec. 6, respectively. Additional charges against Shub were then dropped. Common Pleas Judge Edwin Jones instructed the jury Dec. 7 to find the 5th defendant, Helen Nicholas, not guilty of interfering with a fireman, whereupon Special State Prosecutor John Hayward moved to drop the remaining cases, and all 20 were dropped for lack of evidence. (Rupe was given a 6-month sentence Jan. 21, 1972.)

U.S. Atty. Gen. John N. Mitchell had announced Aug. 13, 1971 that no federal grand jury would be empaneled to investigate the shootings. Mitchell said that "there is no credible evidence of a conspiracy between National Guardsmen to shoot students on the campus." He also said that "there is no likelihood of successful prosecutions of individual Guardsmen." But Elliott L. Richardson, who replaced Mitchell as attorney general, announced Aug. 3, 1973 that the Justice Department was reopening its investigation of the case because of "the need to exhaust every potential for acquiring facts relating to this tragedy."

The Justice Department's Aug. 1971 finding contrasted with a private report, released July 22, 1971, which was published with funds from the Department of Law, Justice & Community Relations of the United Methodist Church's Board of Christian Social Concerns. That report, written by Peter Davies of New York, said a small group of Guardsmen had agreed to "punish" the students and had opened fire on signal. Davies cited a "monumental accumulation of testimony and photographs which support the theory that the shooting was planned and carried out with the intent to kill, maim or injure students." He based the 227-page analysis on testimony already on public record. Through the Methodist Church board, the report was submitted to the Justice Department a month before it was made public. It was released to the public because the department made no response to its "appeal" for an "immediate and thorough" federal investigation. Davies asserted that "a few Guardsmen, perhaps no more than 8 to 10," from Troop G of the 107th Armored Cavalry, had decided to shoot at students "at an opportune moment." He said most of the Guardsmen involved in the shooting "did indeed fire in reaction to those who triggered the shooting by their willful firing."

A federal grand jury in Cleveland Mar. 29, 1974 indicted 8 former members of the Ohio National Guard in connection with the shootings. The Guardsmen were technically charged with violating the civil rights of the students. While the indictment said all 8 Guardsmen had fired in the direction of demonstrators, 5 were accused of firing the rifle shots that resulted in the deaths. The 5 were James D. McGee, William E. Perkins, James E. Pierce, Lawrence A. Shafer and Ralph W. Zoller. The other 3—Mathew J. McManus, Barry W. Morris and Leon H. Smith—were charged with firing pistols and shotguns that resulted in injuries. The 8 pleaded not guilty Apr. 4.

Wall Street Construction Workers Battle Students

Helmeted construction workers broke up student antiwar demonstrations in New York City's Wall Street May 8, 1970. 70 persons were injured in the fighting, including 3 policemen. The workers, yelling "All the way U.S.A." and "Love it or leave it," then stormed City Hall and forced officials to raise to full staff the U.S. flag that had been placed at half staff in mourning for the students killed at Kent State University.

At a news conference May 9, Mayor John Lindsay, appearing with Police Commissioner Howard R. Leary, charged that New Yorkers had "witnessed a breakdown of the police as the barrier between them and wanton violence." He said violence by "marauding bands of construction workers" had been appalling and charged that police had failed to contain it.

2,000 construction workers and their supporters again marched through Wall Street May 11. Enough police were on hand to control the demonstration, but several bystanders were punched and kicked. The workers carried signs saying "Lindsay is a bum" and "Impeach the Red Mayor." Lindsay praised the police May 11 for acting "alertly, skillfully and professionally" to control the crowds.

Construction workers again gathered on Wall Street May 12 across police barricades from about 1,000 antiwar students from a dozen graduate business schools of Eastern universities. The students wore short hair, coats and ties and claimed they voiced opposition to the war from the "Establishment."

Massive Crowd Protests in Capital

A crowd estimated at 60,000 to 100,000 demonstrated in Washington, D.C. May 9 in a protest hastily organized after Pres.

Nixon announced U.S. troop movements into Cambodia and planned on a more massive scale after the deaths at Kent State. Although more than 5,000 troops had been placed on alert, the mass protest was peaceful. But after the rally, organized by the New Mobilization Committee to End the War in Vietnam (New Mobe), police used tear gas to disperse small bands of demonstrators who roamed through the streets causing disruptions and throwing rocks.

The rally began at noon and stretched through several hours of speeches and songs while the temperature climbed to 90°. As the rally began to break up at about 3 p.m., some 700 persons bearing coffins draped in black marched to Arlington Cemetery. Other more militant protesters, some carrying rocks and sticks, moved towards the Justice and Labor Department buildings. 30 persons tried to turn over one of a string of buses blocking off the White House area. After 5 p.m. police began to use tear gas to disperse the young demonstrators.

More serious disturbances occurred early the next morning. Protesters set fire to a car and truck and stoned police and firemen on the George Washington University campus. After leaving the campus, students caused disruptions at the Washington Monument, and a bomb exploded at the headquarters of the U.S. National Guard Association. Police arrested about 375 persons, mostly at the university.

Police Shotguns Kill 2 at Jackson State

2 black youths were shot and killed by police during a night of violence outside a women's dormitory at Jackson State College in Jackson, Miss. the night of May 14, 1970. Those who died were Phillip L. Gibbs, 21, a junior at Jackson State, and James Earl Green, a high school senior. 9 others, all black, were wounded. Gibbs was found dying in front of the women's dormitory. Green was found beside a Jackson State dining hall across the street. Witnesses charged that about 40 highway patrolmen lined up and riddled the women's residence hall with shotguns from a distance of 30 to 50 feet.

Jackson city police were quoted as saying that the patrolmen had opened fire only after they had come under sniper fire from the dormitory. Students denied the report. The Associated Press quoted Dr. John A. Peoples Jr., president of Jackson State, as telling a student assembly, "We have witnessed 2 of our brethren slain wantonly and determinedly. This will not go unavenged."

How the violence started was not clear. The incident was reported to have begun when stones and bottles were hurled at passing white motorists on a street adjacent to the school. Jackson State students attributed the disorders to non-students. After the police were called in, someone set fire to a parked vehicle near the campus. The students then milled in front of the residence hall shouting at police. Moments later the police opened fire.

The Mississippi United Front, an umbrella organization of 30 civil rights and antipoverty groups, announced May 17 that it would move to provide protection for students and other black groups across Mississippi. A cochairman of the Front said, "We are determined that from now on, when we suspect that law enforcement officers are hell-bent on killing some black folks, they'll be doing it at some risk to their own lives."

Atty. Gen. John N. Mitchell, following a 2-day inspection in Jackson, warned the nation's law enforcement officers May 21 to "Keep their cool" during civil disorders. In a statement released in Washington, Mitchell said he was stepping up the Justice Department's investigations into the shootings at Jackson and Kent State University and the shooting of 6 Negroes during a night of racial disorders in Augusta, Ga. May 12. Mitchell said: "I would remind all law enforcement agencies, whether they be local police, state police or National Guardsmen, that the first requirement of professional law enforcement officers is the protection of the public." He acknowledged that provocations often accompanied civil disorders, but he said police "have a responsibility to keep their cool and to utilize only such minimum force as is required to protect the safety of the general public, the bystanders and themselves."

A new confrontation that threatened to again pit Jackson State College students against Mississippi policemen was narrowly averted May 23 when a key Nixon Administration official flew to Jackson from Washington at night to calm rising tensions and arrange a compromise between the 2 groups. Jerris Leonard, assistant attorney general in charge of the Justice Department's Civil Rights Division, arrived in Jackson at 4 a.m. after the department learned that Mississippi police were preparing to move onto the Jackson campus to remove the scarred panels of the women's residence hall, which bore the marks of the police bullets. Jackson State students had maintained a constant vigil since the shooting, claiming that evidence might be destroyed if the panels fell into the hands of officials whom the students said were responsible for the police shooting. The students retreated after they were told that the wall panels would be taken as evidence by FBI agents rather than by Mississippi officials.

The President's Commission on Campus Unrest held 3 days of hearings in Jackson Aug. 11-13. Jackson Police Lt. Warren M. Magee, who had led city and state police involved in the shooting, said Aug. 11 that the firing on the students was contrary to his orders. Highway Patrol Inspector Lloyd Jones testified Aug. 13 that the patrolmen had no orders to fire, but he said there had not been enough time to issue such orders. Charles Snodgrass, state patrol personnel officer, said Aug. 13 that he and 2 other officials had investigated the actions of patrolmen involved and had concluded that they had acted properly.

The commission said Oct. 1 that the Jackson State shooting was "clearly unwarranted." The report contained a harsh indictment of Mississippi law enforcers. The panel said "a significant cause" of the deaths and injuries was "the confidence of white officers that, if they fire weapons during a black campus disturbance, they will face neither stern departmental discipline nor criminal prosecution or conviction." The panel said it had been unable to determine the truth of reports that firing by snipers had prompted the shooting. The report said "the most favorable reading of the evidence" in support of the sniper theory "indicates that at most 2 shots were fired from one window" in the student dormitory that was the target of firing by "more than 20" highway patrolmen and "several" city policemen. The commission said that "a broad barrage of gunfire in response to reported and unconfirmed sniper fire is never warranted." But the commission also criticized students and other blacks for "vile verbal abuse" directed at the police and for deliberately increasing tensions. The panel said that "spreading false rumors, urging rock-throwing, burning, and other violence, and taking violent action to focus attention on student concerns are deplorable and completely unjustified."

U.S. Judge Harold Cox discharged a federal grand jury in Jackson Dec. 11 after it failed to return any indictments in the case. (A county grand jury, convened in Jackson in July, had commended state lawmen for their actions in the Jackson disorders. The county jury had indicted a black youth on charges of inciting to riot, but Mississippi dropped the charges against him in August.)

2 Kansas Youths Die in Street Disorders

Kansas Gov. Robert Docking declared a state of emergency in Lawrence, Kan. July 21, 1970 and ordered state troopers to help quell street disorders that left 2 youths dead and one policeman seriously wounded. The disorders had begun July 16 in Lawrence, home of the University of Kansas, after a black teen-ager was shot. He was identified as Rick Dowdell, 19, a former Kansas student. Lawrence police said he was shot in an exchange of gunfire during a traffic chase.

Following Dowdell's death there were several firebombings July 17-20 and a sniping incident in which a policeman was seriously wounded while cruising through the college town's black neighborhood.

The 2d youth killed was shot July 20. He was identified as Harry Nicholas Rice, 18, a Kansas student. According to police, Rice was shot while participating in a disturbance near the university. The police said there was no information as to who shot Rice.

Lawrence City Manager Buford Watson Jr. told newsmen July 21 that he attributed the disorders to "the war" and "the other things" that seemed to disturb the nation.

Nixon & Agnew React to Campus Violence

Pres. Nixon May 1, 1970 contrasted the "bums . . . blowing up the campuses" with the "kids" fighting the war in Vietnam, who, he said, were "the greatest." Speaking informally with civilian employes at the Pentagon, where he attended a briefing on Cambodia developments, Nixon said: "You see these bums, you know, blowing up the campuses. Listen, the boys that are on the college campuses today are the luckiest people in the world, going to the greatest universities, and here they are burning up the books, storming around about this issue. You name it. Get rid of the war there will be another one. Then out there [in Vietnam] we have kids who are just doing their duty. They stand tall and they are proud. . . . They are going to do fine and we have to stand in back of them."

Earlier remarks by Vice Pres. Agnew on college turmoil had stirred dispute. Addressing a GOP fund-raising dinner in Hollywood, Fla. Apr. 28, Agnew had referred to students at Cornell University "who, wielding pipes and tire chains, beat a dormitory president into unconsciousness." Cornell Pres. Dale R. Corson, in a telegram Apr. 29, said "no such incident has ever occurred at Cornell" and requested "amends." Agnew's office acknowledged that the incident had occurred not at Cornell but at the University of Connecticut, but it listed a number of violent student activities at Cornell. Corson rebutted these charges as containing "inaccuracies and disrespect for the judicial process."

In a speech at Des Moines, Ia. Apr. 13, Agnew had objected to the admission of unqualified students into colleges "on the wave of the new socialism" in a way that could lower educational values and cause campus disorder. He specifically deplored what he termed a surrender by the University of Michigan to militant black students demanding a 10% black enrollment by 1973. The university's president, Robben W. Fleming, in a commencement address May 2, said: "It is sad to see the Vice President . . . launch superficial attacks on universities for their failure to curb turbulence and for eroding standards by admitting black students. Every study of campus turbulence shows that it is directly related to national policies which are largely beyond the control of universities but which are unpopular with the youth of the country."

Pres. Nixon, in sudden decisions, conferred May 6 and May 9 with student antiwar protesters. The first meeting was at the White House with 6 Kent State University students who had come to Washington to see their Congressman, Rep. J. William Stanton (R., O.). The 2d meeting was a pre-dawn excursion to the Lincoln Memorial to talk with participants in a student protest. The Kent State students had met May 5 with Presidential Assistant John D. Ehrlichman after their meeting with Stanton, who had called the White House. The Presidential invitation followed. The students later reported telling the President the campus unrest was caused by opposition to the Vietnam war, the extension of it to Cambodia and a lack of communication between youth and college administrations and the federal government. They said the President promised a full report on the killing of the four Kent State students "to find out where the errors were made." He also suggested, they related, 4 basic goals that might "minimize" the student dissent—ending the war in Vietnam, avoiding similar overseas entanglements in the future, slowing the arms race and creating a volunteer army.

Pres. Nixon held a televised news conference May 8, using the session to defend the deployment of U.S. troops in Cambodia as a necessary step to shortening the U.S. involvement in the war in Indochina. The President, taking note that his decision had triggered protests on college campuses across the country, said he shared the goals and objectives of his critics but added that time and history would prove his decision "served the cause of a just peace in Vietnam." The President also clarified his May 1 comment on the use of the word "bums" to describe some student demonstrators. He said he regretted that his use of the word was "interpreted to apply to those who dissent." He said "when students on university campuses burn buildings, when they engage in violence, when they break up furniture, when they terrorize their fellow students and terrorize the faculty, I think bums is perhaps too kind a word to apply to that kind of person. Those are the kind I was referring to."

Nixon spoke out Sept. 16 against "the spreading disease of violence" and "its use as a political tactic." Violence and terror, he said, "have no place in a free society. . . . In a system like ours, which provides the means for peaceful change, no cause justifies violence in the name of change." Addressing a campus audience of some 15,000 in the Kansas State University fieldhouse at Manhattan, Kan., Nixon called for "an uncompromising stand against those who reject the rules of civilized conduct and respect for others, those who destroy what is right in our society and whose actions would do nothing to right what is wrong." It was time, he said, "for the responsible university and college administrators, faculty and student leaders to stand up and be counted, because we must remember, only they can save higher education in America. It cannot be saved by government." The President warned against "the acceptance of violence, the condoning of terror, excusing of inhuman acts in a misguided effort to accommodate the community's standards to those of the violent few." He upheld "an atmosphere of reason, of tolerance and of common courtesy" and said that "basic regard for the rights and feelings of others" was "the mark of any civilized society."

The President also pressed these points in a letter to 900 university administrators and trustees, expressing concern over the tendency to lay the blame for campus disorders on federal domestic and foreign policies. "There can be no substitute for the acceptance of responsibility for order and discipline on campuses by college administrators and college faculties," he said, "Those who cannot accept that rule of reason, those who resort to the rule of force have no place on a college campus." The letter, made public Sept. 20, was accompanied by an article written by philosophy professor Sidney Hook of New York University and published in the *Los Angeles Times* Aug. 30. It was recommended by Nixon as "cogent and compelling."

Hook said in the article that it was "noisome hogwash" to contend that "the chief threat of academic freedom today comes from without and not from within." The problem and threat on campus, Hook said, was "academic disruption and violence which flow from substituting for the academic goals of learning the political goals of action." This perverted the purpose of the university from a study of social and political problems into a political effort "agitating for the adoption of partisan political goals,"

Hook argued. He advocated university guidelines for expression of dissent, prompt punishment of violators and resort to civil authority in dangerous, violent campus situations involving "intervention by large outside nonstudent forces."

2 representatives of the American Council on Education (ACE), concerned over recent statements by the President suggesting that college administrators had not accepted responsibility for maintaining order on campus, told Pres. Nixon at a Sept. 25 meeting that the "vast majority of the council's 1,500 member institutions "have made preparations for handling disruption." Sol M. Linowitz, a former U.S. diplomat who headed an ACE committee on campus tensions, and Logan Wilson, president of the council, said a survey of ACE members indicated that "administrators are prepared to act firmly and decisively" to preserve campus order. (Among findings of the ACE poll: an estimated 9,400 "protest incidents" occurred on college campuses in the 1969-70 school year; there was "physical violence" in 230 of the incidents, "property damage" in 410 and arrests in 731; 2/3 of the protests were over external issues, including the war and the environment, and the rest concerned internal university issues.)

Campus violence was a theme of an election campaign speech by Agnew in Grand Rapids, Mich. Sept. 16. Attacking "the general permissiveness that has brought rioting in the streets and on the campuses," Agnew said the working man was "fed up with watching college buildings destroyed in the name of academic freedom."

Nixon, campaigning in Oct. 1970 on behalf of Republican Congressional candidates, called for a vote against dissidents and radicals and those engaging in "obscenities" and violence. Speaking in Columbus, O. Oct. 19, Nixon said that it was time "to draw the line" against terrorism, crime and campus violence. "It is time for the great silent majority of Americans to stand up and be counted," he said. "And I'll tell you how you can be counted—on Nov. 3 in the quiet of the polling booth, if a candidate has condoned violence, lawlessness and permissiveness, then you know what to do."

Nixon and his entourage of GOP campaigners narrowly escaped being hit by eggs and stones hurled by youthful demonstrators following a political speech by Nixon Oct. 29 in San Jose, Calif. It was the most hostile demonstration faced personally by Nixon since he became President. Nearly 2,000 protesters, reportedly students from nearby colleges, confronted the President when he emerged from the San Jose civic auditorium. Just as he was being ushered to his limousine, the first objects were thrown at him by the crowd. At no time was the President struck, but a small stone was reported to have narrowly missed him as he entered his car. The protesters continued to throw objects as Nixon's motorcade wheeled out of the auditorium parking area. 3 windows in one of the press buses were shattered by rocks. Nixon said later in a statement read to newsmen that the "stoning at San Jose is an example of the viciousness of the lawless elements in our society." He said that it was "time to take the gloves off" in talking about such violent actions.

Opposition to Campus Violence

National, state and educational leaders spoke during 1970 in opposition to the violence sweeping the nation's campus communities.

Members of the Illinois House of Representatives, assembled as an extraordinary committee of the whole, met with university presidents and student leaders May 25 to discuss student unrest in the state. The meeting was the result of a resolution introduced by a conservative Republican representative, Webber Borchers, to "request" the university spokesmen to account for the disorders. The legislators, angered by disruption on tax-supported campuses, were told by Rhoten A. Smith, president of Northern Illinois University in De Kalb, that universities were dealing with a "new phenomenon" since the May 4 killings at Kent State University. Smith said that behind the unrest was "a body of student opinion too wide and too serious to be dismissed as 'a few radicals'" and that "force of arms is the least satisfactory way imaginable of dealing with the genuine concern of students about the war and national condition."

Florida Gov. Claude R. Kirk Jr. said May 25 that he had asked the Justice Department to investigate whether campus violence might be caused by a "nationally organized conspiracy of professional agitators with tentacles reaching out to our youth." The governor said his action was prompted by the identification of a girl, in a nationally-distributed photograph, standing beside one of the dead Kent State students as a 14-year-old runaway from Florida.

In a letter to the students, faculty and staff of New York University, Pres. James M. Hester said July 4 that the school would not tolerate extremist efforts to "politicize" the campus. He said the "necessity of criticizing and reforming national policies and our institutions" could not justify "damaging or destroying the very institutions we must improve." Hester said that the university security system had been enlarged and improved and that "it could become necessary . . . to take more prompt and direct action in the future than we have thought desirable in the past."

In a 39-page statement to the President's Commission on Campus Unrest, Sen. Robert C. Byrd (D., W. Va.) said Sept. 9 that college administrators should rid the campuses of radical professors and students and "return to a policy of making our institutions of higher learning once again representative of mainstream America."

In an address to incoming freshmen, Princeton University Pres. Robert F. Goheen said Sept. 9 that the university would not "condone destructive actions or the use of force." He said the campus was "a place for diversity and dissent" but that political activities "must be both voluntary and noncoercive."

About 500 members of the Young Americans for Freedom (YAF), attending a 10th anniversary meeting Sept. 9-12 at the University of Hartford (Conn.), discussed plans to counter radical attacks on campuses and to turn students away from liberal and New Left ideologies. Among strategies discussed were law suits to force universities to stay open or to prevent closings due to radical confrontations; infiltration of student governments and campus publications, which they claimed were dominated by liberals; and distribution of news columns and cartoons to encourage formation of underground antiradical newspapers. Sen. Strom Thurmond (R.,S.C.) warned at the meeting Sept. 11 that the nation faced guerrilla warfare on the campuses.

Albert H. Bowker, chancellor of the City University of New York, told a state legislature committee Sept. 11 that the university would "not countenance those forms of protest which, through violence or the threat of violence, prevent the university . . . from carrying out our legitimate academic mission." At the same hearing, Dr. Harry Porter, provost of the State University of New York, said that a professional security force was being organized on the university's 69 campuses and that the new force would cooperate with state and local police.

Sen. Edward M. Kennedy (D., Mass.), in a speech at Boston University Sept. 14, said that coercive demonstrators "are the hijackers of the university, holding hostage its peace and tranquility." He said violent protesters "must be deterred and repudiated, even—or especially—by those who may share their goals."

Atty. Gen. John N. Mitchell was quoted at a Women's National Press Club meeting in Washington Sept. 16 as saying that violence in the streets and campus unrest were the major political issues of the year and that "this country is going so far right you are not even going to recognize it." The news report, carried in *Women's Wear Daily* Sept. 18, quoted Mitchell as saying that "these stupid kids" were "not informed" about issues, that "the professors are just as bad if not worse" and "don't know anything, nor do these stupid bastards who are ruining our educational institutions." A Justice Department spokesman said later Sept. 18 that the comments attributed to Mitchell, "apparently based on fragmentary and overhead conversations at a social gathering," were "distorted and highly inaccurate."

Study Warns of Crisis on Campuses

The President's Commission on Campus Unrest warned Americans Sept. 26, 1970 of an unparalleled crisis on U.S. campuses that could threaten "the very survival of the nation." Finding a "crisis of understanding" at the base of student violence and violent reaction to campus protest, the panel appealed to Pres. Nixon to "bring us together before more lives are lost and more property destroyed and more universities disrupted." The report was delivered to Nixon by commission chairman William W. Scranton. Speaking to reporters later, Scranton said divisions in the U.S. "are far deeper, far more compelling, and growing far faster than most Americans realize." He added: "Since last spring, up to this minute, there has not been the kind of leadership [needed] to bring about the kind of reconciliation that we're talking about."

In its report, the commission cited divisions in American society "as deep as any since the Civil War." It described an emerging culture of young people opposed to the Indochina war, indignant over racial injustice and impatient with the university itself. The panel said that there was a "growing lack of tolerance" among members of the new student culture and that "many Americans have reacted to this emerging culture with an intolerance of their own." The commission appealed to the nation to "draw back from the brink" and observe a "cease-fire." Describing the threat to the nation's survival, the commission said: "A nation driven to use the weapons of war upon its youth is a nation on the edge of chaos. A nation that has lost the allegiance of part of its youth is a nation that has lost part of its future. A nation whose young have become intolerant of . . . all traditional values simply because they are traditional has no generation worthy or capable of assuming leadership in the years to come."

The panel described as criminals students "who bomb and burn" and law enforcement officials "who needlessly shoot or assault students." "We utterly condemn violence," the report said. "We especially condemn bombing and political terrorism." But the panel warned that "much of the nation is so polarized that on many campuses a major domestic conflict or an unpopular initiative in foreign policy could trigger further violent protest and, in its wake, counter-violence and repression."

The commission urged Nixon to "exercise his reconciling moral leadership as the first step to prevent violence and create understanding." "To this end," the commission said, "nothing is more important than an end to the war in Indochina," which students saw as "a symbol of moral crisis" in the nation that "deprives even law of its legitimacy." In recommendations to government officials, law enforcement officers and university administrations, the commission urged cooperation and planning to handle campus disorders. The commission recommended special training for National Guardsmen and said lethal weapons "should not be used except as emergency equipment in the face of sniper fire or armed resistance justifying them."

Nixon, in a letter to Scranton released Dec. 12, 1970, took issue with the judgment of the commission that "only the President" could offer the necessary moral leadership to heal critical divisions in the country. Nixon's letter was his first public response to the report. Although he applauded some of the commission's conclusions and recommendations, Nixon insisted that the responsibility for maintaining campus peace "rests squarely with the members of that academic community themselves" and not with the federal government. Nixon also questioned the commission's analysis of an alienated "youth culture." The President contended that "the traditional culture of American life has millions of adherents within the younger generation—and neither generation is monolithic." Nixon said that Defense Secy. Melvin R. Laird was reviewing possible changes in National Guard and Reserve Officer Training Corps practices as suggested by the commission and that Atty. Gen. John N. Mitchell was "reviewing the many suggestions pertaining to law enforcement activities within his jurisdiction and the special reports on Kent State and Jackson State." Nixon commented that the commission report "clearly avoided the cliche that the only way to end campus violence is to solve once and for all the social problems that beset our nation."

Disruptions at 85% of High Schools

A study commissioned by the U.S. Office of Education found that 85% of 683 urban high schools surveyed had experienced some type of disruption over the past 3 years. According to the survey, released Oct. 3, 1970, the high schools had reported racial factors involved in a majority of the disruptions characterized as student walkouts, riots or "abnormal unruliness among students." Other types of disruptions reported were teachers' strikes, arson or other property damage, student-teacher physical confrontations, picketing and presence of unruly non-school persons. For the purpose of the survey, prepared at the request of former Education Commissioner James E. Allen Jr., a disruption was defined as "any event which significantly interrupts the education of students."

Dr. Stephen K. Bailey, who had directed the Syracuse University Research Corp. unit that conducted the study, said that the report was an "unsettling story of an unsettling reality" and that the number and seriousness of incidents would "continue to increase unless met head-on with some imaginative program." He said a "widespread and volatile situation" existed in urban high schools.

The study found that racially integrated high schools were more likely to experience disruption than predominantly white or black schools. However, the report said that without even considering moral objections, the solution of segregated schools to cut down on disruptions was unacceptable. The study said: "A segregated educational system would hardly train the young for an integrated future when they become adults."

In integrated schools where the percentage of black students exceeded the percentage of black staff members, the survey found that disruptions were more numerous and more likely to have a racial basis. Field researchers sent to high schools in 19 cities found some evidence of what the report called "black revenge" as a factor in disruptions. The report said: "We note that most urban black young people are fully aware of the long and ugly centuries of disgrace in which they and their kind were oppressed purely on the basis of color."

In dealing with disruptions, the study group concluded, traditional methods—such as suspension, expulsion, in-school detention, referral to parental discipline or police arrest—often produced "perverse and counter-productive results." The study cited examples of experimental programs that had reported some success in limiting disruptions: Berkeley (Calif.) High School, which employed young adult security personnel recruited from the same neighborhoods as the students; Kettering High School in Detroit, which used young, specially trained and well educated policemen; a New York City program of special schools to help disruptive students; and experiments to de-emphasize school "bigness" and "academic rigidities" such as the new John Adams High School in Portland, Ore., organized into "houses" with 300 students each.

Answers to a questionnaire sent to the nation's 29,000 private and public high schools and released Feb. 19, 1970 by the House General Subcommittee on Education showed that 18% of the schools had experienced "some form of student protest" in the 1968-9 school year. Principals of 149 schools reported "riots"; 897 schools experienced boycotts or strikes; 583 had sit-ins; protests through underground newspapers were reported in 754 schools, and protests involving "other tactics" in 1,254 schools.

Terrorist Bombings Widespread in 1970

Terrorist bombings were reported in cities throughout the U.S. during 1970.

Joseph A. Laurita Jr., a West Virginia county prosecutor who had been waging a crusade against organized crime, was injured Jan. 2, 1970 in Morgantown when a bomb wired to his car exploded after he turned the ignition key. Laurita sustained arm and leg injuries. Laurita, who had been elected to the Monongalia County prosecutor's office in 1969 after waging a strong law and order campaign, had been investigating local gambling activities.

Nearly 1/3 of Denver's school buses were destroyed or damaged Feb. 6 when at least 12 dynamite bombs exploded under their gas tanks while they were parked overnight in a fenced school lot. Some school officials indicated they believed the explosions were the work of whites opposed to the city's arrangement of busing schoolchildren to achieve racial balance. Denver's acting fire chief said the bombs had been tied together, and in his opinion "it was a strictly professional job."

Reacting to a series of San Francisco-area bombings that later resulted in the death of a police sergeant, Gov. Ronald Reagan asked U.S. Atty. Gen. John Mitchell Feb. 18 to investigate the "cowardly acts of terrorism and destruction." Reagan said Berkeley had suffered "from a long series of violent confrontations planned by mindless revolutionaries who are dedicated to the overthrow of our democratic system." 2 bombs had exploded Feb. 13 in a

Berkeley police station parking lot, injuring 7 policemen and destroying 3 autos. Sgt. Brian V. McDonnell, 45, died 2 days after he was injured when a time bomb exploded Feb. 16 outside a San Francisco police station. Other bombs went off the same evening at 2 Berkeley department stores, but no damage was caused, and police Feb. 17 found a bomb in an Oakland paint factory. 500 Berkeley residents held a rally Feb. 25 to present a petition requesting a crackdown on "revolutionary and subversive organizations." The petition had 15,000 signatures.

A series of dynamite explosions demolished a New York townhouse in the Greenwich Village area Mar. 6, killing at least 3 persons. Police said revolutionaries had been operating a bomb factory in the 4-story building. 2 young women, one of them the daughter of a Midwest radio-station president who owned the building, were reported to have fled the house as the first explosions rocked the building. Police and firemen sifting through the rubble Mar. 7-17 found the remains of 3 persons, one of whom remained unidentifiable. One of the victims was identified as Theordore Gold, 23, believed to have been a leader of the 1968 student strike at Columbia University and a member of the militant wing of the radical Students for a Democratic Society (SDS). A 2d victim was identified as Diana Oughton, 28, a member of the militant Weatherman faction of the SDS. The 2 girls who fled the building were identified as Cathlyn Platt Wilkerson and Kathy Boudin.

Scores of buildings were evacuated in New York Mar. 12 after a series of explosions caused extensive damage in 3 mid-town skyscrapers. There were no injuries as the explosions shattered windows and walls at the home offices of Socony Mobil, General Telephone & Electronics and International Business Machines (IBM). A terrorist group calling itself "Revolutionary Force 9" claimed credit for the bombings. The group said in a letter that the 3 companies had been hit because they were "enemies of all life."

All Washington, D.C. public schools were evacuated briefly Mar. 13 after school administrators said they had received more than a dozen telephoned bomb threats. The area's 190 schools were quickly emptied, but there were no explosions.

2 small incendiary devices exploded in 2 Manhattan department stores Mar. 21, causing minor damage. One person was injured.

At least 15 persons were injured Mar. 22 when a small bomb exploded on the dance floor of a New York nightclub, the Electric Circus.

One man was killed and several others injured Mar. 28 when an explosion ripped through a New York apartment on the Lower East Side district. Police said later that they found several live bombs and a cache of bomb-making devices and materials while sifting through the debris.

Saboteurs bombed a high-voltage power line near Berkeley Apr. 13, causing a one-hour blackout on the campus.

An explosion of 20 to 30 sticks of dynamite ripped through the 34-story Louisiana State Capitol building in Baton Rouge Apr. 26, shattering windows, peeling marble slabs from the chambers' walls and shattering desks in the senate chamber. No one was injured in the blast. A Baton Rouge newspaper disclosed Apr. 27 that it had received an anonymous letter linking the blast to the killing of 3 Negroes by Louisiana policemen. The note said: "This is partial payment for the murder of 3 of my black brothers. Crimes against black people will not be tolerated. 3 dead pigs—Dunaway, Coates, Normand." United Press International reported that the 3 names referred to 3 Louisiana policemen: Wilfred D. Dunaway, Luther Wesley Coates and Jimmie B. Normand. A 2d blast Apr. 26 demolished the air-conditioning facilities for the Baton Rouge Country Club.

At least 7 persons were injured June 9 when a bomb rocked New York City's central police headquarters. Glass, bricks, mortar and other debris were blown across the adjacent streets as the explosion heavily damaged the 2d story of the 5-story building. The *N.Y. Times* and the Associated Press said June 10 that they had received letters from Weatherman, a splinter faction of the Students for a Democratic Society (SDS), who claimed credit for the bombing.

Bombs damaged 2 Bank of America branches June 19 in Berkeley, Calif. The explosions shattered dozens of windows but did little structural damage. No one was injured. (A fire that officials said was of "very suspicious" origin gutted a Bank of America branch near the Irvine campus of the University of California Oct. 26. The burned building had been painted with various epithets, some reading "Death to the Pigs" and "All Power to the People.")

A bomb explosion caused an estimated $200,000 worth of damage June 29 to a science building on the Drake University campus in Des Moines, Ia.

A bomb explosion July 1 shattered windows and destroyed reference material at the University of California's Center for South & Southeast Asia Studies in Berkeley.

New York City police reported July 5 that a security policeman had uncovered 11 firebombs placed under 5 police cars in a fenced-in parking area. The police said the molotov cocktails had not exploded because they had been constructed with defective timing devices.

3 persons were injured July 7 in New York City when a pipe bomb exploded at the Haitian consulate. A police inspector said damage was "minor." 2 hours later explosive devices were found at the Portugese and South African government offices in New York City. The 2 bombs were defused by the police.

Phillip J. Lucier, 49, president of the Continental Telephone Co., was killed in a St. Louis suburb July 24 when a bomb exploded in a car seconds after he entered it.

3 explosions rocked the Camp McCoy Army base in Sparta, Wis. July 26, after an unidentified caller told camp authorities that a bomb had been planted on the base. No one was injured by the explosions, which short-circuited the camp's electrical power.

A dynamite blast caused $500,000 in damages to the old Federal Office Building in Minneapolis Aug. 17. The building was headquarters for military induction in the area.

A wooden building used as the temporary headquarters for the Burlington, Mass. police was damaged Aug. 26 after a firebomb was tossed inside it. The incident was one in a series of attacks against the police in Burlington, a community of 22,000 northwest of Boston.

An early morning explosion tore apart the Army Mathematics Research Center at the University of Wisconsin (Madison) Aug. 24 and killed Dr. Robert Fassnacht, 33, a post-doctoral researcher. The blast destroyed most of the contents of the building, including a $1½ million computer. The explosion occurred at 3:42 a.m., 2 minutes after Madison police had received an anonymous phone call warning that a bomb had been planted at the center. Fassnacht had stayed late at the center to finish a research project in low-temperature physics. 4 other persons were injured by the explosion, which destroyed trees and autos near the building and shattered windows 10 blocks from the campus. Edwin Young, university chancellor, said Aug. 25 the explosion "ruined the life work of 5 physics professors and wiped out the Ph.D. theses of 2 dozen graduate students." (Madison had been the scene of unrest and a series of bombing incidents in recent years. The Mathematics Research Center had been the frequent target of antiwar demonstrators, who objected to research on campus under contract to the Army. However Dr. J. Barkley Rosser, director of the center, said

Aug. 24 that the research was in applied mathematics and had "nothing to do with national defense.")

Leaflets distributed in Madison Aug. 25 contained an explanation of the bombing offered by "We who understand and support the demolition of the Army Math Research Center." It charged that research at the center "has killed literally thousands of innocent people" and concluded, "if the military suppresses life and freedom, . . . we must suppress the military." Similar motives were reported Aug. 27 in *Kaleidoscope,* an underground campus newspaper. The paper said it had received a statement by phone from "The New Year's Gang," which claimed responsibility for the bombing as "part of a worldwide struggle to defeat American imperialism." The name reportedly stemmed from an unsuccessful attempt to bomb an Army ammunition plant in Baraboo, Wis. Jan. 1. The statement said that unless demands were met by Oct. 10, the group would take "revolutionary measures of an intensity never before seen in this country . . . open warfare, kidnapping . . . and even assassination." The newspaper said the explosion had gone off 2 minutes ahead of schedule and added that the gang "regrets the death of Robert Fassnacht."

The FBI Sept. 2 filed charges of conspiracy to bomb, sabotage and destruction of government property against 4 fugitives: Karleton Lewis Armstrong, 22, a former chemistry major at the university; his brother Dwight Alan Armstrong, 19, a high school dropout; Leo Frederick Burt, 22, a student at the university; and David Sylvan Fine, 18, who had been on the staff of a Students for a Democratic Society (SDS) publication at the University of Delaware. The FBI cited a letter from Fine to a friend postmarked Aug. 28 New York City. The letter said Fine and Burt were headed toward Canada. It contained a document labeled "Communique from the underground number one—the Marion Delgado Collective." (Marion Delgado was a mythical revolutionary child popularized in the SDS publication *New Left Notes.*) The document was an elaboration of the statement reported by *Kaleidoscope.* All 4 fugitives were indicted on murder charges Sept. 1, 1971.

Karleton Armstrong, arrested in Canada in 1972 and extradited to the U.S., pleaded guilty Sept. 28, 1973 to a reduced charge of 2d-degree murder. He was sentenced Nov. 1 to an "indeterminate" prison term not to exceed 23 years.

District Court Judge Fred Nelson of Tulsa, Okla. suffered burns and lacerations Aug. 25 when a bomb exploded as he started his car outside his home.

A bomb exploded Sept. 4 in St. Paul, Minn. at a Union Oil Co. tank storage field. The blast caused little damage. Hours earlier, Army experts had disarmed a bomb at St. Paul's Midway National Bank. The bomb had been discovered following a tip to police.

A statue of a policeman in Chicago's Haymarket Square was demolished Oct. 5 by a small bomb. It was the 2d time the statue had been bombed, and, as in the first instance (in 1969), Weatherman claimed responsibility.

A series of explosions Oct. 8 hit a courthouse in San Rafael, Calif., an ROTC building on the University of Washington campus in Seattle and a National Guard armory in Santa Barbara, Calif. A 4th bomb was found and disarmed in a building at the University of California in Berkeley by an Army bomb squad. No injuries were reported in the explosions, 2 of them preceded by telephone warnings, but property damage was extensive. The bombings were believed by police to be the work of Weatherman. They came less than a day after a tape-recorded message, purportedly made by Bernardine Dohrn, a fugitive Weatherman leader, was played at a news conference in New York. The message warned that a fall offensive by young revolutionaries was about to begin "that will spread from Santa Barbara to Boston, back to Kent [State] and Kansas."

A virus research center at the Stanford Research Institute in Irvine, Calif. was demolished Oct. 18 by a blast that also destroyed a nearby greenhouse. The center had been a target of revolutionaries in 1969.

A time bomb exploded Oct. 22 outside a church in San Francisco, showering nails and bits of steel shrapnel on mourners who had gathered for the funeral services of a patrolman slain in a bank holdup. No one was injured in the blast, which ripped a hole in the church's wall.

2 dynamite explosions Nov. 1 damaged a military induction center in Fresno, Calif. and the office of the *Fresno Guide*, a conservative triweekly newspaper.

5 buildings were hit by dynamite blasts in Rochester, N.Y. Oct. 12. The bombings damaged 2 downtown public buildings, 2 Negro churches and the home of a white union official. One person sustained minor injuries.

An early-morning blast Oct. 14 ripped through Harvard's Center for International Affairs in Cambridge, Mass. The bomb exploded shortly after 1 a.m., when the center was closed. The blast, which injured no one, was preceded by a phone caller who warned campus police "to get the janitor out of there. This is no joke." Responsibility for the bombing was claimed by the "Proud

Eagle Tribe," which identified its members as "revolutionary women."

3 persons were injured in an explosion Dec. 11 in the University of Kansas (Lawrence) computer center. The explosion came 3 minutes after a phone call warned that a bomb was set to go off.

A firebomb exploded Dec. 15 in the Army Reserve Officers Training Corps offices on the University of Connecticut (Storrs) campus. Officials said there was modest damage to ROTC records. (An apparent firebombing had damaged the headquarters of the antipoverty agency in nearby Bridgeport Dec. 14.)

6 persons had been arrested in New York City Nov. 2 on charges of conspiracy to make bombs and commit arson and murder. Bronx County District Attorney Burton B. Roberts, who announced the arrests, said he had reason to believe that 4 of the suspects were "connected with the Weathermen." Although the SDS faction had been linked to recent bombings in New York and elsewhere, Roberts said none of the charges grew out of actual bombings. He said the 6 were seized in raids on 3 different apartments, where police discovered books on explosives, materials to make bombs and maps of major buildings in New York and Chicago. Those arrested were Donald Cavellini, 27, of New York; his twin brother, William, of Somerville, Mass.; Jefferson Bernard, 19, of Syracuse, N.Y.; Mrs. Beth Katz, 27, Timothy Doyle, 28, and his mother, Mrs. Mary Doyle, 54, all of New York. Roberts said William Cavellini and Mrs. Doyle were not connected with Weatherman.

The Justice Department announced that a federal grand jury in Miami had indicted 3 members of the Black Afro Militant Movement Dec. 16 in connection with 3 bombings in March and May. Jerome P. Trapp, Alfred Featherston and Charles Riley Jr. were charged in connection with a May 5 firebombing of the computer center at the University of Miami (Coral Gables) and a firebombing of a store and attempted firebombing of a lumber yard in Miami Mar. 13.

(2 gunmen, armed with a submachine gun and a shotgun, had set off bombs in a police station, a bank and a parking lot in Danbury, Conn. Feb. 13 as a diversionary tactic while they robbed a downtown bank of $40,000. The robbers then drove their getaway car 2 blocks away, then blew up the car and transferred to another car. The police reported that 26 persons were slightly injured during the blast at police headquarters. 2 brothers were arrested separately Mar. 7 and charged with the bombings and bank robbery. John Russell Pardue, 27, was apprehended in Danbury, while his

brother James Peter, 23, was arrested by FBI agents in Rockville, Md.)

Nixon & Other Officials Seek Weapons Against Bombing

Pres. Nixon asked Congress Mar. 25, 1970 to set severe penalties, including death, for the illegal use and transportation of explosives. He said he was asking for harsher federal laws to stem "an alarming increase in the number of criminal bombings in the cities of our country." In a White House statement, Nixon said recent bombings were "the work of political fanatics" who must be dealt with as the "potential murderers they are." He proposed in his legislation that any individual "engaged in the transport or use of explosives" in violation of the proposed laws "be made subject to the death penalty if a fatality occurs." The President said his purpose for bringing crimes linked with bombings under federal jurisdiction was to assist state and local governments combat the "multiplying number of acts of urban terror." Nixon also joined the Justice Department in asking Congress that "molotov cocktails," homemade bombs made with gas-filled bottles, be included in the categories covered by existing antibombing laws.

The Gallup Poll reported Apr. 22 that most Americans would crack down particularly hard and impose stiff penalties on persons convicted of terror bombings, hijacking and inciting riots. The poll reported that in a survey conducted Mar. 13-15, 78% of those interviewed would give terrorist bombers jail terms ranging from 10 years to death. (6% said they would impose the death sentence on convicted "bombers.") A majority of 59% would impose sentences ranging from 10 years to death in cases of sky piracy. (4% said they would impose the death penalty.) Americans, the poll said, were more lenient when it came to sentences for convictions stemming from inciting to riot. Of those interviewed, 43% said they would impose sentences of less than 10 years. (2% surveyed said they would ask for the death penalty.)

The Nixon Administration announced July 21 that it would present to Congress a new explosives-control act to combat the sharp rise of bombings in the U.S. The proposed law would require federal licensing of all persons manufacturing or dealing in explosives, positive identification of retail buyers and a statement on how they proposed to use the materials. Interior Secy. Walter J. Hickel, who announced the Administration's proposal, said the law was needed to deal with a wave of bombings that had killed 40 persons, injured 384 and caused property damage estimated at $22 million in the past 15½ months. The proposal was drawn up by a special White House panel. The Administration proposal would also expand federal authority to arrest anyone connected with thefts or illegal use of explosives.

2 Congressional subcommittees held hearings July 15-22 and heard city, state and federal law enforcement officials testify that political, terrorist and criminal bombings had reached crisis proportions in some U.S. cities and on some college campuses. Nearly all of the officials who appeared before the Senate's Investigations subcommittee and the House's Judiciary subcommittee July 15 said federal legislation was needed to curb the sharp rise in bombings. Eugene T. Rossides, assistant secretary of the Treasury, said July 15 at the opening of the Senate subcommittee hearing that "from Jan. 1969 to April of this year . . . this country suffered a total of 4,330 bombings, an additional 1,475 attempted bombings and a reported 35,129 threatened bombings." Rossides said bombs had caused "at least 40 deaths and at least $21.8 million of property damage in the last 15 months." New York City Police Commissioner Howard R. Leary told the Senators July 16 that since Jan. 1969 there had been 366 bombing incidents in New York City, including those "of municipal and federal banks, religious houses of worship and commercial buildings as well as residential buildings used as 'bomb factories.' " Leary said the bombings, especially those involving police station houses, had grown to such an extent that New York police could not guarantee the safety of persons visiting district police stations.

After charges by librarians from several cities that Internal Revenue Service (IRS) investigators were compiling lists of persons who had checked out books on explosives, Treasury Secy. David M. Kennedy said July 29 that no agency in his department "is undertaking any general investigation of readers of books." In a letter to Sen. Sam J. Ervin Jr. (D.,N.C.), Kennedy said he would allow investigations of what books a particular suspect had withdrawn from libraries. The charges had come to light during the 89th annual conference of the American Library Association. In a report issued July 2, the association's Intellectual Freedom Committee pledged legal support to any librarian willing to contest subpoenas for book withdrawal records. A report by the editor of the Southern Regional Council publication *South Today,* released July 8, charged that IRS officials "have been quietly visiting libraries for at least 2 months" to obtain names of persons checking out books on explosives and "books loosely described as 'subversive' or 'militant.' " Reese Cleghorn, in the report written for the

publication, said the IRS probe "is believed to be the nation's
first coordinated effort to gather intelligence information that
makes Americans suspect because of what they read."

Officials of 9 cities agreed Sept. 4 to join in a war on bombings
that had affected each of the cities. The agreement came out of a
meeting of mayors and other city officials in Omaha, Neb., called
by Mayor Eugene Leahy of Omaha following an Aug. 17 bombing
in which one city policeman was killed and 7 others injured. Leahy
said the cities planned to exchange information gathered by local
law enforcement agencies on activities of what they called revolutionary groups and on narcotics traffic. Mayors attending the
meeting included Thomas Urban of Des Moines, Ia.; William D.
Dyke of Madison, Wis.; Charles S. Stenvig of Minneapolis; Robert
LaFortune of Tulsa, Okla.; Paul Berger of Sioux City, Ia.; and Sam
Schwartzkopf of Lincoln, Neb. Other officials at the meeting were
Police Chief George Seaton of Denver and City Attorney Daniel
Klas of St. Paul, Minn.

Nixon ordered a new crackdown on terrorist bombings Oct. 9,
less than 24 hours after a series of explosions rocked 2 military
installations and a courthouse on the West Coast. White House
Press Secy. Ronald L. Ziegler, who was with Nixon when he announced the crackdown, said "the President pointed out that these
bombings are further evidence of the need for speedy Congressional
action on the bombing legislation that he has submitted."

The Senate Oct. 8 passed as part of an anticrime package a bill
that would increase the penalties for the unlawful use of explosives
and for terrorist bombings.

Weathermen Declare War on Establishment

The *N.Y. Times* May 25, 1970 published excerpts from a statement that claimed to be a "declaration of war" issued by the
Weatherman faction of the SDS. The statement, received by the
Times' Chicago bureau, was identified by the senders as a transcript of a tape recording by Bernadine R. Dohrn, a leader of the
group.

The statement warned: "Within the next 14 days we will
attack a symbol or institution of Amerikan [a radical spelling
used to suggest Nazi-like oppression] injustice. This is the way we
celebrate the example of Eldridge Cleaver and H. Rap Brown and
all black revolutionaries who first inspired us." (While there was
no obvious Weatherman attack within the specified 2 weeks, a
dynamite time bomb exploded in the New York City police

headquarters June 9, and the Associated Press received a hand-written communication, signed "Weatherman" and dated June 10, claiming that the group had planted the bomb because "the pigs in this country are our enemies.")

The declaration also claimed that an unidentified body recovered after a March explosion in a New York townhouse was that of Terry Robbins, a Weatherman who had been a radical leader at Kent State University in Ohio in 1968 and who had been named in a Chicago indictment that grew out of the Oct. 1969 "Days of Rage" demonstrations by the group.

The statement claimed that the 12 Weathermen indicted in Chicago, except those killed in the explosion, "move freely in and out of every city and youth scene in this country." The declaration claimed there were "several hundred members of the Weatherman Underground. ... In every tribe, commune, dormitory, farmhouse, barracks and townhouse where kids are making love, smoking dope and loading guns—fugitives from Amerikan justice are free to go." The statement said that Weatherman was "adopting the classic guerrilla strategy of the Vietcong and the urban guerrilla strategy of the Tupamaros [a Uruguayan revolutionary organization] to our own situation here in the most technically advanced country in the world."

The *San Francisco Chronicle* said July 28 that it had received a letter, signed "Weatherman Underground," that warned Atty. Gen. John N. Mitchell: "Don't look for us, dog: we'll find you first." The letter was described by the senders as a "3d communication," apparently referring to the May "declaration of war" and the June 10 letter claiming credit for the bomb explosion in New York police headquarters. The letter, dated July 26 and also received by the *N.Y. Post,* said, "Everywhere we see the growth of revolutionary culture and the ways in which every move of the monster-state tightens the noose around its own neck."

A federal grand jury in Detroit had indicted 13 Weatherman members July 23 on charges of conspiracy to commit bombings through a nationwide underground of terrorists. By July 25, 5 of the defendants had been taken into custody. 4 of those at large, including the top Weatherman leadership, were already being sought on fugitive warrants under an indictment in connection with the Chicago "Days of Rage" demonstrations. The indictment charged that the conspiracy had been born at a Dec. 1968 meeting in Flint, Mich. The charges traced the bombing plot through a Feb. 1970 meeting in Cleveland and alleged bombmaking that resulted in the New York townhouse explosion in March.

The indictment charged: "It was part of the conspiracy that the defendants would organize a 'central committee' to direct underground bombing operations . . .; that this group would be assigned to Berkeley, Calif.; Chicago, Ill.; New York, N.Y.; and Detroit, Mich.; that clandestine and underground 'focals,' consisting of 3 or 4 persons, would be established; that the 'focals' would be commanded by the 'central committee' in the bombing of police and other civic, business and education buildings throughout the country."

Named as defendants in the indictment were Mark W. Rudd, 23; Bernadine Dohrn, 28; William Ayers, 25; and Kathy Boudin, 27. All 4 had been named in the "Days of Rage" indictment, as was another defendant, Linda Sue Evans, 23, who had been arrested in New York earlier in the year and released on bail. Also charged was Cathlyn P. Wilkerson, 26, who had been named as co-conspirator in the Chicago indictment and had disappeared after the New York townhouse explosion. Besides Miss Evans, defendants taken into custody by police were Russell T. Neufeld, 23, arrested in Chicago July 23; Dianne Marie Donghi, 21, arrested in New York July 23; Robert G. Burlingham, 24, who surrendered in Boston; and Jane Spielman, 23, who surrendered in New York July 25. The other defendants were Ronald D. Fliegelman, 26; Naomi E. Jaffe, 27; and Larry D. Grathwohl, 23.

The grand jury cited 21 "overt acts" in carrying out the conspiracy but connected the defendants with only one actual bombing attempt, an abortive attack on a police association building in Detroit in March. Rudd was quoted as saying in a Cleveland speech Feb. 4 that "the Weathermen were going underground and would commit acts of assassination and bombings of police and military installations."

A statement signed by Bernardine Dohrn and reported by the *N.Y. Times* Dec. 24 suggested a Weatherman movement toward a "cultural revolution" as an "alternative direction" to the "tendency to consider only bombings or picking up a gun as revolutionary." The statement had been distributed by the Liberation News Service and had appeared in a number of campus and underground newspapers. The statement said: The New York townhouse explosion had "forever destroyed our belief that armed struggle is the only real revolutionary struggle." "It is time for the movement to go out into the air, to organize, to risk calling rallies and demonstrations, to convince that mass actions against the war and in support of rebellions do make difference." Above Miss Dohrn's name, the statement bore the words "Weather Underground," in contrast to the words "Weatherman Underground" identifying previous statements. The switch was attributed to feminist influences in the movement.

Hoover of FBI Charges Kidnap Plot, Case Ends in Mistrial

FBI Director J. Edgar Hoover, testifying before a Senate Appropriations subcommittee Nov. 27, 1970, said that the FBI had uncovered a radical plot to kidnap a high government official. Hoover alleged that Philip F. and Daniel Berrigan, 2 Roman Catholic priests then in prison for destroying draft records, were leaders of the group, which he identified as the East Coast Conspiracy to Save Lives.

The FBI director said that the "anarchist group," composed of Catholic priests, nuns and laymen, if successful in the kidnaping, "would demand an end to United States bombing operations in Southeast Asia and the release of all political prisoners as ransom." He also said the group "plans to blow up underground electrical conduits and steam pipes serving the Washington, D.C. area in order to disrupt federal government operations." During his testimony Hoover said intelligence sources indicated that a White House aide had been intended as a possible victim of the plot. He later told reporters that other federal officials and foreign diplomats were potential targets.

William M. Kunstler and the Rev. William C. Cunningham, attorneys for the Berrigans, immediately branded Hoover's testimony as "a far-fetched spy story." They said if Hoover "had the evidence he claims to have," his duty would be to "see that the Berrigans and their alleged co-conspirators are prosecuted." In a statement issued by Kunstler and Cunningham, the Berrigans said Nov. 28 that Hoover was "over-generous" in naming them as leaders of the alleged plot. They said that "at Danbury," the federal prison in Connecticut in which they were incarcerated, "we have neither the facilities nor personnel to conduct such an enterprise."

6 self-acknowledged members of the East Coast Conspiracy to Save Lives said Nov. 30 that the Berrigans had never belonged to their 11-member group and that they had never considered kidnapping or sabotage. At a Washington, D.C. news conference, the 6 said the group had been inactive since Feb. 1970, when members had "liberated" draft files in Philadelphia and General Electric Co. records in Washington. The 6 included 3 Catholic priests, 2 nuns and a former student.

Philip Berrigan and 5 others were indicted Jan. 12, 1971 on charges of conspiring to kidnap Henry A. Kissinger, assistant to the President for national security affairs, and of plotting to blow up the heating systems of federal buildings in Washington. The indictment was delivered by a federal grand jury in Harrisburg, Pa., near the federal prison at Lewisburg where Berrigan was imprisoned during part of the alleged conspiracy. Also named as co-conspirators but not indicted were Daniel Berrigan and 6 others. The indictment stated that "dynamite charges were to be detonated in approximately 5 locations" in Washington underground tunnels on Washington's Birthday in February. It said that Philip Berrigan and the Rev. Joseph Reese Wenderoth, 35, of Baltimore, also indicted, had investigated the city tunnel system as part of the plot. The indictment said the conspirators planned to kidnap Kissinger the next day. Besides Berrigan and Wenderoth, the 4 others indicted were the Rev. Neil Raymond McLaughlin, 30, of Baltimore; Anthony Scoblick, 30, of Baltimore, a former priest; Eqbal Ahmad, 40, a fellow at the Adlai Stevenson Institute of Public Affairs in Chicago; and Sister Elizabeth McAlister, 31, of Marymount College. Along with Daniel Berrigan, the following persons were named co-conspirators: Sisters Beverly Bell, 43, and Marjorie A. Schuman, 47, both of Washington; William Davidon, 43, a professor at Haverford (Pa.) College; Thomas Davidson, 25, of Washington; Paul Mayer, 39, of Edgewater, N.J., a former priest; and Sister Joques Egan, 52, reported to be a member of the Religious Order of the Sacred Heart of Mary in New York.

A federal grand jury in Harrisburg, Pa. issued a new indictment Apr. 30, 1971 against Philip Berrigan and 7 others on charges of plotting to kidnap Kissinger and to blow up heating tunnels in government buildings. The indictment superseded the one returned Jan. 12. The new indictment named 2 additional defendants and broadened the charges to include a series of draft board raids. Attached to the indictment were 2 letters, allegedly exchanged by Berrigan and Sister Elizabeth McAlister. The letter attributed to Sister Elizabeth described a plan "to kidnap—in our terminology make a citizen's arrest of—someone like Henry Kissinger." Berrigan's alleged reply contained criticisms of the idea but added, "Nonetheless, I like the plan." The indictment charged that Sister Elizabeth transmitted the letter in August 1970 to Berrigan in the federal prison in Lewisburg. The letter said that after the kidnaping was accomplished, the group would "issue a set of demands," including a halt to U.S. use of B-52 bombers over North Vietnam, Cambodia and Laos and "release of political prisoners." The letter said Kissinger would be held "for about a week" during which he would be tried and the trial filmed for the news media. The letter said, "There is no pretense of these demands being met, and he would be released after this time with a word that we're nonviolent as opposed to you who would let a man be killed . . . so that you can go on killing." The reply attributed to Berrigan objected that the plan was too "grandiose" and suggested ways to "weave elements of modesty into it." It also warned of the precedent of a kidnaping: "the first time opens the door to murder—the Tupamaros [guerrillas] are finding that out in Uruguay." The 2 new defendants in the indictment were John Theodore Glick, 21, then serving an 18-month sentence in federal prison (Ashland, Ky.) for a 1970 raid on federal offices in Rochester, N.Y., and Mary Cain Scoblick, 32, of Baltimore, a former nun. 3 persons, listed as unindicted co-conspirators in the original indictment, were not named in the new document. Those dropped were Daniel Berrigan, Thomas Davidson, and Paul Mayer, a teacher at the New York Theological Seminary.

After a trial that opened in Harrisburg Feb. 21, 1972, a mistrial was declared Apr. 5 after the federal jury reported itself unable to reach a verdict on the charges of conspiracy to kidnap Kissinger, blow up Washington heating tunnels and raid draft board offices. But the jury found Berrigan and Sister Elizabeth guilty of smuggling contraband letters at the Lewisburg federal prison. The government dropped the conspiracy charges Sept. 5, 1972.

Urban Rioters Clash With Police

Disorderly mobs and urban rioters clashed with police in several violent episodes in 1970. United Press International (UPI) reported June 18 that a confidential Justice Department report had forecast potential disturbances in the black areas of the nation's densely populated urban centers during the summer of 1970. According to UPI, the report was leaked to the press by a Justice official. Based on a nationwide survey, it said that widespread hostility between young blacks and the police, increasing access to arms and growing support for the Black Panthers had increased the chances for summer disturbances.

About 100 South Carolina state troopers Mar. 3 routed a mob of angry whites, wielding ax handles and baseball bats, who stormed buses transporting black schoolchildren to a formerly all-white school in Lamar, S.C. About 200 white men and women rushed the buses, smashing windows, after they rolled up to deliver 39 students to Lamar High School. The troopers drove the whites away from the buses by lobbing tear gas into the crowd long enough to get the children safely into the school. The mob then rushed the empty buses and overturned 2 of them. After a final fusillade of tear gas was fired in their midst, the mob dispersed. Several black children received minor injuries from flying glass and the effects of the tear gas. Several troopers and members of the mob also suffered from the effects of the gas fumes. A spokesman for Gov. Robert E. Mc-Nair said later that the troopers would have opened fire with their pistols "if the tear gas had not worked as effectively as it did."

Police dressed in riot gear and carrying fixed bayonets patrolled the streets of River Rouge, Mich., a predominantly black industrial suburb of Detroit, Apr. 29 after 2 nights of firebombings and lootings Apr. 27-28. Police from 14 neighboring communities were called in to stop the disorders which threatened to overflow into downtown Detroit. The violence had erupted after a racial confrontation turned into a fight between black and white youths at River Rouge's high school. The police broke up the fight with tear gas, but bands of youths roamed the area, stoning police cars and shattering windows. 17 people were injured as a result of the fight, and 29 persons were arrested.

6 black men were shot and killed and 20 other persons wounded May 12, during a night of racial violence in Augusta, Ga. marked by looting, burning and sporadic sniper fire. Police said 5 of the 6 killed were shot by the police. The 6th died of gunshot wounds from an unknown origin, police reported. 1,200 National Guardsmen patrolled the streets of Augusta May 13 after being mobilized by Gov. Lester G. Maddox. According to city officials, at least 50 fires raged unchecked as sniper fire and blockades by bands of Negroes kept firemen from the blazes. A citywide curfew was ordered into effect May 13 by Mayor Millard Beckum as police were unable to contain the disorders. The violence had erupted after several thousand Negroes staged a march through downtown Augusta to protest the death by beating May 9 of a Negro youth in a county jail. The march, which had been peaceful, escalated as bands of Negroes began setting fires, breaking windows and looting storefront windows. Autopsies at the State Crime Laboratory in Atlanta May 15 confirmed an earlier report that the 6 slain men had been shot in the back with buckshot. Dr. Irvine Phinizy, a physician with the county coroner's office, who had said in a preliminary report May 13 that the six were shot in the back, asserted that the autopsies showed that "all of the bullets entered the bodies from the rear." The *N.Y. Times* and *Washington Post* reported May 16 that according to witnesses, at least 3 of the 6 dead Negroes

were unarmed bystanders not involved in the rioting. According to the witnesses, the police did not fire in self defense. They said none of the 6 slain men were carrying firearms.

200 armed National Guardsmen were dispatched to Athens, Ga. May 13 to quell disorders that erupted after a group of demonstrators were tear-gassed by Athens policemen. Police arrested 72 protestors after warning them they would be jailed if there was any attempt to march in Athens. The racial unrest was triggered by dissatisfaction among leaders of both the black and white communities over a school board integration plan scheduled to go into effect in September.

All junior and senior high schools in Syracuse, N.Y. were shut down May 14 as scattered racial disorders that began May 13 continued. One black youth was shot and 6 others injured during the 2 days of disorders that spread to the fringes of the down-town business section.

About 150 blacks stormed through the downtown area of Lake Providence, La. May 17, hurling bricks through store windows. The disorders were reported to have been touched off after 2 black candidates were defeated in a local election. Lake Providence, which had a population of 5,781 and a 2-1 Negro majority, had elected a white mayor by 600 votes and re-elected the white marshal by 300 votes.

One black man was shot by a Hot Springs merchant May 17 as bands of Negroes rampaged through a predominantly black section of the Arkansas city, hurling bricks and looting goods from smashed storefront windows.

51 persons were arrested in Rahway, N.J. May 21 following a racial clash May 20 in the Rahway high school that precipitated fighting in the streets. Mayor John C. Marsh, who had ordered a dusk-to-dawn curfew after the disorders, eased the curfew May 21 after a quiet day in the city of 35,000 and in the 1,600-student high school. Rahway officials said the damage caused by the disorders was relatively light, although 2 establishments suffered losses after firebombs had been ignited.

State troopers were sent into Jackson, Ga. May 24 to quell disorders that began after a fight between a white man and a Negro. A police spokesman said two Negroes were arrested during the disorders, in which 2 fires were set and some damage to downtown stores was reported.

Firebombings gutted 2 tobacco warehouses in Oxford, N.C. May 26, and the ensuing blazes destroyed an estimated $1 million worth of tobacco. Police were unable to quell the sporadic violence that had plagued Oxford since the first week of May. 3 other Oxford business establishments were destroyed by firebombs May 25. The first outbursts of violence broke out when a Negro was shot to death. 2 whites were arrested and charged with murder, but black groups protested the police handling of the investigation. Many of Oxford's blacks, including the slain man's widow, staged a 40-mile march from Oxford to Raleigh May 23-24 to protest what they called inadequate protection to Oxford's black community.

Bands of black youths used hit-and-run tactics to elude police in Melbourne, Fla. May 28 during the 2d consecutive night of racial disorders in the city's 40-block black district. The disorders were quelled late May 28 when armed policemen moved into the area and arrested 60 persons. The violence had started after leaders of Melbourne's black community had failed May 27 to get a hearing before the city council to present grievances about the lack of employment opportunities for black workers. When they returned to their community, other residents began to overturn cars and smash store windows.

A week of racial disorders in Alexandria, Va. May 29-June 5 left one youth dead and scores of stores looted. Alexandria was also plagued by a rash of fires, one of which caused extensive damage to the boyhood home of Confederate Gen. Robert E. Lee. The disorders began May 29 when Robin Gibson, 19, a black youth, was shot to death by a white employe at a grocery store in Alexandria's black district. After the shooting, about 200 blacks congregated near a lot to protest Gibson's death and to assail the decision to free his alleged murderer on $10,000 bond. A car was overturned and set afire, triggering other blazes in the area. A clash between the youths and police was avoided after older Negroes from the district calmed the youthful crowd.

Scores of residents of the Brownsville section of Brooklyn, N.Y., bitter over the vast accumulation of uncollected refuse littering the area's streets, sidewalks and vacant lots, touched off a wave of disorders June 12 that included looting and at least 3 fires ignited by arsonists. Firemen summoned to quell the blazes were harassed by young residents who bombarded them with garbage and rocks. The outbreak had started after 2 men were arrested for dumping garbage into the street and setting it afire. Soon after the 2 men were apprehended by police, other residents dumped more refuse into the streets, also setting it afire.

At least 4 firemen and 3 policemen were injured June 14, in the predominantly Puerto Rican East Harlem area of New York

City as hundreds of youths roamed an 11-block area, smashing windows, setting rubbish fires and looting stores. The disorders had begun after a massive outdoor rally called to protest the arrest of a leader of the Young Lords, a militant Puerto Rican organization, had brought an influx of youths into East Harlem. The demonstration was disrupted as bands of youths fanned out from the protest staging area and moved into other streets. After the firemen had succeeded in putting out the larger blazes, police moved in to quell the disorders.

A dusk-to-dawn curfew for the black neighborhoods of Miami, Fla. was lifted June 19 after 300 volunteer black peacemakers succeeded in ending disorders that had plagued Miami for 3 days June 16-18. The peacemakers walked through the ghetto streets urging residents to end looting, firebombing and rock throwing that had erupted June 16 after an angry crowd had accused a store owner of selling them inferior quality goods. The police reported more than 60 persons arrested and 13 persons wounded by gun-fire.

5 consecutive nights of street disorders began in New Brunswick, N.J. July 21 when bands of youths roamed through the business district, smashing windows and besieging a police station house. Police reported that 93 persons had been arrested during the disorders, 75 for violating a curfew. About 18 of those arrested were charged with inciting to riot, possession of incendiary materials and refusing to obey police orders.

Several thousand youths, angered by the refusal of a rock group to play at a free afternoon concert, spilled out of Grant Park in downtown Chicago July 27 and battled police for 6 hours with rocks, bottles and chunks of street asphalt. A light rain helped put an end to the disorders. Police reported that more than 150 youths had been arrested. At least 25 persons, including 10 policemen, were hospitalized for minor injuries. One youth was wounded when the police fired a volley of shots to disperse a band of rock-throwing youths. The disorders began after a horde of youths, part of the estimated crowd of 75,000 that had gathered for the free concert, swarmed onto the stage and scaled the steel towers holding the loudspeakers. The featured band, Sly and the Family Stone, refused to play while the youths were on the stage. Police moved in to clear the stage and were greeted by a hail of rocks and bottles from some youths in the crowd.

One person was shot to death and 25 others wounded in 6 days of street violence July 29-Aug. 3 in Hartford, Conn. A city-wide curfew, imposed July 31 by Mayor Antonina P. Uccello, helped bring the disorders to an end Aug. 3. Hartford, whose population of 155,000 included about 50,000 blacks and 20,000 Puerto Ricans, had been plagued by racial disturbances for the past 4 summers. The violence broke out July 29 in 3 sections of the city. Puerto Ricans, reported to be angered by the acquittal of a white police-man who had been charged with shooting the driver of an allegedly stolen car, broke windows and looted stores in Hartford's South Green section. In the Charter Oak Terrace section of the city, sim-ilar violence erupted. Disturbances were also reported in the city's North End section. Witnesses and police offered opposing views in the death of a 28-year-old Puerto Rican Aug. 1. Hartford police said the slain man, Efraim Gonzales, was shot by a sniper while he was walking along a street. 2 of the victim's brothers said they saw a policeman fire at Gonzales after a 2d officer had fired tear gas at them as they walked along the street. Police denied this and said they were using only birdshot in their weapons. A Hartford hospital said the slain man had died of 2 bullet wounds. Hartford police arrested seven men at the Black Panthers' headquarters Aug. 2, charging that much of the sniper fire during the disorders had been traced to the building, which housed the Panthers' office. One of those arrested was charged by police with firing a rifle at a policeman.

The fatal shooting Aug. 6 of a black woman by policemen touched off 3 nights of racial violence in Lima, O. More than 500 National Guardsmen patrolled the streets Aug. 6-8, and a citywide dusk-to-dawn curfew helped end the disorders Aug. 8. There were conflicting reports about the fatal shooting Aug. 6 of Mrs. Chris-tine Ricks, 45. Police said they were trying to arrest a black youth when Mrs. Ricks grabbed a policeman's pistol and "emptied the gun at the officers." Police said Mrs. Ricks was fatally shot when police returned her fire. Black residents charged that police shot Mrs. Ricks when she tried to intervene in what they said was a police beating of a black youth.

4 white boys and one black youth were shot and wounded in 2 apparently related incidents Oct. 5 and Oct. 7 outside an integrat-ed high school in Pontiac, Mich. A 2d black student was hit by a car near Pontiac Central High School Oct. 7 as white and black youths continued a 2-day battle with bottles and rocks. Tensions among the white and black communities in the industrial city were reported high partly as a result of a court decision ordering deseg-regation of Pontiac's public schools. The first shooting took place soon after 4 whites and about 20 black youths began fighting near the school. According to a police account, the 4 whites in the fight began running when at least one black youth produced a

pistol and began firing at them. All 4 were wounded, one seriously. The Oct. 7 shooting of a black student occurred during a fight near the school that, at one point, involved about 500 participants and spectators. Police used tear gas to rout the youths.

Trenton, N.J., public schools were shut for 2 days Oct. 29-30 because of racial disorders stemming from the city school board's decision to implement a student busing plan. The board voted Nov. 1 to reopen the schools, and a dusk-to-dawn curfew that had been imposed on Trenton Oct. 29 was ordered relaxed by Mayor Arthur J. Holland. The violence had erupted Oct. 29 when fighting broke out between 100 black and white youths at a school in the city's predominantly Italian section. The fighting spread into the downtown district when bands of black youths surged into the area, hurling bottles at policemen and breaking store windows. State troopers joined local police and county detectives in bringing the disorders to an end. More than 200 persons were arrested during disorders. More than 25 persons were reported injured, including 2 policemen.

Several carloads of armed blacks riddled the police station in Cairo, Ill. with hundreds of rounds of gunfire 3 times in 6 hours Oct. 24-25. No policemen were wounded, and the attackers were repulsed after each assault. This was the first outbreak in racially-plagued Cairo since Sept. 1969, when racial disorders had flared in the all-black Pyramid Courts project. After the police had beaten back the 3d attack, Cairo Mayor A. B. Thomas said, "We do not have racial troubles. We do not have civil rights activities. What we have had tonight in Cairo is open armed insurrection." According to police, the first attack began the evening of Oct. 24 shortly after a grocery store owned by a white family across the street from the Pyramid project was burned. Sniper fire prevented firemen from fighting the blaze. After the fire, 15 to 18 blacks, dressed in Army fatigues and armed with rifles, drove to police headquarters and opened fire. 2 hours later the blacks returned and again sprayed the station house with bullets. The 3d attack occurred in the early morning hours Oct. 25.

A black soldier home on leave was shot and critically wounded Nov. 8 as clashes between blacks and whites continued in Cairo. The Nov. 8 night of violence was also marked by the burning of the city's largest lumberyard, which was owned by a white businessman who had been involved in the racial conflict. The soldier, Wiley Anderson, 21, suffered 5 gunshot wounds. Police said they did not know who shot him. A spokesman for the United Front, a black militant organization, said Anderson was wounded by snipers firing into the Pyramid project. The blaze that gutted the Cairo Lumber Co. was believed by the city's fire chief to have been touched off by an arsonist. It caused an estimated $100,000 damage to the company, owned by Robert Cunningham, a leader of a white vigilante group that had been forced to disband in 1969 under pressure from the state government.

2 days of racial disorders in Daytona Beach, Fla. Nov. 7-8 left a dozen stores damaged by firebombs. The police said no arrests were made and no one was injured. The Associated Press reported that the arrest of 19 persons following a march through the city's downtown streets was responsible for the violence. United Press International said the disorders started after a black youth was shot and wounded at a gas station.

4 days of sporadic sniper fire and burnings in Henderson, N.C. Nov. 5-8 had erupted in the aftermath of a dispute over the county's school desegregation policies. A fireman was killed during the disturbances Nov. 7 when a gun he was carrying fell to the pavement and discharged, fatally wounding him in the head. Dissatisfaction in Henderson's black community over a school desegregation plan for Vance County was believed to have been the underlying cause of the outbreak. Black leaders had staged protests in Henderson for weeks over the decision by school officials to reopen an all-black school in the community. Black spokesmen charged that the board was trying to evade desegregation by reopening the school. The board agreed to shut the school and bus its students to desegregated schools. Following the board's decision, black youths demonstrated at the board offices for the hiring of a black athletic coach and a black assistant principal.

Police & Prison Guards Attacked

2 Negroes, reportedly members of a small extremist group, were charged June 29, 1970 with attempting to murder Detroit policemen after they had wounded 3 officers June 28 in what the police described as an ambush on the city's East Side. The 2 men, Lawrence White Jr., 26, and Michael Anderson 22, were reported to be members of the National Committee To Combat Fascism. 3 other men were charged with illegal possession of weapons.

A Plainfield, N.J. policeman died July 1 from a gunshot wound he sustained June 30 while aiding firemen at a blaze who had come under sniper fire in the city's predominantly black West End district. City officials said that the fire was "deliberately staged" to lure police into a sniper ambush. The slain patrolman,

Robert M. Perry, 22, died at a Plainfield hospital following surgery. His partner, Robert G. Beck, who was also wounded when they responded to the firemen's call for assistance, was listed by the hospital in good condition with a leg wound.

29 guards and 84 inmates were injured July 4 when a riot marked with racial overtones erupted in the Holmesburg Prison in Philadelphia. Philadelphia Police Commissioner Frank L. Rizzo said the riot, which lasted 3 hours, "was a complete racial problem." According to prison officials, the riot started during a lunch hour when a black inmate assaulted a white guard. Other guards tried to stop the fighting but were attacked by inmates brandishing table legs, meat cleavers and makeshift pitchforks. According to Rizzo, "about 20 white inmates were viciously beaten" by the black prisoners. The trouble at the 74-year-old prison ended when the men were driven back to their cellblocks.

A black militant leader sought in connection with the Aug. 17 death of an Omaha policeman surrendered to police Aug. 27 in Omaha. David L. Rice, minister of information for the National Committee to Combat Fascism, had been sought in the slaying of Ptl. Larry D. Minard. Minard, 29, was killed and 7 other Omaha policemen injured when he touched a satchel that police said had been filled with an explosive and rigged as a booby trap. The 8 policemen had been lured to a vacant house in Omaha's predominantly black Near North Side district by a phone caller who said a woman had been heard screaming in the house.

Detective James A. Alfano, assigned to the Chicago police Gang Intelligence Unit, died in a Chicago hospital Aug. 17 after he had been gunned down in an ambush on the city's South Side. Alfano, 30, was the fourth Chicago policeman slain by riflemen in the city's black wards since mid-June. Chicago police said Aug. 18 that they had arrested 4 members of "Main 21," the ruling body of the Black P. Stone Nation, a confederation of 60 black street gangs centering around the old Blackstone Rangers. One of those held, Charles E. Bey, 23, identified himself as the vice president of the Nation and a member of "Main 21." Bey was charged with conspiracy to commit murder in connection with Alfano's slaying. Alfano had been fatally wounded Aug. 13 when a rifleman fired a shot into Alfano's unmarked police car.

One policeman was shot to death and 6 others wounded Aug. 29-31 in Philadelphia in a series of gun battles with members of the Black Panthers and a splinter group of another black militant organization. Police Commissioner Frank L. Rizzo said Aug. 30 that the Aug. 29-30 shootings, which resulted in the death of a policeman and wounding of 3, had been attributed to a group called "The Revolutionaries," which he said had plotted to murder policemen. The 3 other officers were wounded Aug. 31 when police staged raids at dawn on 3 Black Panther centers in search of a suspect wanted in connection with the earlier shootings. Gunfire was exchanged during 2 of the raids before the police used tear gas to rout the centers' occupants. 14 persons were arrested by police and arraigned on charges of assault with intent to kill and weapons charges. Rizzo said warrants for the raids had been obtained on the basis of information supplied by a suspect held in connection with the Aug. 29 slaying of Sgt. Frank Von Colln, 43. Von Colln was murdered in an isolated outpost in a public park after he had dispatched 2 other officers to investigate a report that a patrolman had been shot near the park. 2 other policemen had been wounded Aug. 30 when 2 men opened fire on their police cruiser and fled.

15 members of a black militant organization affiliated with the Black Panthers were arrested in Detroit Oct. 25 and charged with murder and conspiracy to murder in connection with the shooting death of a black policeman and the wounding of another. The 15, all members of the National Committee to Combat Fascism, were arrested after a 9-hour confrontation with police during which the police wheeled up an armored carrier and faced the blacks, who were pointing high-powered rifles out of the building that housed their offices. There was no gunfire as 12 of the 15 militants surrendered peacefully. They were accompanied out of the building by Detroit's acting mayor, the police commissioner, 3 city councilmen and black community leaders who served as mediators during the tense standoff. The 3 other militants were routed when police lobbed tear gas canisters into the group's headquarters. The 7 men and 8 women arrested were charged with first-degree murder and conspiracy in the Oct. 24 death of patrolman Glen Edward Smith, 26. According to the police account, Smith was killed by a shotgun blast fired from the committee's headquarters. A 2d policeman, Marshall Emerson Jr., was wounded by the blast. Police and members of the militant organization agreed that the shooting of the patrolmen and the subsequent arrest of the 15 was triggered by an incident involving the sale of Black Panther literature on a street corner. The committee issued a statement alleging that 2 officers, without provocation, began to beat up 2 youths distributing the literature. The committee said that a crowd gathered and that when the patrolmen fired into the crowd, someone in the gathering returned the gunfire.

Nearly 3,000 policemen from 25 states had converged on Washington Oct. 14 for a noon-time rally on the steps of the Capitol to protest the increase in armed attacks on lawmen. The president of the Fraternal Order of Police (FOP), John H. Harrington, exhorted the policemen to bring pressure on their representatives in Washington for legislation to give the police more power and reverse court decisions that he said "aid and abet criminals." Harrington blamed the Supreme Court and the American Civil Liberties Union (ACLU) for violence by radical groups against policemen. Harrington, a 30-year veteran of the Philadelphia police, said that there was a national conspiracy by radical organizations to murder lawmen. He accused the Court and the ACLU of actions serving to coddle outlaws and extremists. Earlier, before the House Internal Security Committee, holding hearings on the Black Panthers, Harrington charged that "Communist-backed" radical groups, like the Panthers, Students for a Democratic Society and Weatherman, were trying to terrorize Americans and topple the government. He blamed radicals for the murder of 20 policemen since January.

Atty. Gen. John N. Mitchell Oct. 23 discounted the idea that there was a national conspiracy hatched by the left to murder policemen. He told interviewers, however, that "constant repetition" of radical dialogue "has brought about more attacks upon police."

FBI Director J. Edgar Hoover told a Senate appropriations subcommittee Nov. 27 that the Black Panthers had been "directly responsible" for killing 11 policemen and wounding 64 others in the past 4 years.

(Burton I. Gordin, executive director of the Michigan Civil Rights Commission, had been shot to death Mar. 20 in a downtown Detroit garage.)

San Rafael Judge Killed, Angela Davis Acquitted

Superior Court Judge Harold J. Haley, 65, and 2 black San Quentin convicts were killed Aug. 7, 1970 in a gun battle following an attempted escape and kidnapping at the San Rafael, Calif. courthouse. Jonathan Jackson, 17, who had brought the guns used to force the judge and 4 other hostages out of the courtroom, was also killed in the shootout.

Marin County officials filed charges of kidnaping and murder Aug. 15 against Ruchell Magee, 31, a San Quentin convict who was in the courtroom as a witness and had been wounded in the gun battle. The same charges were brought against Angela Davis, 26, a black militant and Communist recently ousted from the University of California (Los Angeles) faculty. Police said Miss Davis had bought 4 guns brought into the courtroom by Jackson, identified as her frequent companion and bodyguard. Miss Davis and Jackson were both involved in raising money for the defense of the "Soledad Brothers," 3 blacks, one of them Jackson's brother, charged with killing a white guard at Soledad state prison. Police were investigating the possibility that the kidnaping was part of a black militant plot to exchange hostages taken at the San Rafael courthouse for the release of the Soledad Brothers, a theory supported by a reported quote from one of the kidnappers: "We want the Soledad Brothers freed by 12:30 today."

(The murdered guard at Soledad prison had been found dead Jan. 16, 3 days after 3 black convicts, in the midst of a prisonyard melee, had been shot to death by a guard. George Jackson, 28, and 2 other inmates were charged with the guard's murder. Black Panther leader Huey P. Newton and the Soledad Brothers Defense League held that the 3 convicts had been chosen for the charge because of their militancy.)

The 2 convicts killed in the courthouse shooting were James McClain, 37, on trial before Haley on a charge of stabbing a San Quentin guard in 1969, and Arthur Christmas, 27, another witness at the trial. Deputy District Attorney Gary W. Thomas, prosecutor at the trial and one of the hostages, was seriously wounded, and Maria Elena Graham, a juror who was also taken hostage, was wounded in the arm. The 2 other hostages, both women jurors, were not injured.

The gun battle began after the hostages were taken out of the courtroom—Haley with a sawed-off shotgun taped to his neck —and forced into a rented van in the courthouse parking lot. The courthouse was surrounded by 100 law officers—sheriff's deputies and San Quentin guards. The shooting began when one of the prison guards tried to halt the van. Witnesses were divided as to whether the firing first came from the gunmen or the guard who tried to halt the van. James W. Park, San Quentin associate warden, said Aug. 8 that prison policy was that "we will not let a prisoner here escape with a hostage. ... Once you allow a hostage situation to work, then you'll be plagued with it forever, like airliner hijackings."

At a double funeral in an Oakland, Calif. church Aug. 15, Black Panther leader Newton eulogized Jackson and Christmas as "the first of a new breed of freedom fighters." He said: "When laws no longer serve the people, ... it is the people's right and the people's duty to free themselves from the yoke of such laws."

Angela Davis was seized by FBI agents Oct. 13 in a midtown New York City motel. Arrested with Miss Davis was David R. Poindexter Jr., 36, who was charged with harboring a fugitive. She was acquitted by a Santa Clara County jury in San Jose, Calif. June 4, 1972 of all charges of mueder, kidnapping and conspiracy in the case.

Panthers & Other Black Militants

The Black Panther Party's chapter headquarters in Jersey City, N.J. was set afire Jan. 20, 1970 after it had been partially doused with gasoline. According to a spokesman for the party, shortly after the fire had been extinguished, the building was raked by gunfire. Jersey City deputy police chief Patrick McGee estimated that about 30 shots had been fired, all apparently from outside the store-front headquarters. No one was injured.

White and black clergymen in Toledo, O. succeeded Apr. 11 in easing tensions between city administrators and officers of a newly formed Black Panthers chapter after Toledo's mayor called the Panthers the "Ku Klux Klan of the black community." Mayor William Ensign made the remarks after he was told that members of the Panthers were patrolling the streets of Toledo's ghetto areas and carrying rifles. After meeting with members of 2 ministerial groups, Ensign conceded that he was not justified in comparing the Panthers to the Klan "as remembered by the black community."

The National Association for the Advancement of Colored People (NAACP) announced June 13, that it would give $50,000 to a citizens' panel created in Dec. 1969 to study the clashes between the Black Panthers and police in cities across the country. The NAACP indicated that it was donating the funds to keep the panel in operation. The group had not conducted hearings. Lack of funds and a special request by a top Nixon Administration civil rights official prompted the group, headed by former Supreme Court Justice Arthur J. Goldberg and NAACP executive director Roy Wilkins, to delay the start of the investigation.

75 armed Massachusetts state troopers arrested 19 blacks in New Bedford July 31 during a raid on what police said was the city's Black Panther headquarters. All 19 were charged with conspiracy to commit murder and conspiracy to anarchy. The arrests followed 3 nights of disturbances and sporadic sniper fire July

29-31 in the troubled community. Police said 3 women, including a 15-year-old, were among the 19 arrested. New Bedford Police Capt. Harry Kenyon said a number of those arrested were not New Bedford residents. Mayor George Rogers said "this bears out our contention some time ago that the violence had been fomented by revolutionaries and self-styled leaders who are not representatives of the community." While the raid was in progress, police conducted a house-to-house search for weapons used in the scattered sniping incidents.

The leader of a local black militant organization was fatally shot July 27 by Houston police riflemen perched atop a church roof during a gun battle that left 4 other persons wounded. Carl Hampton, 21, chairman of Peoples Party 2, died in a Houston hospital several hours after the shooting. Houston Police Chief Herman Short said that the policemen had opened fire only after they had been fired upon from the street below. They had been on the roof maintaining a surveillance post overlooking Peoples Party headquarters, site of 2 nights of turbulence. Police identified Hampton and Roy B. Haile Jr. as the gunmen who had fired at the police on the roof. According to the police, Haile, 24, was a member of the Students for a Democratic Society (SDS). Police said the 3 others wounded had come from inside Peoples Party headquarters during the shooting. The shooting took place in the area of a July 26 rally by blacks to protest the arrests of 2 youths who had been picked up carrying weapons near party headquarters. The arrests were reported to have triggered the shooting incident.

Explosions & Rap Brown's Disappearance Delay Trial

The trial of black militant H. Rap Brown on charges of arson and inciting a 1967 Maryland riot was delayed by changes of venue, explosions and Brown's failure to appear Mar. 16, 1970 in court in Bel Air, Md.

The pretrial hearings had begun in Bel Air Mar. 9 but were adjourned Mar. 10 for one week after 2 Negroes, one of them a close friend of Brown, were killed when an explosive device shattered their car 2 miles from the Bel Air courthouse. The 2 men were identified as Ralph E. Featherstone, a leading black militant and an associate of Brown, and Thomas (Che) Payne, a former civil rights worker in Mississippi and Alabama. Maryland Gov. Marvin Mandel Mar. 14 released police and medical findings indicating that Featherstone and Payne were killed after they had accidentally detonated explosives they had been transporting in the car. The data included a preliminary report from the FBI and detailed findings by the Maryland police and state medical officials. There was speculation, however, that Featherstone and Payne were killed by whites who thought Brown was in the car at the time of the explosion.

A 2d explosion Mar. 11 shattered part of the Cambridge, Md., courthouse, the original site for Brown's trial. The trial had been transferred to Bel Air from Cambridge in 1968 at the request of a county prosecutor who said he was convinced Brown could not have an orderly and impartial trial in Cambridge. The change of venue was granted over the objections of Brown's defense attorneys. The trial resumed Apr. 20, 1970 in a new city and with the defendant still absent. Brown's chief defense counsel, William Kunstler, told the court in Ellicott City, Md. that he still did not know where his client was. The trial had been moved to Ellicott City after the explosions.

Puerto Rican Militants Arrested After Church Seizure

More than 100 members and sympathizers of the Young Lords, a group of Puerto Rican militants, ended an 11-day occupation of a church in New York City Jan. 7, 1970, surrendering to unarmed sheriff's deputies. The group had seized the Methodist church in East Harlem after regular Sunday services Dec. 28, 1969, demanding free church space to operate a free-breakfast program for ghetto youths. Police then cordoned off the building, but no move was made to oust the militants.

Dr. Wesley Osborne, district superintendent of Methodist churches in New York, said he had joined with church officers in seeking a court injunction ordering the Young Lords and their sympathizers out of the building. New York State Supreme Court Justice Hyman Korn Jan. 2 granted a preliminary injunction ordering the Young Lords to vacate the church, but the group refused to comply with the order. Korn Jan. 3 signed a citation ordering the Young Lords to appear in court and explain why they should not be held in contempt of court for disregarding the Jan. 2 injunction. Following talks with their attorneys, the Young Lords agreed to leave the church Jan. 7. Police arrested 105 persons, taking them to the State Supreme Court building for arraignment. New York State Supreme Court Justice Saul S. Streit Feb. 24 quashed the contempt charges against the 105 members of the Young Lords. The charges were dropped after the group reached agreement with city officials and the church to operate a day care center in the church for ghetto youths.

ANTIWAR PROTESTS & CIVIL STRIFE (1971)

Street, Campus & Prison Violence

Massive antiwar protests, terror bombings, campus turmoil and violent unrest in U.S. cities continued through 1971.

Nationwide demonstrations against a U.S.-supported South Vietnamese campaign in Laos in Feb. 1971 were accompanied by violence from California to Massachusetts. Hundreds of thousands of marchers massed in cities from Washington, D.C. to San Francisco in opposition to the conduct of the war. Thousands were arrested in Washington following disorders and vandalism by roaming bands of demonstrators. Arrests blocked raids on Selective Service Offices.

Terror bombings in the U.S. reached new intensity in 1971. A bomb exploded in the Senate wing of the Capitol building in Washington, and firebombs destroyed 10 school buses in Pontiac, Mich. The International Association of Chiefs of Police reported (in 1972) that the 2,054 U.S. bombing incidents in 1971 had set a record in the history of the nation. The 2,543 bombs brought death to 18 persons and injured 207. 13 of the dead were killed by explosive bombs, 5 by firebombs. 55% of the bombings were in political protest and juvenile vandalism. 22% were in revenge, various other protests and harassment of law-enforcement agencies. Manufacturing and commercial establishments were the chief targets. Casualties were largely civilian rather than police. The bombers' favorite weapon was the firebomb. The reports indicated that bombers were drawn from both the political right and the political left.

Police clashed with black militants in North Carolina, Louisiana and Tennessee. A farm labor contractor was charged with the slaying of 23 farm workers in California. Protests and violence marked the opening of newly desegregated schools in the South. 42 inmates and hostages died in a massive prison uprising in Attica, N.Y. The National Advisory Commission on Civil Disorders reported that urban conditions had worsened since 1968.

Laos Campaign Protested

Nationwide demonstrations Feb. 4-15, 1971 in opposition to U.S. support of a South Vietnamese incursion in Laos were accompanied by violence on 5 campuses. The protests were the most widespread since the reaction to the invasion of Cambodia in May 1970. The initial protests, however, did not reach the level of dissent in past years.

An explosion at the Armed Forces Induction Center in Oakland, Calif. Feb. 4 broke 200 windows and tore doors off their hinges. A message received by the *Oakland Tribune* and signed "the Bay Bombers" read: "This is our reply to the invasion of Laos, in Cambodia, in Thailand, in Vietnam, and to the Pentagon's 'protective retaliation' policies." The Atlanta induction office was bombed Feb. 13, and Bucks County, Pa. draft files were burned Feb. 15 in Bristol. A Reserve Officers Training Corps building was damaged by fire Feb. 5 following an antiwar rally at the University of California at Santa Barbara. 14 young people, identified as members of the Philadelphia Resistance, broke into the South Vietnamese embassy in Washington Feb. 8. There was no damage and the protesters left after arrests were made.

A protest and march by 4,000 demonstrators in Boston led to 14 arrests as windows were broken and 2 policemen were injured. Violence also broke out in Baltimore, where a protest by more than 300 demonstrators ended in rock and bottle throwing during which 6 policemen were injured, windows were broken and 23 persons were arrested. About 1,500 demonstrators protested Feb. 10 near the Berkeley campus of the University of California; 2 persons were arrested as some protesters clashed with police. Several hundred protesters occupied the Social Science Building for several hours at the University of Wisconsin. There were 6 arrests and some window breaking in Washington as 1,000 protesters marched from George Washington University to the White House.

At Stanford University, where protests and window breaking that began Feb. 7 caused $13,500 in damage, 70 demonstrators occupied the computer center Feb. 10. As protests continued at Stanford the next day, 2 persons were shot by an unknown assailant as they stood near the office of the Free Campus Movement, a conservative group.

3 offices in the Columbia University School of International Affairs were wrecked by antiwar protesters Feb. 12; a student and 3 policemen were injured slightly and one student was arrested.

Antiwar Demonstrations

A series of "teach-ins" at U.S. colleges and universities to mobilize antiwar activity was started Feb. 22, 1971. At a Harvard session, attended by 1,500 students, speakers urged the students to avoid violence and to organize political pressure campaigns against the war. Militant students failed in an attempt to disrupt the meeting.

Hundreds of thousands of marchers massed in Washington (where the number of demonstraters was estimated at 200,000 to 500,000) and San Francisco Apr. 24 and held peaceful rallies urging Congress to bring an immediate end to the war in Indochina. Although radicals seized control of the speakers' platform for a portion of the West Coast rally, there was none of the violence and large-scale arrests that marred some of the previous mass protests against the war. As in the past, most of the protesters were young, with high school and college students making up the largest contingent. However, more adults participated than in former antiwar rallies. There was only a sprinkling of blacks in the Washington protests, organized by the National Peace Action Committee (NPAC), but minorities, particularly Mexican-Americans, played a major role in the West Coast demonstration.

By contrast with the April demonstrations, 12,000 persons were arrested in antiwar protests in Washington May 3-5. The more than 7,000 detained May 3 constituted a record for the city. The demonstrators, conducting large-scale civil disobedience protests designed to close down the capital, were organized by the Peoples Coalition for Peace & Justice, particularly the coalition's radical Mayday Tribe constituent. Washington police had prepared for the threatened disruptions by ordering 30,000 protesters out of West Potomac Park in a pre-dawn raid May 2. The demonstrators' permit to use the park was canceled, according to District of Columbia Police Chief Jerry V. Wilson, because of "numerous and flagrant" violations of the permit and "rampant" use of drugs. Later, government and city officials and demonstration leaders credited the failure of the protesters' aim to close down the city to the clearing of the park and dispersal of the demonstrators. With a mandate from Pres. Nixon to keep the city "open for business," the 5,100-man Washington police force, backed by federal troops, used tear gas and made mass arrests May 3 to keep traffic moving and to prevent the demonstrators from reaching their announced target, the Pentagon. 4,000 federal troops were deployed in the city, some of them transported by helicopter to the Washington Monument. Other forces included 1,400 National Guardsmen and Park and Capitol police.

In Washington's May 3 operation, the police arrested 2,000 of the protesters by 8 a.m., successfully stifling an attempt to tie up traffic at targeted bridges leading into Washington and at downtown traffic circles. Dr. Benjamin Spock was one of the earliest arrested as he, with 300 others, tried to march to the Pentagon. Lacking jail facilities, the police detained thousands outdoors in the Washington Redskins football practice field near Robert F. Kennedy Memorial Stadium. Throughout May 3, protesters, splintered into small groups, roamed through the city and blocked intersections, using their bodies, trash cans, and disabled or parked cars. Chased by police, they regrouped on other corners. There were no reports of looting or window-breaking, but some property damage resulted from the protesters' tactic of slashing the tires of cars. In a few incidents, rocks were thrown at police, but such violence was rare as compared with other disruptive protests. There were 155 reported injuries of police and protesters. Police used their nightsticks, aiming mostly at protesters' legs, but some of those arrested were treated for head injuries. Mayday leader Rennie Davis, speaking at a mid-afternoon press conference shortly before he was arrested on conspiracy charges, agreed that the protest had failed. He said, "We want to make clear that we failed this morning to stop the U.S. government." (FBI agents arrested Davis for conspiring to keep federal employes from their jobs and to violate the civil rights of others. Similar charges were lodged against John Froines, who was arrested May 4.)

The protesters in Washington changed their tactics May 4 and did not attempt to block the heavily guarded bridges leading into the city. 2,000 more were arrested during the day—most of them during a rally at the Justice Department. Others were arrested throughout the day as police scattered groups of protesters, but without the sweeping arrests and tear gas used May 3. More than 1,000 demonstrators were arrested May 5 after they had forced officials to close the Capitol to visitors.

A court battle developed May 3-5 as attorneys challenged the mass-arrest procedures used by the Washington police. Public defenders, representing thousands detained in the Redskin practice field, charged in a *habeas corpus* petition filed May 3 that many of those detained were "non-demonstrators who without notice were swept off the sidewalk by police without just cause" in "dragnet" fashion. Superior Court Judge Harold H. Greene ruled May 4 that the police must release those arrested May 3 who were not charged with a specific offense. A federal appeals court panel May 5 upheld Greene's finding that the police had illegally detained protesters May 3. Police Chief Wilson May 5 denied published reports that the Justice Department and White House had decided on the mass arrest procedures. Wilson said, "The decision to temporarily suspend the use of field arrest forms [citing specific offenses] and to immediately arrest all violaters of the law was mine and mine alone."

The Mayday Tribe had explained its goals and philosophy in a "tactical manual" read by protesters gathered in West Potomac Park to prepare for the protests. According to the manual: "Mayday is an action, a time period, a state of mind and a bunch of people." "The aim of the Mayday actions is to raise the social cost of the war to a level unacceptable to America's rulers. To do this we seek to create the specter of social chaos while maintaining the support or at least toleration of the broad masses of American people." The tactic chosen was nonviolent civil disobedience in order to keep a broad base of support and in order to lessen "the likelihood of coming into violent conflict with the GIs who will be ordered to disperse us and who we wish to win on our side."

Nationwide demonstrations May 5 paralleled the Washington protests as antiwar groups proclaimed a "moratorium" on business as usual. Protesters estimated at 20,000 to 40,000 gathered in Boston, and 10,000 rallied in New York City in the largest of numerous antiwar protests held outside of Washington. While most of the protests were peaceful, police used tear gas to disperse thousands of University of Wisconsin protesters in Madison and thousands of University of Maryland students who blocked traffic near their College Park, Md. campus. In San Francisco, protesters clogged the streets, and 76 demonstrators were arrested after a confrontation between police, armed with nightsticks, and protesters, armed with rocks. In Seattle, a protest march by 3,000 youths was dispersed by police. Other disruptions and arrests occurred during protests in Waukegan, Ill., Lakewood, Colo., Rochester, N.Y. and in Minneapolis, where 10 students and the chaplain from Macalester College (St. Paul) were arrested for blocking the entrance to the federal building. 3 firebombs broke the windows of a building at Arizona State University (Tempe), and a small explosive device went off in the Chico, Calif. branch of the Bank of America. (A bomb had shattered windows at the Bank of America's Santa Cruz, Calif. branch May 1, in an incident reported to be the 35th assault on properties of the bank within the past 15 months.)

Demonstrators estimated at 2,000 to 4,000 staged a sit-in that completely surrounded the John F. Kennedy Federal Building in Boston May 6 in the 2d consecutive day of antiwar protests in the city. Officials reported 130 arrests. At one point, police charged the crowd of protesters. Numerous injuries were reported, none serious. Antiwar protests continued at the University of Maryland in College Park May 6-10. National Guardsmen, who had left the area after helping quell disruptions May 5, returned May 7 and used tear gas against 2,000 protesters. Gov. Marvin Mandel declared a general state of emergency May 7 and imposed a curfew. The Guardsmen remained on campus through May 10. There were 63 arrests in the 4 days.

Atty. Gen. John N. Mitchell said May 13, 1971 that some leaders of the antiwar demonstrations in Washington had backgrounds of "Communist association." Mitchell told newsmen that Communists and Communist sympathizers "have been part of the leadership and makeup of every mass demonstration." Asked how important to the protests was Communist leadership, Mitchell answered: "Important enough to be one of the major stimulants in bringing these people to Washington." "Communist sources" had provided "some of the resources that have been used for some of these demonstrations." Mitchell again praised Washington police for what he said was an "outstanding job in keeping the city open" during the May 3-5 protests.

Figures made public May 18 by Arnold M. Malech, executive officer of the District of Columbia Superior Court, showed that the court had dismissed charges in 712 of the first 1,999 Mayday antiwar demonstrator cases to be processed. In another 420 cases, the district corporation counsel's office had decided not to file charges, and the corporation counsel had decided not to prosecute another 131 of those arrested. 588 persons were found guilty, but only one of these defendants was convicted after a trial. Almost all those found guilty—584 persons—pleaded no contest to disorderly conduct charges. 3 others pleaded guilty. In 93 of the initial cases, those arrested chose to forfeit collateral posted on their release rather than stand trial or enter a plea. Of those who pleaded guilty or no contest, 347 were released on the basis of time already spent in jail, 218 were given suspended sentences and 22 were fined.

The U.S. Court of Appeals for the District of Columbia, ordered the Washington corporation counsel May 26 to suspend prosecution of persons arrested during the Mayday demonstrations unless there was "adequate evidence to support probable cause for arrest and charge." The city prosecutor said May 27 that about 2,500 of the remaining cases would be dropped. The appeals court was ruling on an emergency appeal brought May 24 by the American Civil Liberties Union (ACLU), which argued that most of those arrested May 3-5 had been illegally detained.

Superior Court Judge Charles W. Halleck, in a commencement address prepared for St. Joseph's College (Rensselaer, Ind.) and released in Washington May 29, charged that D.C. police and prosecutors chose "order at the expense of citizens' rights" in their handling of the Mayday protests.

FBI Blocks Draft Raids

FBI agents and local police foiled Selective Service office raids in federal buildings in Buffalo, N.Y. and Camden, N.J. by arresting 25 persons late Aug. 21 and early Aug. 22, 1971. Both groups were associated with the Catholic Left. FBI officials, in announcing the arrests Aug. 22, made no direct connection between the 5 arrested in Buffalo and the Camden defendants.

Officials in Buffalo said the 5 young men and women had ransacked files in both the draft and U.S. Army Intelligence offices in the federal building. A statement by the Buffalo defendants, made public through a New York antiwar group Aug. 23, indicated their aim was to confiscate military intelligence and draft records. The statement said it was "our duty before God and man" to act against "these records that help make the Vietnam war possible." One of the defendants, Charles Lee Darst, 22, was the brother of David Darst, a "Catonsville [Md.] 9" draft-raid defendant who had died in an auto accident while appealing his sentence. The others were Jeremiah D. Horrigan, 21; James Martin, 25; Ann Masters, 26, and Maureen C. Considine, 21. All 5 were indicted on conspiracy charges Sept. 30.

40 FBI agents were stationed at the Camden Post Office Building for hours preceding the 4 a.m. arrests Aug. 22. The government said that an informer who had "provided reliable information to the FBI on at least 12 occasions" had infiltrated the group. 20 were arrested in Camden at the time of the raid, some still on the premises of the federal building, which included offices of the Selective Service board, Army Intelligence and the FBI. The defendants included John Peter Grady, 46, described by the bureau as the "ringleader and mastermind" of the plot. Grady had served as co-chairman of the Catonsville 9 Defense Committee. Also arrested were 2 Catholic priests: the Rev. Peter D. Fordi, 34, a New York Jesuit and member of the East Coast Conspiracy to Save Lives; and the Rev. Michael J. Doyle, 36, assistant pastor of St. Joseph's Pro-Cathedral in Camden. A 4th defendant was the Rev. Milo M. Billman, 39, a Lutheran minister. 2 others, Rosemary Reilly, 22, and Robert Glenn Good, 22, had been involved in a

recent draft protest in the office of Selective Service Director Curtis Tarr. In addition, these 2 defendants had been charged with contempt in a Harrisburg grand jury investigation of an alleged conspiracy to kidnap Henry Kissinger: Paul Bernard Couming, 23, and John Swinglish, 27. The others arrested Aug. 22 were Michael John Giocondo, 42; Joan Reilly, 23; Kathleen Mary Ridolfi, 22; Robert W. Williamson, 21; Terry Edward Buckalew, 20; Anne Cunham, 23; Lianne Moccia, 21; Francis Mel Madden, 32; Barry James Mussi, 22; Sarah Jane Tosi, 19; Margaret Mary Inness, 26; and Keith William Forsyth, 21. A 21st defendant, Dr. William A. Anderson, 36, an osteopath, surrendered Aug. 23.

28 persons were indicted by the grand jury in Camden Aug. 27. The 7 not already arrested, including 2 Catholic priests, the Rev. Edward J. Murphy, 34, and the Rev. Edward J. McGowan, 36. The others were Martha Shemeley; Anita Ricci, 22; Eugene F. Dixon, 37; Frank Pommersheim, 27; and a woman only identified as "Jamette" or Jane Doe. All the defendants were charged with conspiracy to burglarize a government office, steal public records and interfere with the Selective Service System. 21 were also charged in counts involving actually breaking into the building. McGowan surrendered to the FBI Sept. 9.

The Rev. Joseph O'Rourke, 33, a New York Jesuit involved in raising bond for the defendants, said Aug. 23 that "well over one million" files had been destroyed in antidraft activity in the country. A Selective Service spokesman said that the records could be replaced. The official said there had been "5 or more" raids each month in 1971, down from 168 raids in 1970. He said such raids had cost the government $1.16 million in the fiscal year 1969-70.

U.S. Capitol Bombed

A powerful bomb exploded in the Senate wing of the Capitol at 1:32 a.m. Mar. 1, 1971, 33 minutes after a phone warning that the blast would occur as a protest against the U.S.-supported Laos invasion. The explosion, in an unmarked, out-of-the-way men's lavatory, damaged 7 rooms. There was some damage as far as 250 feet away. No one was injured. The phone message to a Capitol operator warned: "This building will blow up in 30 minutes. You will get many calls like this, but this one is real. Evacuate the building. This is in protest of the Nixon involvement in Laos." A preliminary estimate by the Capitol architect's office calculated damages at more than $300,000.

Pres. Nixon and members of Congress expressed shock, coupled with concern over the security of the Capitol. Sen. George S. McGovern (D., S.D.), in one of the few statements to connect the bombing with the U.S.' Indochina policy, blamed "our Vietnam madness" for the "barbaric" action. He said: "The massive bombardment we are continuing year after year against the peoples of Indochina has its counterpart in the mounting destruction of humane values in our own land. ... It is not possible to teach an entire generation to bomb and destroy others in an undeclared, unjustified, unending war without paying a terrible price in the derangement of our society."

In letters postmarked Mar. 1 after the bombing and sent to the *N.Y. Times*, the *N.Y. Post* and the Associated Press, a group calling itself Weather Underground claimed responsibility for the bombing. The letters, mailed from Elizabeth, N.J., said: "We have attacked the Capitol because it is, along with the White House and the Pentagon, the worldwide symbol of the government which is now attacking Indochina."

Capitol Police Chief James M. Powell testified Mar. 2, at hurriedly called hearings of a Senate Public Works subcommittee, that 200 to 300 bomb threats had been received at the Capitol in the past few years.

Leslie Bacon, 19, was arrested in Washington Apr. 27 as a material witness "with personal knowledge" of the bombing. After her arrest, Miss Bacon was flown Apr. 29 to Seattle where she appeared before a federal grand jury, which Justice Department officials said was investigating the bombing and other matters "relating to national security." Miss Bacon's arrest was made public Apr. 28 when her lawyers appeared before a federal judge in Washington to argue that the arrest warrant be quashed and the $100,000 bail reduced. The arrest came in an FBI raid of a youth commune where she lived with members of the Mayday Tribe, which was then organizing antiwar protests in the capital. At the Washington court hearing, an FBI agent said information indicating that Miss Bacon had knowledge of the Capitol bombing came from an undercover government informer. Asked if she was suspected of participating in the bombing, the agent answered, "Yes."

At a Seattle court hearing May 3, U.S. Attorney Stan Pitkin said the grand jury there was investigating such alleged crimes as interstate travel to promote a riot, interstate transportation of explosives and destruction of government property. Seattle had been the scene of more than 30 bombings over the last two years. Miss Bacon's lawyers said that she was not asked before the Senate jury

about the Washington bombing until her 2d day of testimony, May
1. Reporting that she denied any knowledge of a plot to bomb the
Capitol, Jeffrey Steinborn, one of her attorneys, denounced the
probe May 1 as "a general fishing expedition into antiwar politics."
Miss Bacon refused to answer questions and pleaded the 5th Amendment for the first time during her testimony May 2, when the questioning turned to a Dec. 4, 1970 attempt to bomb a New York
bank. Government attorneys, in a hearing May 3, sought a court
order to force her to testify about "her participation in plans to
bomb" the bank; the bank bombing attempt had been thwarted
when undercover policemen arrested 6 persons, allegedly as they
were planting the bomb. (At the New York indictment of the 6
bomb plot suspects Dec. 8, 1970, it had been alleged that they had
planned the blast as the first of a "series of heavy actions against
the Establishment.") U.S. District Court Judge W. Boldt in Seattle
May 6 ordered Miss Bacon to answer questions about the New
York bombing attempt. He upheld the government's argument that
Miss Bacon could not refuse to answer questions about the bombing
because she had waived her 5th Amendment rights in the matter
when she previously testified willingly about her part in the bomb
plot. Miss Bacon's lawyers said May 6 that she had testified before
the Seattle grand jury on the New York bombing, as ordered, but
had refused to answer other questions. In a statement read by her
lawyers, she said that she had taken part in the early planning of
the New York bombing but "withdrew from all plans more than
a month before the actual attempt."

Leslie Bacon was sent to jail in Seattle May 19 for contempt.
Miss Bacon was jailed for disobeying a court order to answer
questions about her movements Mar. 1, the day of the Capitol
bombing, despite a government offer of limited immunity from
prosecution.

The 6 defendants in New York had pleaded guilty Mar. 18 to
conspiracy to firebomb or dynamite a branch of the First National
City Bank and 5 other buildings, including one that contained the
offices of Pres. Nixon's former law firm, Mudge, Rose, Guthrie &
Alexander. They had been arrested outside the bank on information supplied by an undercover patrolman who drove them to the
site. Before the sentencing of 5 of the defendants May 7, Assistant
District Attorney Kenneth Conboy cited 169 bomb attempts in
the city in the past 2 years. The defense pointed out that the
defendants had been careful to avoid the possibility of injuring
bystanders and that they had acted for political motives. State
Supreme Court Justice Harold Birns, in imposing sentence, said the

conspirators' "political beliefs in no way mitigate the enormity of the crime." The youngest of the defendants, Christopher Trenkle, 20, was ordered to take a psychiatric examination before sentencing. 3 defendants—Richard R. Palmer, 40, identified in the indictment as a Weatherman "recruiter"; Sharon Krebs, 33; and Martin Lewis, 25—received the maximum sentence of 4 years each. The remaining 2, sentenced to 3 years each, were Joyce Plecha, 26, and Claudia Conine, 23. Miss Bacon was arraigned in federal court in New York June 29 on charges of conspiring with the other 6 to bomb the New York bank. The charge was based on her testimony in Seattle.

Klansmen Charged in Michigan School Bus Bombing

Arsonists slipped through a chain-link fence Aug. 30, 1971 and set firebombs that destroyed 10 school buses parked in a school lot in Pontiac, Mich. The buses were part of the city's school-bus fleet, which was to be used to help carry out a court-ordered integration plan that required extensive busing. The plan, which would involve the crosstown busing of 8,700 school-children, had evoked widespread community opposition.

FBI agents arrested 6 Ku Klux Klan members Sept. 9 in connection with the bombing. The Klansmen were charged with plotting at a statewide meeting of the Klan in July to blow up the buses. Specifically, they were charged with conspiracy to violate the public education section of the Federal Civil Rights Act, to violate federal bomb statutes and to obstruct federal court orders.

One of the 6 charged was Robert E. Miles, 40, who was described as the grand dragon of the Michigan Realm of the United Klans of America. The 5 others arrested were Wallace E. Fruit, 29; Alexander J. Distel Jr., 28; Dennis C. Ramsey, 24; Raymond Quick Jr., 24, and Edmund Reimer.

An affidavit filed in U.S. court in Detroit Sept. 10 charged that the Klansmen had also planned to "knock out" a power station in the Pontiac area as a diversion for a full-scale mortar attack on the city's 90-bus fleet. The affidavit also disclosed that an unpaid undercover agent had been involved with the Pontiac group of the Klan and had reported to the FBI on its activities.

(A fire that police said was intentionally set off by a chemical Feb. 4 1971 had gutted a 2-story office building in Charlotte, N.C. that housed the law offices of Julius L. Chambers, 36, who was representing the black plaintiffs in a Charlotte school desegregation case before the Supreme Court. The fire was described as one of a series of attacks against Chambers, his firm and his family.)

Student & Allied Violence

Mayor James M. Corbett of Tucson, Ariz. declared a curfew and martial law after a 3d consecutive night of violence Jan. 23, 1971 near the campus of the University of Arizona. 6 police officers were injured and 41 persons arrested Jan. 23 during an outbreak of firebombing and window-breaking. Officials attributed the trouble to "street people" who demanded that a portion of the campus be made a "people's campground" and that the city drop proposed ordinances against hitchhiking, loitering and panhandling. Order was reportedly restored Jan. 24. Campus officials said Jan. 25 that only about 40 of the 148 persons arrested since Jan. 21 were students at the university, which had an enrollment of 25,000 students.

2 policemen and a student were shot dead Mar. 11 during a riot on the University of Puerto Rico campus at Rio Piedras, a suburb of San Juan. The rioting broke out following fights between members of student radical groups advocating Puerto Rican independence and cadets of the university's Reserve Officers Training Corps unit. Those killed were Jacinto Gutierrez, 21, an ROTC cadet; Maj. Juan Mercado, commander of a special police riot squad; and Miguel Rosario, a member of the riot squad. Some 50 others, including police, students and professors, were wounded by gunfire or rocks thrown by both sides. Following the campus violence, radical students went through Rio Piedras, attacking stores associated with the U.S. and starting fires. Police arrested 64 people Mar. 12 in connection with the rioting. The campus was closed following the riot.

The Rio Piedras campus battle apparently began when an ROTC cadet appeared on campus in uniform. The ROTC program had been a source of friction since 1967. (In Mar. 1970, an ROTC building at the university was sacked and burned and a coed was shot and killed.) The 2 radical student groups involved in the riot were the Federation of Students for Independence (FUPI) and the youth organization of the Puerto Rican Independence party.

Humberto Pagan Hernandez, 20, a 3d-year student, was arrested Mar. 17 and charged with first-degree murder in the slaying of Mercado. 6 men and a woman were charged Apr. 10 with rioting and malicious damage in connection with violence in a business district near the University of Puerto Rico following the campus riot. 5 of those charged were listed as students at the university.

Students at Merritt College in Oakland, Calif. seized and held the college's administration offices for 2 days but left Mar. 17, minutes before 100 policemen arrived on campus.

A fire, which police attributed to arsonists, destroyed the administration building at the Santa Cruz campus of the University of California Apr. 8. Police said that arson had caused blazes at these other institutions: the Fletcher School of Law & Diplomacy at Tufts University (Medford, Mass.), where a blaze Mar. 21 caused $75,000 damage; the University of Hawaii (Honolulu), where a Mar. 5 fire caused by gasoline splashed around a campus building followed a fire the week before at an ROTC building; and Cornell University (Ithaca, N.Y.), where a Mar. 17 fire damaged a classroom used by the Air Force ROTC unit.

A crowd of 2,000 black and white students gathered at the home of the president of the University of Florida in Gainesville Apr. 15, demanding his resignation and protesting what they called the school's "racist" policies. The incident, during which Pres. Stephen C. O'Connell and his family left his residence under police escort, followed the arrest and suspension of 67 members of the Black Student Union during a sit-in outside O'Connell's office. After the arrests and suspensions were announced, black and white students had held a protest rally that police dispersed with riot sticks and tear gas.

About 70 students seized and occupied a dean's office at Vassar College in Poughkeepsie, N.Y. Apr. 22 in protest against the school's faculty hiring and tenure policies and against the administration's decision not to rehire 6 lecturers and assistant professors because they had not produced sufficient scholarly research.

Police and sheriff's deputies confronted 500 demonstrators near the University of California at Berkeley May 15 in a clash that resulted in 40 arrests and a number of injuries. The protesters, marking the second anniversary of the "People's Park" battle, were responding to student newspaper editorials urging an assembly to "rededicate" the park. In the clash, which involved some young people of high-school age, police used tear gas and putty-like bullets (designed to control crowds) to disperse roving bands that threw rocks and bottles at police. Earlier some protesters had pulled down part of the fence surrounding the park. The campus newspaper, *The Daily Californian,* had published an editorial May 11 saying: "For 2 years our boycott of the park has stood witness to the blood that flowed there. It is time we honored that blood with action—we must take back the park."

Panthers & Other Black Militants

Police opened fire Jan. 12, 1971 on the Black Panthers' head-quarters in Winston-Salem, N.C. with pistols, shotguns and rifles after 2 youths had pinned officers down with gunfire from the building. The 2 youths surrendered shortly after the 45-second police fusillade. No injuries were reported. Police had been called to the Panthers' center to investigate the theft of a truckload of meat. A delivery truck driver told police his truck had been stolen and was seen outside the Panthers' building. Police lobbed tear gas into an open window, and seconds later the first shots rang out from the 2 youths inside. Police said the meat, guns and 150 rounds of ammunition were found inside the building.

Firemen summoned to battle 2 blazes in a black housing project in New Orleans were repulsed Jan. 12 by residents who forced them out of the area with a continuous shower of rocks and bottles. 2 buildings used by the Black Panthers as offices burned. The fires, which police said were started by firebombs, erupted in the Desire Housing Project, site of numerous racial clashes during 1970. A New Orleans TV station said an anonymous phone caller had claimed that the fires had been set in retaliation for the arrest of blacks in the Desire project area.

11 black members of the Republic of New Africa were charged with murdering a Jackson, Miss. policeman, Lt. W. L. Skinner, who was fatally wounded in a gun fight that erupted Aug. 18 when police raided the headquarters of the black separatist group to serve 3 of its members with fugitive warrants. An FBI agent and another Jackson policeman were also wounded in the 20-minute exchange of gunfire. Skinner died Aug. 19 of head wounds. Immediately after his death, murder charges were filed against the 11 blacks. The 11 were also charged Aug. 22 with treason. The treason charges were filed under an old state law that declared it illegal to participate in armed insurrection against the state. Among those held was Imari Abubakari Obadele, the group's president. Obadele said in a statement released Aug. 22 that his group regretted that Skinner had been killed. He criticized the Jackson chief of police and the FBI for raiding the offices, saying that "any warrant can be delivered to us peacefully provided one or 2 black lawyers are present."

The House Internal Security Committee said Aug. 23 that while the Black Panthers posed a physical danger to the nation's policemen, they were "totally incapable of overthrowing our government by violence." The 4 Republicans on the committee indicated, however, that they objected to the moderate tone of the report. Reps. John M. Ashbrook (O.), John G. Schmitz (Calif.), Fletcher Thompson (Ga.) and Roger H. Zion (Ind.), contended that the majority report did not give "a clear understanding of the Black Panther Party as a subversive criminal group using the facade of politics as a cover for crimes of violence and extortion." The majority report was defended by Rep. Richardson Preyer (D.,N.C.), who headed a subcommittee that heard former Panthers testify about the party. Preyer said in a separate report that it would be easy to write "a real zinger of a report" that would provoke greater public outrage, but it might also help revive the party by making martyrs of its leaders. The majority report said that "the Black Panther Party, through its deliberately inflammatory rhetoric and through the actual arming and military training of its members, had contributed to an increase in acts of violence and constitutes a threat to the internal security of the United States." The report added, however, that the committee did not believe that the Panthers "constituted a clear and present danger to the continued functioning of the U.S. government of any other institutions of our democratic society."

5 Die in San Quentin Jailbreak Attempt

George Jackson, one of the 3 black convicts known as the "Soledad Brothers" (charged with killing a Soledad Prison guard), was shot and killed Aug. 21, 1971 as he attempted to escape from the California State Prison at San Quentin. 2 other convicts and 3 prison guards were killed during the escape attempt. Order was restored by prison guards, state highway troopers and sheriff's deputies about 2 hours after the break effort had begun.

According to prison authorities, Jackson was killed by a tower guard atop one of the observation towers as he dashed across the prison yard. Another convict accompanying Jackson surrendered in the yard after Jackson was shot. Jackson, 29, was the oldest and most widely known of the Soledad Brothers. (He had published his prison memoirs in Nov. 1970.), Jackson and the other 2 Soledad Brothers, John W. Cluchette, 28, and Fleeta Drumgo, 26, had been incarcerated in San Quentin's maximum security cellblock awaiting trial on murder charges in connection with the death of a guard at the Soledad State Prison in Jan. 1970. The 3 had been serving at Soledad on burglary sentences.

Prison officials said that after order was restored following Jackson's death Aug. 21, guards returned to the cellblock area where the uprising had erupted and found in Jackson's cell the bodies of 2 slain guards, a wounded guard and a dead prisoner. Another guard and another prisoner were dead in the corridor, where there were also 2 more wounded guards. Both of the dead inmates were white. The slain guards' throats had been slashed. Later, prison guards found the probable weapon—a razor blade fitted into the handle of a toothbrush. The 2 dead prisoners' throats were also cut. No reason was established for their deaths. Louis S. Nelson, warden of San Quentin, said Aug. 22 that Jackson was carrying a gun when he made his break attempt.

Stephen M. Bingham, 29, a white lawyer and the last man to visit Jackson before he was slain, was formally charged *in absentia* Aug. 31, 1971 with murder in the deaths of the 2 convicts and 3 guards during Jackson's attempted breakout. Bingham was accused of smuggling a gun into the prison visiting area and giving it to Jackson. San Quentin authorities said Jackson used the gun to force his way out of a maximum security cellblock. (Under California law, Bingham's alleged complicity made him equally guilty with the perpetrators of a capital crime.) Bingham was indicted by a grand jury on murder charges Oct. 1, as were 6 black San Quentin convicts. They were also charged with conspiracy to escape by violent means, conspiracy to possess a firearm and conspiracy to kidnap correctional officers. In addition to Bingham, those indicted were Fleeta Drumgo, one of the 2 surviving Soledad Brothers, Hugo A. Pinell, John Larry Spain, Willie Tate, David Johnson and Louis N. Talamantes. The indictment charged that Bingham gave Jackson an automatic pistol and clips during a visit shortly before Jackson made his breakout attempt. Jackson used the gun, the indictment charged, to kill Jere P. Graham, one of the prison guards. The indictment said the others slain "were killed by members of the conspiracy."

Warden Louis S. Nelson of San Quentin Prison told the *Los Angeles Times* Sept. 30 that Jackson was killed by a prison guard who was trying to hit him in the legs. But the account given by San Quentin prison officials of how Jackson died took on a new dimension Sept. 21 when a revised autopsy showed that Jackson was shot in the back, not through the top of the head as first reported. In the preliminary autopsy report, issued Aug. 23—2 days after Jackson was shot—Marin County coroner Donovan O. Cook had said that the fatal bullet had penetrated the skull and exited from the lower region of the back. According to the new autopsy, completed Sept. 7 but not made public until Sept. 21, Jackson was shot in the lower back, and the bullet traveled up through the body and exited through the skull.

(Police Sgt. John V. Young, 45, was killed at his desk in San Francisco Aug. 29 when 2 black men fired repeated blasts from shotguns into the Ingleside police station. Homicide Lt. Charles Ellis speculated Aug. 30 that Young's death was one of a series of retaliatory acts for Jackson's death. Other acts tentatively linked by police to Jackson's death were the bombings of several public buildings and a branch of the Bank of America. Among buildings bombed were 2 State Department of Corrections offices in San Francisco and Sacramento. Police said a phone caller shortly before the San Francisco blast said the bombing was "in defense of George Jackson.")

Gov. Ronald Reagan Sept. 9 ordered the agency in charge of California's penal facilities to look into recent violence at several prisons to counter what he described as efforts to "distort the facts" of the San Quentin break-out attempt. In ordering the probe, Reagan laid the blame for the recent violence at state institutions to "self-proclaimed, revolutionary forces" in and out of the prisons. He said part of the trouble at the prisons could be traced to changes in the composition of the prison populations. He said that "many of these incidents also result from the fact that our correctional institutions contain a greater percentage of violent offenders than ever before."

Attica Prison Uprising Brings Death to 42

Nearly 1,500 state troopers, sheriff's deputies and prison guards staged an air and ground assault Sept. 13, 1971 to put down an uprising by 1,200 inmates at the Attica Correctional Facility in Attica, N.Y. 38 persons—29 prisoners and 9 guards and civilian employes held as hostages by the rebellious inmates —died when lawmen stormed the prison in upstate New York. One guard who had been injured when the insurrection broke out Sept. 9 died of head injuries Sept. 11, and 3 more inmates died of their wounds Sept. 15, 23 and 25. 3 of the convicts had been killed by other inmates, who slashed their throats. The death toll thus reached 42. 28 hostages were rescued by the invading troopers.

The decision to send armed troopers into Attica was made after 4 days of taut negotiations between the rebels and state correction authorities had failed to bring an end to the revolt. New York State Commissioner of Corrections Russell G. Oswald gave the order to have the lawmen move in. Gov. Nelson Rockefeller strongly defended Oswald's decision Sept. 15. Rockefeller announced that a "distinguished panel of impartial visitors" would be named to guarantee the constitutional rights of Attica's prisoners.

Most of the prisoners killed in the troopers' onslaught died from the attackers' gunfire. But at least 2 of the dead inmates were reported to have been slain by other convicts. Early reports by prison officials said most of the slain hostages died when convicts slashed their throats. Other hostages were said to have been beaten and stabbed to death. However, a medical examiner said Sept. 14 that official autopsies had showed that the 9 hostages had died of gunshot wounds. Dr. John F. Edland, who performed 8 of the post mortems, said "there was no evidence of slashed throats." Oswald later confirmed that all of the hostages had died of bullet wounds.

Major events of the Attica uprising:

Sept. 9—The insurrection began shortly after 8.30 a.m. when a group of prisoners refused to form into work details. The revolt spread as prisoners, mostly blacks, began breaking windows, burning bedding and office furniture. The rebellious convicts, numbering about 1,000, seized 32 guards and civilian employes as hostages. Later the inmates issued a list of 15 demands that included coverage by state minimum wage laws, an end to censorship of reading materials and no reprisals for the revolt. Twice during the day Oswald met with groups of inmates in an unsuccessful effort to secure the release of the hostages. At one negotiating session, the convicts said they wanted specific visitors to see the conditions at Attica. Among those listed were William M. Kunstler, the militant civil rights attorney, and Huey P. Newton of the Black Panthers. No shots were fired during the day, but prison guards fired rounds of tear gas into the cell block area held by the insurgents.

Sept. 10—Negotiations between Oswald and rebel leaders continued at an impasse. The convicts repeated their demands but added new ones asking for "speedy and safe transportation out of confinement to a non-imperialistic country" and a federal takeover of the prison. One of the prisoners' demands was granted when a U.S. judge signed an injunction insuring that no administrative reprisals would be taken against them. The prisoners rejected the injunction as "meaningless." Attica authorities granted another demand by permitting outsiders sought by the convicts to enter the prison to witness negotiations and view prison conditions. Among those observers were Rep. Herman Badillo (D., N. Y.), Tom Wicker, an associate editor of the *N.Y. Times,* and Clarence B. Jones, publisher of the *Amsterdam News.*

Sept. 11—The uprising claimed its first victim when a guard died of head injuries sustained when the revolt broke out. Officials said William Quinn had been injured fatally when convicts threw him from a 2d-floor window in the prison. Bobby G. Seale of the Black Panthers arrived at the prison to join the 23-member observer committee. The snag in the negotiations was said to be over the rebels' demand for complete amnesty and the authorities' unwillingness to grant it.

Sept. 12—The observer committee asked Gov. Rockefeller to intervene, but he declined. Rockefeller said that "I do not feel my physical presence on the site can contribute to a peaceful settlement." Bobby Seale left the prison, saying that officials would not let him take part in negotiations unless he tried to talk the convicts into surrendering.

Sept. 13—Shortly after the lawmen recaptured control of the prison, Rockefeller issued a statement saying that the uprising had been brought on by the "revolutionary tactics of militants." Rockefeller announced that he had ordered a "full investigation of all the factors leading to this uprising, including the role that outside forces would appear to have played." Rockefeller spoke to Pres. Nixon twice during the day, and according to a White House spokesman, the President "expressed his support for the actions" that Rockefeller took.

Gerald Warren, deputy Presidential press secretary, said in Washington Sept. 14 that Nixon stood by his support of the manner in which Rockefeller had handled the situation even after it was learned that the hostages had not died of knife slashings as first reported.

Vice Pres. Agnew accused the "radical left" and the nation's news media Sept. 27 of trying to turn the Attica revolt into "yet another cause celebre in the pantheon of radical revolutionary propaganda." In a speech to the International Association of Chiefs of Police, meeting in Anaheim, Calif., Agnew said that instead of paying tribute to 633 lawmen killed in the U.S. in the past 10 years, there had been "inordinate attention focused on the self-declared and proven enemies of our society." "Only by the total inversion of all civilized values can those among the militant inmates which killed a guard and slashed the throats of fellow inmates during the period of their holdout be termed heroes in a struggle for human life and dignity," Agnew said. He attacked the news media for giving wide currency to "the most inflammatory and baseless charges" of convicted criminals and their sympathizers. In a signed article in the *N.Y. Times* Sept. 17, Agnew had said he believed that the "approbation given extremists by some responsible leaders of both races has nurtured the roots of violence such as occurred at Attica . . ." Agnew praised Rockefeller for acting "courageously" to end the confrontation at the prison. He said that those who would have had Rockefeller act otherwise "have yet to learn the paramount lesson of our century: that acquiescence to the demands of the criminal element of any society only begets greater violence."

Other Prison Violence

2 inmates of the Illinois state prison in Pontiac were shot by guards and 7 others were injured during a 4-hour riot Oct. 3, 1971. 5 guards were reported injured. The riot was laid to a fight between inmates allied with 2 rival Chicago street gangs, the Black P Stone Nation and the Disciples.

A riot Oct. 4 at the Dallas (Tex.) jail involved more than 500 prisoners. One inmate died en route to a hospital shortly after the riot. 2 convicts and 2 jailers were injured during the disorders. The rebellion was put down by policemen using high pressure water hoses.

Urban Disturbances

One man was killed and 50 injured Jan. 31, 1971 when a Mexican-American rally in East Los Angeles turned into a battle with Los Angeles County sheriff's deputies. Gustave Montag Jr., 24, died after being shot as 6 deputies fought off a barrage of rocks thrown by some 600 youths. The rally, attended by about 3,000 Mexican-Americans, had been organized by the Chicano Moratorium Committee in protest against alleged police brutality during and since an Aug. 1970 riot when a Maxican-American newspaper columnist was killed by a tear-gas projectile. A hearing into the death of the columnist, Ruben Salazar, ended with the district attorney's refusal to prosecute the policeman who fired the tear gas.

During the Jan. 31 violence, 90 persons were arrested. Damage from fires was estimated Feb. 1 at $194,000. 56 buildings were damaged. A federal marshal, stationed at the rally as an observer, said Feb. 1 that the riot was "definitely started by agitators" and seemed to have been a "planned operation." Rosalio Munoz, head of the Chicano Moratorium Committee, said that the deputies "took the law into their own hands." (3 deputy sheriffs, guards at the Los Angeles central jail, were fired Feb. 4 on charges that they sprayed a crowd-control chemical on prisoners who had been arrested during the Jan. 31 riot.)

2 persons were shot to death during 4 days of racial violence in Wilmington, N.C. Feb. 5-8. Order was restored Feb. 8, but 600 National Guardsmen continued to patrol the streets Feb. 9 to prevent further outbreaks. The unrest was linked to a church being used by black students who were boycotting Wilmington's public high school. The first of the 2 slayings took place Feb. 6 when a 19-year-old black youth was shot by a policeman who said the boy had pointed a shotgun at him. Black residents charged that the youth was shot as he helped move furniture from a home threatened by a nearby fire. The 2d victim was a 57-year-old white man shot outside the church. He had been armed with a pistol.

Racial tensions, fueled by reports that 2 policemen had beaten a Puerto Rican man, led to a week of sporadic looting and fire-bombing by Puerto Rican youths Aug. 16-23 in Camden, N.J. Calm was restored Aug. 24. 4 persons were injured during the disorders and more than 200 arrested. The rioting stemmed from demands from Camden's Puerto Rican community that the 2 patrolmen be suspended. Leaders of the Puerto Rican neighborhoods also pressed for a greater voice in the local government. Mayor Joseph M. Nardi suspended the policemen Aug. 21, "solely for the purpose of avoiding further pain in the city."

Throughout the Southern and Border states, most school districts reopened newly desegregated schools with a minimum of disruption in the fall of 1971. In Chattanooga, Tenn., a bomb damaged a high school Sept. 6, but city and police officials insisted that they had found no relationship between the explosion and the opening of the city's schools. (The school had been the scene of racial disorders during 1970.) A dynamite bomb damaged 2 classrooms in a vacant school Sept. 1 in Columbus, Ga. In Kannapolis, N. C., an elementary school was damaged by 8 firebombs, but schools remained open Sept. 4.

City authorities and Puerto Rican youth leaders in Hoboken, N.J. Sept. 6 negotiated a truce ending 2 days of disturbances marked by window smashing and looting. Hoboken police said 42 persons had been arrested and 8 policemen injured during the disorders. The Puerto Rican youths accepted the informal truce after Hoboken officials agreed to release 35 Puerto Ricans arrested during the disturbances. Among the charges against the 35 were disorderly conduct, assaults on policemen and assault with a dangerous weapon. The trouble had begun Sept. 4 when word spread through the city's Puerto Rican community that police were beating 2 Puerto Rican brothers accused of assaulting a merchant with a knife. A crowd of Puerto Ricans marched on police headquarters. Fighting erupted when police tried to hold back the demonstrators.

A black high school student was killed and 3 policemen wounded during 2 nights of racial unrest in Lubbock, Tex. Sept. 9-11. Mayor James H. Granberry and the city council agreed to drop a dawn-to-dusk curfew Sept. 11 after black leaders complained that intensive police patrolling of Lubbock's black neighborhoods increased tensions. The disorders had broken out Sept. 9 after a 16-year-old black student was shot in the heart by a white classmate in an argument over a pack of cigarettes. 3 Negroes were charged Sept. 10 with intent to murder after a sniper shot a patrolman in the neck.

H. Rap Brown Shot & Captured in New York

H. Rap Brown, the fugitive black militant leader who disappeared in May 1970, was shot and captured by police in New York Oct. 16, 1971. Brown, 28, was shot twice in the stomach as he and 3 other men tried to make their getaway after they had robbed a bar. 2 policemen were wounded in the exchange of gunfire.

According to police, Brown was one of 4 or 5 men who robbed 25 customers of a Manhattan bar at gun point. When the suspects came out of the bar, police said, they saw a policeman and opened fire. During a run-and-shoot gunbattle that ensued, 50 policemen joined the chase. Brown's 3 companions were arrested in a building a few blocks from the West Side bar they allegedly held up. Brown was shot and captured on the roof of the same building.

Convicted of armed robbery Mar. 29, 1973, Brown was sentenced May 10 to 5 to 15 years in prison.

Charges of inciting to riot and arson stemming from racial disturbances in Cambridge, Md. in 1967 were dropped against Brown Nov. 6, 1973. Instead, Brown pleaded guilty to a misdemeanor charge connected to his failure to appear for trial in the case in 1970. Judge James MacGill of the Howard County (Md.) circuit court sentenced Brown to one year in prison to run concurrently with the sentence he was already serving in New York State.

24 Farm Workers Found Slain in California

Farm labor contractor Juan V. Corona, 37, was arraigned June 2, 1971 in Yuba City, Calif. on murder charges in connection with the slaying of 23 men whose bodies were found buried in peach orchards on the outskirts of Yuba City. Corona pleaded not guilty to 10 counts of murder at the arraignment. The charges listed the 10 bodies dug up by sheriff's deputies May 26, the day Corona was arrested. (A 24th body was dug up from a crude grave in the peach orchards near Yuba City June 2. The police said only that it was found in the same general area where the other 23 victims had been found.)

Almost all of the bodies were believed to be those of itinerant farm workers who drifted in and out of the Sacramento Valley during the farming season. A few were identified as rootless members of Yuba City's Skid Row community. The murdered men were middle-aged, ranging from 40 to 60. Most had been clubbed in the back of the head. The first of the bodies was found May 20 in a shallow grave near the Feather River.

Corona was linked to the slayings by 2 sales receipts found in the grave of a victim who had been dead less than 48 hours. Corona had also been questioned in connection with the disappearance of one of the murdered men. Corona had a history of mental illness. He had been committed to a state mental hospital near Yuba City for 3 months in 1956 at the request of his brothers. Doctors at the hospital diagnosed him as a schizophrenic but later discharged him as cured.